Building Your Ideal Private Practice

A Guide for Therapists and
Other Healing Professionals

Building Your Ideal Private Practice

*A Guide for Therapists and
Other Healing Professionals*

Lynn Grodzki

W.W. Norton & Company
New York • London

The first quote on page v is reprinted with permission of the publisher. From *A Simpler Way,* copyright 1996 by Margaret Wheatley and Myron Kellner-Rogers, Berrett-Koehler Publishers, Inc., San Francisco, CA. All rights reserved.

For information about permission to reproduce selections
from this book, write to
Permissions, W. W. Norton & Company, Inc., 500 Fifth Avenue,
New York, NY 10110

Composition and book design by Paradigm Graphics
Manufacturing by Haddon Craftsmen

Library of Congress Cataloging-in-Publication Data
Grodzki, Lynn.
Building your ideal private practice: a guide for therapists and
other healing professionals / Lynn Grodzki.
p.   cm.
"A Norton professional book."
Includes index.
ISBN 0-393-70331-2
1. Psychotherapy—Practice. 2. Mental health counseling—Practice. 3.
Psychotherapists—Marketing. I. Title.

RC465.5 .G76 2000
616.89'14'068—dc21   99-058069

W. W. Norton & Company, Inc., 500 Fifth Avenue, New York, N.Y. 10110
www.wwnorton.com
W. W. Norton & Company Ltd., 10 Coptic Street, London WC1A 1PU

6 7 8 9 0

There is a simpler way to organize human endeavor. It requires a new way of being in the world. It requires being in the world without fear. Being in the world with play and creativity. Seeking after what's possible. Being willing to learn and be surprised.

—Margaret Wheatley and Myron Kellner-Rogers,
A Simpler Way

I have learned that if you build a successful person, they, in turn, will build a successful business.

—Jackie Nagel, business coach

Contents

Acknowledgments

To be a good business coach it helps to have great clients, and I have been especially blessed in this area. I want to extend my appreciation to the hundreds of talented therapists I have had the pleasure to coach. Asking for help can be particularly forbidding for those who make a career out of helping others, so I feel privileged to have had so many therapists place their trust in me. To respect the confidentiality of the coach-client relationship, I have changed names and identifying details when using case studies, unless given specific permission to do otherwise.

As a first-time author, I relied on the guidance of Susan Munro and Deborah Malmud, my editors at Norton, who believed in the importance of this book and offered me clear direction and expert advice. My circle of encouragement includes many people who supported my efforts in many, many ways and I thank them all. I am most deeply grateful to my husband, Tad, a patient reader and rigorous editor of countless drafts. He maintained a loving, stable, always motivating presence and was, in effect, a wonderful coach himself.

Building Your Ideal Private Practice

*A Guide for Therapists and
Other Healing Professionals*

Part I

Preparation

1

The Blueprint

You're in private practice, or ready to start one. You love the work you do with your clients. But today, loving your work and being a talented professional isn't enough to insure the success of your practice; you also need to be an enthusiastic, talented businessperson. As a business coach who specializes in helping therapists and other healing professionals achieve success, I want to show you how to build an *ideal practice*—one that is both highly profitable and personally satisfying *at the same time.*

The notion of having an ideal practice that is simultaneously profitable and satisfying may seem like a pipe dream when you are wondering whether your practice can withstand yet another slowdown in client referrals, increasing professional competition, or an unpredictable economic marketplace. Overcoming the challenges you currently face in order to build a thriving practice means knowing what to *do,* but more importantly, it means knowing who to *be.* By who to *be,* I mean taking a frank look at yourself and making some necessary shifts in your thoughts, feelings, and behaviors so that you become an alert, savvy, skillful businessperson. From this position it is easy and natural to take the steps to create the private practice you desire—your ideal practice.

My goal is to help reinforce your business awareness by showing you ways to strengthen your emotional, cognitive, and strategic capacities. During the past four years I have coached over six hundred "therapists" of all professions—a diverse range of practitioners including physicians, psychologists, social workers, counselors, personal coaches, nurses, energy healers, chiropractors, massage therapists, physical therapists, acupuncturists, and body workers. (For the sake of simplicity, throughout the book

I will use the terms *therapist* and *therapy* generically to connote a wide variety of professionals and their professions. When I use these terms, please know that I am speaking to you, regardless of the nature of your professional training.) In the process, I have learned one undeniable fact: How your practice performs is an accurate reflection of you, as the owner. It will be strong where you are strong and weak where you are weak. Taking an honest, careful look at your existing practice will show you precisely where you need to make changes within yourself. My job is to show you how. Throughout the book, I will show you how you can make changes:

- *emotionally,* by developing the right kind of internal and external professional support;
- *spiritually,* by designing a compelling business vision that upholds your integrity;
- *cognitively,* by adopting an entrepreneurial, antisabotage mindset;
- *strategically,* by identifying and implementing the actions that generate a flow of referrals, boost profits, and add value to a small practice; and
- *creatively,* by charting a course to keep you and your practice on the cutting edge of your profession.

If you are like many other therapists I coach, you will notice that the more you change in these directions, becoming a stronger businessperson, the more your practice improves, becoming more profitable, organized, and resilient. You will attract quality clients, retain them longer, and run a smoother operation. Your list of complaints will shrink as you resolve your business problems with less stress. You may find that with your practice in such good shape, you relax and do your best work ever as a therapist. All of this is a natural progression, based on making specific changes within yourself that get reflected in your business and your craft. Along the way, you will probably recognize that you have refined your ability to stay focused and remain optimistic, even when others worry. And these days, in the workshops and classes I teach, I meet too many talented professionals who feel very worried.

I hear this worry at the start of every practice-building workshop, when I ask the therapists attending to introduce themselves. "Share the major challenge you face regarding private practice today," I request. Then I hear a lot about what is going wrong:

> "I've tried everything I can think of and my practice is still not growing."
>
> "I need more clients who can pay my full fee."
>
> "I hate the idea of having to market my services."
>
> "I think I do good work—why can't I maintain a full practice?"
>
> "I'm doing okay today, but what about next month?"
>
> "The competition in my area is fierce. I can't keep up."
>
> "I'm brand-new and I feel totally overwhelmed—how do I even get a practice started?"
>
> "Managed care has cut my income in half—I'm desperate."
>
> "I'm worried that I'll have to compromise who I am and what I value in order to make a living."
>
> "I'm not business-minded and I'm not making enough money."

As participants continue to speak, I see others in the audience begin to nod their heads in agreement as, one by one, they voice their concerns: isolation from peers, the breakdown of traditional referral networks, increased paperwork, and stagnant fees. Some, at the beginning of their careers, wonder how they'll be able to make a living; others with more time in practice refer nostalgically to the "good old days" when private practice seemed so much easier.

> "I feel frightened. I've been in practice a long time. I do good work and I hate having to change what has worked well for me. It's not much fun to be a therapist today. I'm thinking of leaving the profession."
>
> "I'm afraid of losing clients if I increase my fees. My overhead is up, my profits are down. I don't understand how to make money at this business."
>
> "At every professional meeting I go to, I hear people talking about how it's only going to get harder to survive in private practice. I'm scared. This is taking a lot more work than I thought. Maybe I'm just not cut out for owning my own business."

There is a heaviness in the room, an undercurrent of hopelessness and frustration.

"Why do you think you are facing these particular challenges at this particular time?" I ask.

Now everyone comes alive, ready to offer opinions. Some lament the public's negative perception of their profession; some berate themselves for not knowing more about how to run a small business. Others cite territorial battles that pit groups of practitioners against each other, the lack of public awareness about their areas of expertise, or too little support from their professional community about practice-building. Many point to the destructive effects of managed care.

As I listen to the group wrestling for explanations to their dilemma, two themes emerge. The first theme, voiced by therapists who run their business within a medical model, speaks to the dramatic shift in current market forces. If you rely on insurance or managed care to fund your services, you are well aware of this shift. Everything about the way your business operates is changing. I call this the "Oz" syndrome. In the movie *The Wizard of Oz,* a tornado is bearing down on Dorothy and her dog, Toto. Unable to get to the root cellar for protection, they huddle in the farmhouse. The tornado lifts the house into the air and carries it a long way, until it crashes down, depositing them in a new land. Dorothy and Toto crawl out of the house and look around. The film, up to this point photographed in black and white, has now turned to Technicolor. The landscape is surreal and fantastic. Dorothy shakes her head and utters that classic phrase: "We're not in Kansas anymore, Toto."

Those who operate within a medical model similarly find themselves bewildered by the new, chaotic economic landscape managed care has wrought. Gone are the days when generous insurance adequately subsidized therapy sessions. Today a therapist in private practice faces the choice of working under contract for a profit-minded insurance company and accepting whatever fees and conditions the company decrees, or finding clients who pay out of pocket.

You may see this development as either the good news or the bad news for therapy. From my viewpoint, as both a psychotherapist in full-time practice for over a decade and as a business coach, I see the increasing restrictions that managed care puts upon therapists as potentially good news for the profession of therapy, *if* these restrictions encourage frustrated therapists to step away from the managed-care model of business altogether and eliminate their dependence on insurance payments.

I believe that as more therapists in private practice decide to operate outside of managed care, the profession of therapy will shift away from a medical model, and therapy will become primarily a service-oriented business. Over time, therapists will learn to be more fluent within the business landscape; as a result, the profession of therapy may finally emerge from the shadows and come into the light, achieving a greater level of acceptance from the general public.

Up until now, therapy has been a misunderstood, mysterious profession. We therapists speak about our work using jargon and citing psychological theories that the general public often finds confusing. But if therapy becomes a fee-for-service business, therapists will be forced to explain, in clear language, what therapy is, how it really works, and all the benefits it produces. More responsibility will shift to each therapist in private practice to become an educator as well as a clinician.

If you accept the model of a therapy practice as a service business, you will become more businesslike in your approach. You'll learn to articulate who you are and what you do in words that the average person can understand. You'll connect more with your public, finding out what people really want and what they will gladly pay to receive. You'll need to produce tangible results. If therapy competes in the marketplace as a service business, the mystery, taboo, and vagueness of our work may finally be replaced with a broader public understanding of the value, importance, and logic of therapy, including psychotherapy, alternative medicine, and other forms of mind/body/spirit healing. When this happens, therapy will be publicly recognized as a necessary, at times profound, educational method that teaches us how to be more fully human and live an optimum life. For this reason, I believe that the market forces that are shifting therapy out of a medical model into a personal-growth business model are potentially good news for the profession.

But you will only see this as good news if you enjoy operating your own business. This brings me to the second theme: Why do therapists face so many challenges in private practice today and why are therapists of two minds when it comes to running their own businesses? Do you believe that working in a helping profession precludes you from combining personal satisfaction with financial success? If so, you are struggling with a split in your psyche in regards to your practice. Let me demonstrate how this split works.

WHY THERAPISTS FAIL IN BUSINESS

Can you remember why you became a therapist? When I interview therapists about their choice of vocation, I am reminded that the root Latin word for vocation is *vocare,* meaning *to call.* Many therapists felt called to their profession. Often they had a personal experience with therapy that profoundly changed their lives; they chose the profession in order to pass on their healing experience to others. This was true for me. I left a successful career in the family business to go back to graduate school at some sacrifice, because I really wanted to become a therapist. Therapy had changed my life so dramatically that I wanted to help others in a similar way. In my workshops and classes I often ask therapists how they felt called to become a therapist, and many touching, wonderful stories emerge. As they speak about their calling the room fills with love, their love for their profession.

Then I remind therapists that one definition of business is "profit-making," and ask how many felt called to make profit. Usually this request is greeted with startled laughter. No one in the room has a touching story to share about *that.* They didn't become therapists in order to be in business. Recently when I asked a group of therapists to give me a word that described their feelings about business, one brave soul stood up and said, "Would *hate* be too strong a word?"

Now do you understand the split in your psyche with regard to private practice? You may love working in your profession, but hate working in your business. You may feel that your role as a therapist conflicts with your role as a businessperson. This split makes sense in light of our cultural stereotypes about business; in our society, we hold a stereotype about the kind of person who succeeds in business. This person is ruthless, manipulative, loves power, and places the need to win above the need to relate well to others. Think of the maxim, "It's nothing personal, it's only business," which is often used to justify callous business behavior.

This stereotype poses a problem for therapists. We know, first and foremost, that our work is highly personal. A successful outcome in therapy rests on the personal relationships we create with our clients. For this reason, we tend to excel in the skills of insight, listening, and empathy. We want to heal others, not harm them. Anything that threatens building good relationships with our clients threatens our clinical results. So we may believe that paying too much attention to our business makes us cold and hard, that is, untherapeutic.

The split between therapy and business becomes evident in the way that therapists make peace with their mixed feelings about business, saying, "You have to take the pros with the cons." The "pros" refers to the sense of freedom and self-determination that comes from being your own boss. Having a private practice offers a wonderful degree of autonomy and independence not found as an employee. The "cons" mean the inevitable tasks any practice requires, including organizing, marketing, practice management, setting and keeping business boundaries, networking, budgeting, setting fees, collecting fees, raising fees, and overseeing policy—basically keeping the business growing. This notion of the pros versus the cons illustrates a core problem that many therapists don't understand: Learning to love operating your business ultimately will allow you to be a better therapist and to work at your craft with a higher level of integrity. Unfortunately, I see many wonderful, talented professionals failing in private practice in small and large ways, as they wrestle with this internal conflict. As their practices flounder or stay marginally profitable, therapists wonder where they have gone wrong.

A STRONG PRACTICE

Four years ago I attended a course on marketing for therapists. Over one hundred therapists filed into a hotel conference room on a snowy morning and listened for six hours as the speaker gave lots of ideas and how-to advice. I thought it was comprehensive, uncomplicated business advice, but I noticed how many therapists ended the day looking confused and disheartened. Some left the room early, but I couldn't tell if that was due to the snowy conditions or their difficulties with the content of the class. Months later, each participant received a list of the names and addresses of all those who had attended. I invited those in my local area to come to an informal focus group. My idea was to serve coffee and bagels and hear how the participants were doing in their practices.

Thirty therapists came to talk. None could point to substantial change in their practices as a result of the course. Most said they hadn't been able to use the marketing ideas to their satisfaction. They might have tried one or two techniques but they soon gave up when the results weren't as promising as they had hoped. They rejected many ideas as being "not quite right" for themselves, but didn't know what to do instead. They didn't have the necessary skill sets to address their current business problems and found themselves mired in negative thinking. As I listened and probed for more information, I felt concern for these therapists, who desperately wanted to improve their practices, but still didn't have a systematized approach that worked.

I decided then and there to design a program targeted to therapists like those sitting in my office—trained, experienced clinicians who were getting nowhere with traditional marketing approaches. As I thought further, I recognized that those thirty therapists were missing three essential elements to running a successful business:

1. *They lacked some key personal qualities that help you succeed in business.* No matter how much information or advice I might give you about business strategies, if you are lacking in these qualities you will not be able to consistently bring in clients, achieve your financial goals, or set good practice policies. I understood that a business coaching program for therapists would have to begin with a focus on personality—shifting who you need to *be,* not just what you need to *do* in order to have a successful business.

2. *These therapists did not know enough about business.* They didn't know basic business concepts, much less the innovative ideas that are

shaping the market today. They needed a very adapted form of business coaching—one that would use metaphors and anecdotes they could relate to, those tailored to their specific needs and sensibilities. They also needed to learn a series of step-by-step marketing, financial, and administrative strategies that directly enhance a therapy practice. If knowledge is power, their practices were severely underpowered.

3. *They didn't recognize how to bring craftsmanship into their businesses, how to polish an ordinary practice and make it shine.* Many of them worked too hard without results, spinning their wheels in the wrong direction. They needed to know some tricks of the trade, those finishing touches that experienced, successful therapists use to make the business of therapy easier.

I realized I had three categories of coaching to do with therapists, to help them put these elements in place. The first category I called *preparation.* It represents the key personal qualities and mindset that prepare you, the owner, emotionally, mentally, and conceptually to become a strong business person capable of building an ideal practice. The second I called *building blocks.* It includes all of the hands-on tools, strategies, plans, and essential information that result in a profitable, well-run business. The third I called *finishing touches,* those finely honed, craftsman-like touches that add sparkle and distinction to a practice.

Unconsciously, I drew on the terms of construction—preparation, building blocks, and finishing touches—to organize my thinking about practice-building. This makes sense when you know that I am married to an architect, and as a result hear a lot about building and design. But I have seen that over time, this metaphor has helped the therapists I coach to recognize the many similarities between building a strong house and building a prosperous, lasting private practice. I am going to expand this metaphor by walking you through the five steps of building a house and then show you how each step contains an important message for you about how to build or re-build your therapy practice. These five steps are your blueprint, and constitute a solid approach to practice-building whether you are starting a new practice from scratch, renovating or diversifying an existing one that needs attention, or simply insuring that a well-functioning practice continues to stay strong over time.

A WELL-BUILT PRIVATE PRACTICE

Here are the five basic steps of building a house:

1. Assess the site.
2. Draft the design.
3. Lay the foundation.
4. Erect the framework.
5. Add the finishing touches.

Now let me show you how each of the five steps relates to building your ideal practice.

ASSESS THE SITE

Building a house requires preparation. Long before the builder ever picks up a hammer and nails, the owner and architect have a number of steps to take. They visit the property where the house will stand and look at the lay of the land, seeing how to position the house. A house can sit many ways on one site. Some ways will offer maximum support for the building; some will cause it to slide and shift. The architect and owner walk over every inch of the site, measuring carefully and looking at site plans to make sure that the ground is strong. They don't want to encounter any unfortunate surprises that will undermine the finished house. The earth needs to be level, with weak areas shored up in order to have a solid surface that can hold the weight of the building.

To build a strong practice, you need sufficient support underneath you, as the business owner, to keep you emotionally level, thinking straight, and feeling capable. We will assess how well prepared you are to withstand the emotional stresses and strains of running a business. Without enough positive support you may shift and tilt, lose your commitment to your business plan, or find that an underlying weakness in your resolve erodes your best efforts.

Chapter 2 begins the preparation, showing you how to get ready to make some changes—in this case becoming a better business person—by becoming an "ideal business coaching client." (In chapter 2 I also show you how to use this same preparation technique with your clients, helping them to become "ideal therapy clients" so that they can get the most out of their therapy with you.)

Chapter 3 explains in detail how you can create a powerful internal and external emotional support system to manage the sometimes bumpy nature of private practice. I will teach you two effective techniques to help you ride out the inevitable ups and downs, including how to lessen negative beliefs that block you from following through on your business goals.

Message for the therapist: To build a lasting business, put sufficient emotional and professional support in place.

DRAFT THE DESIGN

The design for a house is both a vision and a working plan. As a vision, it incorporates the dreams and needs of the owner. A poor design means the owner will feel unsatisfied living in his own home. A good design will enhance the owner's well-being and let him function well. A great design inspires the owner, bringing an element of spirit into the dwelling. As a working plan, it instructs the builder on specifically what to do and how to do it.

The best design for your private practice is a business vision. Properly drafted, your business vision is much more than a daydream—it's a living, breathing picture of your future. In chapter 4 I will take you through the *aligned vision process,* a unique method of creating a vision that I developed specifically for therapy business owners. This will help you to align the direction of your future practice with your integrity values. You will learn how to identify trends affecting your practice and to pinpoint your strengths as a therapist. Having an aligned business vision will help you to know what decisions to make to have an ideal practice and give you a detailed plan for moving forward.

Message for the therapist: Design an aligned business vision that gives your practice direction and purpose.

LAY THE FOUNDATION

The larger the building project and the more difficult the site, the deeper the foundation needs to be. The foundation provides the reinforce-

ment that the house needs to stand straight and last over time. Even if you
are not building a new home but renovating an existing one, the first place
to check before starting to build is the foundation. A poor foundation will
cause a house to sink; walls may crack. A strong foundation means the
house will endure, with few problems, for a long time.

You need a strong, underlying foundation to help you firmly establish
your practice. Your foundation is your ability to think like a businessperson—staying focused, optimistic, and resolute. With this thinking in place,
your practice will stand straight. In chapter 5, I will show you how to
develop an entrepreneurial mindset—to see opportunity instead of problems and to stay focused on the future of your business, instead of the past.
We will look at what you can do to overcome the barriers the public faces
in using your services and how to tap into a powerful resource, your "inner
entrepreneur."

Message for the therapist: Develop a strong foundation for your practice
by adopting an entrepreneurial mindset.

ERECT THE FRAMEWORK

With the site prepared, the design in hand, and the foundation in place,
the builder begins to erect the framework of the house. Each board is mea-
sured, cut, and nailed into place. The steps of construction are logical and
methodical. The builder looks for the most efficient ways to carry out the
architect's design. As each room in the house gets constructed, it represents a series of thoughtful choices about the allocation of materials,
money, space, and resources.

As you may know, there are many frameworks you can use to build a
private practice. There is no one "right" way to set up a practice; it's only
a question of finding *your* ideal way. To help you make your own thoughtful choices about the construction of your practice, I will give you over fifty
proven, practical strategies and action steps and show you how to custom-
design a business plan, generate an abundance of referrals, expand, diversify, add value, set good policies, make more money, and even build a
practice you can sell when you decide to retire. Each strategy is based on
a logical, methodical process, adapted for a therapy business.

Chapters 6 through 10 include all the practical "how-to" ideas, illustrated by case examples, so that you understand how to implement each strategy. I will give you ideas that you can use to improve your business immediately or as part of your long-term plan for sustained growth over several years. And unlike others who write about marketing a business, I include only those marketing techniques that preserve the relational qualities between you and potential clients. I avoid all "push marketing" ideas that are too promotional and hard-sell for the business of therapy; instead, I suggest ways to use "pull marketing," techniques that allow you to naturally attract great clients and opportunities.

Message for the therapist: Build your practice your way—erect a framework that results in your ideal practice by choosing from dozens of practical, effective strategies.

ADD THE FINISHING TOUCHES

The finishing touches, called "finish" in the building trade, highlight the craftsmanship of the builder—reflected in the finer choices and detailing that makes a house shine. When you enter a well-built house, the finish is often the first thing you notice. It's important to give time and attention to the small, subtle touches that can have a big impact.

The finish you incorporate into your practice will be the details that set you apart from the crowd and let your practice shine. In times of competition, having a polished practice is one of the easiest ways to insure your success. Chapters 11 through 13 show you how to work smarter, not harder, by shifting your mindset from effort to ease; eliminate the fear-based aspect of your work and stay profitable by doing primarily what you love; become more attractive by modeling the services you offer, as a way to attract better clients; and regard the practice you have built with affection, instead of impatience. You will learn how to move beyond the traditional medical model of therapy toward an innovative personal-growth business model, one of the most important trends you can follow for the future. I will also show you how to hold onto your success by becoming highly self-motivated, so that you maintain your ideal practice over time.

Message for the therapist: Take your practice from ordinary to extraordinary by implementing the finishing touches that make a big impact on clients.

Throughout this book you will find case examples, anecdotes, exercises, guided imagery, and practical advice. I have also provided a pre- and post-test for you to take, so that you can track your progress and see measurable results as you learn how to:

- take some calculated risks to get your practice positioned in today's economic marketplace
- shift your business mindset from uncertainty to assurance
- sharpen your analysis of your professional situation
- develop a clear, effective business vision
- articulate your "basic message"—the essence of what you have to offer as a therapist
- avoid promotion and selling yourself—marketing that often doesn't work for therapists—and instead adopt "relational" marketing, which educates and engages new clients
- understand the wide range of business strategies that work best for a therapy business
- set and achieve your desired business goals
- ensure that your work continually adds value to your clients' lives
- create a "circle of encouragement" that supports and inspires you throughout your practice-building efforts

This last point is very important to remember. In times of great anxiety, we tend to feel isolated and cut off from our peers. In the midst of our fears about surviving financially, we jealously guard information and referral sources. We forget that these are the moments when we most need energy and support from our colleagues, so we can all come through the tough times together. Paradoxically, many of the easiest ways to build a practice (or any other small business) in today's competitive marketplace involve strategies of collaboration.

During each practice-building workshop I lead, I show therapists how to share constructive ideas with the colleagues sitting next to them, so that they can think about their concerns from a broader perspective. Two heads really are better than one. With so much creative energy in a workshop, the emotional atmosphere in the room gets lighter and more energized as the day progresses.

As a workshop breaks up, I overhear people making plans for actions they can take immediately, talking about vision and strategies, exchanging phone numbers, forming support groups. Instead of picturing others in the room as competitors, they are eager to work together as colleagues. I see a group of therapists who feel empowered and in control. Some are thoughtful, still integrating all the new information. Others are talking excitedly, "I can do this. I came in feeling like giving up, but now I'm inspired. I know exactly what to do next." I want you to feel this collegiality too. I will share many stories with you about your colleagues, who are also working to build their practices, so that you will realize that you are part of a larger community of therapists who are learning a new way to function in private practice. You can learn to operate your practice based on a concept of abundance, where there is plenty to go around, instead of deprivation, where you need to defend your few dwindling resources.

Do you feel ready to get started? Let me begin by showing you how to best use me as your business coach.

2

Now You Have a Business Coach

Is there one best way to build a private practice? Some therapists tell me that they built their practices as pioneers—going it alone, suffering some missteps, proceeding by trial and error, reinventing the wheel. Others used the wagon train method of building a practice, following behind a long line of others, walking in the footsteps of known therapists. Both the pioneer and wagon train methods of practice-building have limitations. The pioneer method exposes you to making unnecessary mistakes based on a lack of experience and can be a slow way to build a business. The wagon train method can result in short-sightedness as you mirror the practice methods of your own therapist, or rely on a more experienced colleague to guide you. If you blindly follow a well-worn path that has worked for others, you may miss the crucial ways that it limits your own talent and creativity.

When your goal is to build an ideal practice, one that is custom-designed to offer you high satisfaction and profitability, you need a combination of guidance, information, and choices. One item that directly correlates to private practice success is whether you have had some previous experience in business or a business background.

In fact, recent studies conducted by two West Coast universities show that having good business skills may be the major component to riding out the unpredictable market changes that now affect therapists of all persuasions. Unfortunately, most therapists are lacking in business development; it's an area that is too often overlooked in therapy schools and our professional associations. Graduate programs and professional institutions have traditionally offered therapists many avenues for finding good clinical supervision, but relatively little in the way of business supervision. If you feel that you are lacking as a businessperson, one way to compensate is by hiring a business coach.

A business coach is a cross between a consultant and a mentor, someone who can show you how to improve your practice quickly by bridging the gap between where you are now and where you want to be in the future. A good business coach should motivate and challenge you to create a better business and perhaps, in the process, a happier life.

In sports, coaching is essential to help an athlete develop a winning strategy. The coach shows the athlete how to move forward, overcoming or anticipating obstacles that the player can't see from his or her first-person perspective. The coach urges the athlete to set high goals based on a clear knowledge of the athlete's strengths and a knowledge of the sport, and stands beside the player to say, "You did that pretty well. Now try it this way and see if you can go even further!" For an athlete, having a coach is essential—it can be the difference between success or failure, a long career or being derailed by the unexpected.

As I speak to you through these pages, I invite you to consider me your personal business coach, here to assist you with the business aspects of your practice. Know that I am endorsing your efforts. Every time you master some aspect of your business based on what you will learn in this book, I am cheering for you. I stand behind your goal to have an ideal practice and want you to achieve your personal vision of success. Chapter by chapter, I will challenge you to move forward, stay focused, and persist.

As a practicing therapist, I know firsthand what you may be going through. I built my clinical social work practice as a sole proprietorship in 1988 and continue to operate it successfully today. I love being a therapist in private practice, but I also understand how tough it can be. I recognize what it's like to work in a competitive marketplace, since I live and work in the outskirts of Washington, D.C., an area saturated with therapists. I understand the stress that a private practice can place upon the owner, but I also know how to make a practice grow and stay successful. I can show you what it takes to earn a six-figure income completely outside of managed care, because I have consistently earned in that range for many years. I know how to expand a small practice into a larger one and to create associations with colleagues that benefit everyone. Over the years, I have created a practice that provides me and my clients with high levels of satisfaction, so I can show you how to do that, too.

Rather than offer untested, unproven ideas, I use my own practice as a pilot study every day, trying out new ideas. Then I take these ideas to the therapists I coach in individual sessions or weekly classes, and watch how they use them. I offer these ideas to a larger audience of therapists via workshops and further observe their results. In addition, I have followed a small group of fifty therapists closely for over two years, developing a sense of the strategies that succeed in a therapy business over time and those that don't. I have learned there is no one "right" way when it comes to building a practice. Lots of therapists do a variety of things that work. The trick is having access to enough information and ideas to find what works best for you.

I have conducted interviews with the most successful therapists I know to find out how they did it and to pass their strategies on to you. I have also completed a three-year course in business coaching to be able to offer you a wealth of useful information about business in general. I coach from a model of abundance and collegiality. Some of the people I coach surpass me in their therapy practices, building bigger practices and earning more than I choose to. I love when this happens and applaud their successes. These days, I like having a smaller therapy practice, so that I have time to write and work as a business coach. This helps me to keep in mind the difference between a fulfilling practice and a full practice. I try to help colleagues build a fulfilling practice of their own, letting go of any pressure about measuring up to others.

Now that you have a better idea of the basis of my coaching, I want to turn the focus on you. As your coach, I want you to get off to a strong start in our coaching partnership by getting ready to make some positive changes. The way I'd like you to begin is by becoming my *ideal* business coaching client.

MY IDEAL COACHING CLIENT

As my expertise as a business coach for therapists grew, I became curious about the fact that certain colleagues got great results from my program while others progressed much more slowly, with resistance. After tracking the progress of many participants, I began to understand that those who grasped the material easily and reported the biggest "wins" shared four characteristics. At the beginning of any coaching class or workshop, I could predict who would do well and who wouldn't, using a profile of these characteristics. I call the person this profile represents my "ideal client," because he or she gets the most out of my coaching program. (One of the easiest ways to build an ideal practice is to quickly fill it with ideal clients!)

I decided to see if I could create more ideal clients in every group. I found that just by articulating the ideal client profile to therapists at the beginning of a coaching course, I could increase the percentage of ideal clients in each class. Soon more therapists were "getting it" faster, and the classes became more challenging and fun for all involved. See if you can let yourself move into the role of ideal client so that you can get as much as possible from our time together. Here are the four characteristics that make up the profile:

1. *You are willing to take risks and try new things.* I will ask you to think about your practice in a new way and to take some actions that may be different from your usual method of behaving. (By the way, openness to change is a hallmark of a successful entrepreneur.)
2. *You can let me be the coach.* You may be an expert in your professional role as a therapist, but to get the most out of this book I'd like you to approach the material I offer as a receptive student. I encourage you to learn not only by reading but also by doing, to experiment freely and enjoy participating in the exercises and the field work. Stay curious.
3. *You will adapt any or all of this material in order to make it fit best for you and your situation.* My ideal clients take the initiative to change, alter, or combine any parts of my program in order to get the best results they can in their practices. I actually count on you to do this. From coaching so many professionals I know that this material is useful for a wide range of therapists, physicians, healers, and body workers. If the examples in a chapter seem geared to psychotherapists and you are an acupuncturist, please adapt the idea so that it can be useful to you. If I give you an idea that is not right for your particular style, adapt it freely so that it fits for you. Since I can't be with you to help you redesign the material to insure a perfect fit, I have to rely on your creativity. (When I

teach the course in person, I'm often delighted by the way my ideal clients will take a coaching tip and change it in a way I never would have considered, so that it works perfectly for their practice.)

4. *You understand the 90/10 law.* Ninety percent of my value to you will be outside the time you spend reading this book. I will really be doing my job as your coach when you take the information and ideas and put them to the test in your own professional life. My ideal clients like to take the strategies I offer out into their world, use them, and then report back to me and others about their results.

Each time you learn something new in this book, I want you to think about how you might use it with your own clients. Let's take the concept about ideal clients into your therapy practice. What qualities characterize the clients that you enjoy working with most? Chances are, they will be clients who also get the most out of being in therapy with you, too. Notice that your ideal clients probably mirror some of your own characteristics. For example, my ideal psychotherapy client:

- *Has a sophistication about the process of therapy.* He or she knows the value of not missing sessions, paying on time, following through on assignments between sessions, which makes us able to focus on the issue of their therapy more than the boundaries.
- *Is self-motivated and ready to make lasting change.* Since I have a small practice, I limit myself to working only with serious, committed clients.
- *Values direct and honest feedback from me.* Since I integrate my coaching style into my therapy sessions, I work best with clients who are strong enough to hear direct interpretations.

I want you to create your own profile of your ideal client. Limit it to just a few items, making the criteria inclusive, rather than exclusive. A good profile invites someone into a model therapeutic relationship, instead of pushing someone out. To be most effective, your profile needs to focus on a client's attributes, rather than on data such as age or gender. My ideal client profile is flexible and changes as I change. Yours will, too.

Remember, your profile says as much about who you are as it does about those you would like to attract.

Exercise
Identify Your Ideal Client

Create a profile of your ideal client and share it conversationally with new clients. It will help them understand your approach and your expectations, and show them how to "get their money's worth" or increase the value they receive from their time in therapy. This one step can help you think in a more focused way about the direction of your practice. Fill in these sentence stems:

1. My ideal client appreciates

2. My ideal client values

3. My ideal client understands

4. My ideal client agrees to

Success Takes Time

Just like an athlete, you will need to build up some muscles—business muscles, in this case, which are not about power but about mental and emotional strength—and this takes time. You may feel yourself resisting doing some of the things I suggest. You will may think, *Well, that's interesting, but it's not for me.* Remember that I want you to adapt, rather than dismiss, the suggestions that I make. Rather than rejecting any idea outright, think: *How could I make this of value for my practice?* This will cause you to stretch your metaphorical muscles and discover how you can use each and every idea for yourself, in some way that is right for you.

You may also find yourself needing to increase your patience and per-

severance for managing your business. These are qualities we give gener-
ously to our clients, and but less willingly to our practices. In any business,
perseverance and time make a difference.

For example, among the strategies for generating referrals that I suggest
is a specific way of offering a free workshop to the public. You might think:
I tried giving workshops and it doesn't work, and dismiss the idea. But in
business, as in sports (or in the work you do with your clients, for that
matter), you need to be persistent. Once is rarely enough. Imagine an
athlete who took this approach and decided that if she couldn't hit the ball
far enough the first time, she'd give up. You need to give your ideas enough
time to succeed. When I test out an idea in my practice, such as giving free
monthly workshops, I put the plan in place for a year. Only then will I evaluate how well it has worked. (We'll return to this crucial topic, with specific examples from my own practice and those of other therapists, later in
this book.)

It also takes time to make the shift from doing something awkwardly to
doing it gracefully or elegantly. For example, I request that therapists be
able to verbally state their fee with a smile, as an expression of their
comfort with the amount they charge. Most therapists stumble with this at
first. When we role-play stating their fee in class, they realize the mixed
message that's being sent when they name their fee with any facial expression of guilt, discomfort, or embarrassment. Time and practice make the
difference. You need time to integrate the ideas in this book into your
everyday life and infuse each step with your specific style. Don't give up
too soon.

WORKING ON THE BUSINESS

Michael Gerber, the author of The *E-Myth Revisited,* asks his clients to
spend time working *on* the business, not just *in* the business. As both CEO
and service provider, you need to give equal attention to both areas. You
probably spend countless hours improving your skills as a therapist,
because you have a devotion to your field and want to stay current. Your
business needs the same devotion from you. I request that you consider

the needs of your business as being at least as important as the needs of your clients. A strong practice will allow you to do your best work as a therapist. The reverse will also be true: A weak and floundering practice will drain your energy and adversely affect your clinical work.

You will need to shift from thinking like a service provider working *in* the business (a focus on seeing clients and the day-to-day running of your operation) to thinking like a CEO working *on* the business (a focus on the big picture, taking leadership regarding the future of your practice). How much of your time do you need to set aside each week to work on your business? By the end of this book, you will answer this question for yourself, based on the plan you create. For now, give yourself at least one hour each week, starting this week, to work on the business. Many of you will do more than this and your results will be commensurate with your efforts. Reading this book counts as time spent working on your business. So does following any exercise I outline or field work, when you try out ideas I've suggested.

In my experience coaching hundreds of therapists during the past several years, I have seen that the biggest indicator of practice success is not your years of experience as a therapist. Some new therapists can build a full, dynamic practice in under a year while other experienced, seasoned professionals struggle to fill remaining slots. The biggest indicator is your ability to make a change. It's scary to let go of the way you have always worked in business and try something new. I understand how hard it can be to change your way of doing business as a therapist.

Early in my career, I had an experience that taught me the value of being willing to make change. I let go of a financially successful therapy practice in order to build something that would ultimately bring me more personal satisfaction and more money. I started in private practice sooner than I intended, while still in graduate school. In 1986 I was getting my masters in social work, switching careers from business to therapy. I was also the single parent of a teenage son, who had a long-standing learning disability. For years I had been routinely researching learning techniques, hoping that I could help my son with his school work. Some of the techniques showed great promise. As I shared my enthusiasm about these learning techniques with my peers in graduate school, I began to get a few referrals for learning disabled children who needed a combination of educational and emotional counseling. The parents of these LD children were excited about finding a therapist who could address both their child's poor learning behaviors as well as their emotional blocks. I found that without trying, I had developed a niche of "learning therapy."

I began to have some success stories and by the time I graduated I had the beginning of a small practice. A year later I had nineteen clients to see every week, children and their families who all paid my full fee. These were good, serious clients and I was on my way to building a full practice. But I had a big problem. I did not enjoy the therapy practice I was building. I had left my career in business to return to graduate school to work with adults, not children. Instead, I was working almost exclusively as a child and family therapist. I had little formal training in family therapy and was quickly getting out of my depth. I realized that I was faced with making a big decision about the direction of my practice.

It took another year for me to decide to take a risk and pursue my original vision, changing my practice from top to bottom. Each summer, many of my young clients took a break from therapy to go to camp or on a summer vacation. I chose summer as the time to begin to slowly change my practice. I terminated with some children and began making referrals for others. Then I put all of the toys and games in my office away and started over. Making the change was frightening, but it taught me not to be afraid of rebuilding a practice in order to make things better. The rebuilt practice became more financially successful than the earlier version and, for me, it is infinitely more personally satisfying.

One thing that made it possible for me to change course and rebuild was that I had a strong system of internal and external emotional support in place that I used to calm my anxieties. I want you to have a similar support system in place, so that you can make the changes that serve you best. In the next chapter we will take a look at two powerful methods that that enhance a business owner's feelings of support and optimism, which you can use when you feel uncertain or anxious about your practice.

3

Support and Optimism

I am aware of a pervasive, underlying current of doom and gloom running throughout some of the healing professions. Mental health therapists tell me that they go to professional meetings to find peer support, but leave feeling more distressed than when they walked in. When too many colleagues in a room are dealing with their own fears, the meetings can quickly deteriorate into a forum for sharing horror stories—therapists leaving the business, therapists feeling frustrated and exhausted, or therapists on the edge of bankruptcy.

New therapists often respond to the pessimism with a sense of paralysis, dragging their feet instead of taking steps to get a practice started. More experienced therapists are also not immune to the pessimism and tend to overreact, getting panicked just when they should stay calm and think strategically. In this chapter we will look at what you need to do to rise above feelings of pessimism and fear, so that you can evaluate your current situation and take advantage of the opportunities that exist within any changing marketplace.

The fact that you are operating a business within a changing economic environment doesn't mean that your therapy practice is doomed to fail. The marketplace for all businesses, including the health industry, has been shifting for years due to a globalization of commerce and a movement toward consolidation, downsizing, and re-engineering. There is an advantage in being a small business in a volatile marketplace. Many small businesses do well in times like these because they can be flexible and change course more easily than larger businesses with more overhead. Small companies can find a niche, tap into a consumer need that's overlooked by bigger organizations, or discover a corner of the market just large enough to keep them highly profitable. You need to position your business well, stay open to new ideas, and above all, stay calm.

Staying calm as a business owner requires a strong stomach, a sense of purpose, and a resilient nature. But so do many other aspects of life with which you may be more familiar. Take relationships, for example, an area of life where therapists traditionally have some expertise. It might be easier to understand the nature of a private practice by comparing it to the nature of a relationship.

Several years ago a young woman, newly engaged and quite inexperienced in romantic relationships, came to see me for a psychotherapy consultation. She was terribly anxious.

"What's the problem?" I asked.

"I don't always feel close to my fiance. Sometimes I feel very connected to him, and I can relax. Then I feel more distance, emotionally, so I get tense. I hate the back-and-forth quality of this. I end up terribly anxious and worried whenever I sense even minor distance between us. I'm on a roller coaster between feeling fine and feeling anxious, sometimes several times a day. I just know that when I sense any distance at all, something is wrong."

"I'm curious, what makes you think that sensing distance is a danger signal?"

"I've been told that the way to judge if your relationship is going well is if you feel close to your partner. If I'm not feeling close, I worry we're in trouble."

I decided to educate her a little. "Look, the nature of an intimate relationship is not static. It shifts and changes. You may feel closer one day and less close the next. Nothing is wrong when that happens, within a certain range. This is what a long-term relationship feels like from the inside. Instead of tracking every minor shift in the relationship, I would rather have you explore how to calm your anxiety. You need to develop some stamina so that you can get comfortable with the variable nature of an intimate relationship."

I find myself having similar conversations with therapists about the ups and downs of their practices. The economics of private practice does not follow a linear, flat pattern. We often think that something is wrong when our practice dips, even slightly, and right when our practice rises. But when looked at from a business point of view, the minor ups and downs of a sole proprietorship are not only inevitable, but correct. Nothing is wrong. This is what it looks like and feels like to be inside a small business. The question is, can you calm yourself when your practice acts according to its nature? Can you develop the stamina to handle the natural sway of a small business?

All of the successful therapists I interview insist that their practices do not hold steady at all times. They tell me that they have times when they have unfilled hours and times when they have waiting lists. (The most experienced therapists say they enjoy the "slower" times; they've been in practice long enough to understand that their practice has cycles, and they know they will be busier soon.)

The newer and smaller your practice, the more vulnerable you are to its inevitable rise and fall, both financially and psychologically. As a small business, you have a limited staff, sometimes a staff of one. You, as the owner and therapist, can only be spread so thin. Lots can and does happen to pull your energy away from running your business—life events, family obligations, illness, a difficult caseload, outside projects. Your business responds to your level of distraction, and may go down. Then there will be phases when you have a lot of energy to invest in your business, and then you may see it go up. There is a lag time between actions that you take and the results, so you can't always predict when results will occur. There are many seasonal and marketplace factors that create an up-and-down motion as well. You can't completely control the fluctuation, but you can minimize its effects on the business and on yourself.

Large companies have a marketing staff, a substantial advertising budget, and departments of people who focus on one thing—how to keep the business stable and growing, to minimize the ups and downs. As a small business owner, you can do a piece of that by developing an "ebb and flow" strategy, which you will create in chapter 11. But before we talk about actions to take, you need a way to lessen your own anxiety as the business behaves like a business, moving up and down.

You might compare the situation to being at the helm of a sailboat on the ocean. The smaller the boat, the more you feel the pull of the wind on the sails and the rise and swell of the waves. Larger enterprises have more ballast, more hands on deck to keep things steady. If you are in a small partnership or operate as a sole proprietor, you need a way to stay out of panic mode when those waves get high. This is where optimism, that wonderful quality inherent in the best of entrepreneurs, becomes essential.

Optimism serves several functions for the small business owner. It helps you to focus on the future, more than on the present, which keeps you moving forward. If you are in that small boat in surging seas, you want to keep your eye trained on the horizon, looking for land. If you focus only on your sea sickness and worry, you are lost. Making business decisions based solely on anxiety can lead you in the wrong direction. Sometimes you need to take bold steps and expand, just when you are sensing a downturn. If you give in to your fear and anxiety, you may not be able to take the right steps to move forward.

When you are anxious about your client count you may cling too hard to existing clients and appear desperate to any potential ones. One of the most successful therapists in the Washington, D.C., area told me years ago that the only way for a therapist to do good work was to have a waiting list. That way a therapist could work with a sense of freedom and creativity and be unconcerned about a client leaving. "What if I, as a therapist, don't have a waiting list?" I asked him. He looked at me with some puzzlement, having forgotten that there were therapists less fortunate than he. After pausing for a moment he responded with authority, "Act as if."

Acting as if you are calm, stable, and optimistic when you are really in grave doubt about the future of your practice is great advice, but hard to follow. The best remedies I have found to help therapists "act as if" are the following two methods for calming fears and anxieties. The first is an internal process using a business affirmation, and the second involves developing a professional advisory circle, so that you can elicit the right rather than the wrong kind of support from your peers.

OVERCOMING YOUR BUSINESS ANXIETIES

Joanne is a Ph.D. who has been in private practice for twelve years. Two years ago, she discovered she had cancer. She stopped her practice, terminating some clients and referring others to colleagues, and put all of her considerable energy into getting well. Now she's cancer-free and ready to get back to work, but it's as if she's starting over. She built a practice once. Building it up the second time is possible, but many feelings are coming up that stop her in her tracks.

"I'm doubting myself and my abilities," she says. "There are so many young therapists out there in my community, all eager and enthusiastic. I just don't know if I'm really up to building this practice back. I am surprised at how much fear and reluctance I feel."

I frequently hear about fear from therapists as they struggle to move forward in business, although this is a word that the business community doesn't like to use. At a recent business coaching conference, I talked to a senior coach who specializes in working with high-powered financial analysts. "How do you help your clients deal with their fears about business?" I asked him. "For starters, we never use the word fear," he said. "Most of my clients are men. We use sports terms. We talk about *interference,* a good football term, as in I'm sensing *interference* about meeting my business goals and I am hustling to catch up."

Whatever word you choose to use for it, fear is a common emotion for everyone in business. At the root of our fears are negative beliefs about ourselves or the world. These beliefs feel real, and, what's more, we can point to plenty of validation from the universe about our excuses. Negative thoughts occur to most of us and affect our ability to take risks, become active, and maintain the necessary optimistic perspective. These thoughts may remain quiet as long as we're operating within our comfort zone and dealing with the safe and familiar, but once we decide to do something out of our normal realm, there they are, ready to sabotage our efforts.

Irrational negative beliefs will impede your progress. They will act to paralyze you. You need to be able to envision a business goal and hold it consistently in your mind while you eliminate the irrational fears that weaken your resolve. A colleague of mine met a wealthy developer of hotels who told her how he did this: "Before we ever break ground, I can see the front entrance of the hotel clearly in my mind. Next thing I know, I'm walking up to it." His strategy is clear. Hold the picture of a goal firmly in mind and then take the actions that further the goal. Let nothing dis-

suade you from that picture or from taking the actions. In time, the goal
becomes a reality. You can see how any negative beliefs you currently hold
can block your ability to achieve your goals.

The problem is that we all are capable of having negative beliefs. When
I stretch my comfort zone and go toward a big goal, I have many that
surface. Here are a few off of my personal "hit parade." See if any of these
mirror your own.

- I'm a victim of forces beyond my control.
- That's only true for others, not for me.
- I can't change.
- I am helpless.
- I'm not good enough.
- I'm not worthy.
- I'm not smart enough.
- I don't deserve it.
- I'm all alone.
- I can't trust the universe.
- There is no intelligent universe.
- Life is hard.
- Life is a struggle.
- It'll never work.
- It can't be done.
- I'll go broke.

Negative beliefs are rarely rational; they are fear-based and self protec-
tive, and function to keep us immobile and therefore safe. Often they do
their job too well, effectively preventing us from taking risks, putting ourselves out in front of others, or pursuing a gutsy goal.

You will need a way to overcome your negative beliefs and calm your
anxiety as you follow the instructions in this book that are designed to
encourage you to grow and take some risks. My favorite method is to use
a business affirmation. Although you may have experience with positive
thinking techniques, my method may be different in its intention. This
affirmation process not only trains you to hold a strong, positive business
goal in your mind; it also acts like a garden hoe, digging up the weeds—in

this case your undermining, negative beliefs—and exposing them to the light for examination and, ultimately, removal.

Creating Your Business Affirmation

This affirmation process can help you move forward to accomplish your business actions by calming you and refocusing your attention. But this process can also produce powerful results, far beyond simply soothing a business owner, as you will see in the following example.

I first learned about this affirmation technique from a therapist who uses it as her only method of practice-building. She has enjoyed a full, vibrant practice for twenty years, even though she works in a metropolitan area saturated with therapists. She holds a nursing degree, which is an untraditional degree for a therapist, yet her clients include psychiatrists and psychologists. Clearly she is both gifted and experienced. But she attributes her success in private practice to her regular use of a business affirmation.

She explained to me that whenever her practice falls below twenty-five clients, she schedules an hour a day in her calendar for affirmations. During this time she sits in her office and writes, "I have twenty-five wonderful, serious clients that I am able to help and empower." Then she sits quietly and notices any response from her own mind. Often a negative belief surfaces, in response to the affirmation. She writes down the negative belief and returns to writing the same affirmation. She does this each day, writing page after page of affirmations and the responding negative beliefs. After a few days she notices that her mind quiets, accepting the affirmation as truth. Then, without doing any other action, her phone begins to ring with referrals and her practice fills up again. She has used this as her only practice-building tool for over two decades. She told me she has shared this idea with many younger therapists, but few have followed her advice.

I was happy to learn about this technique and I have used it myself, expanded it, and taught it regularly for the past three years. Some therapists I coach get dramatic results with this—they work with an affirmation consistently and find that without any other behavioral change on their part, their business grows and opportunities spontaneously surface. For example, the week following the introduction of this exercise in my classes, it is commonplace to hear that about 20 percent of the therapists report a sudden flow of referrals coming into their practices. They are often amazed and attribute the referrals to their work with the affirmation. Others have less dramatic results, but talk about a noticeable change in their emotions, saying that using the affirmation helps them to feel calmer and in control. Some therapists follow the instructions to use the affirmation, but don't notice any immediate change (I fall into this camp); I do it for a while and forget about it. Months pass, and then I realize the affirmation I worked with briefly six months ago, "My practice is a pleasure to operate," has become my reality.

"Affirmations make me feel like I am doing something, even when there is nothing more to do," clients tell me. That alone is helpful for anyone operating a small business, because there will often be times you need to wait for your business actions, especially in the area of referrals, to take effect. Try this process, keep some notes about your experience, and watch what happens.

STEP 1. CREATE A BUSINESS AFFIRMATION

Choose an affirmation that you will use for at least ten minutes a day, every day for the next month. The affirmation needs to speak to your particular situation, affirming what you most need or want in your practice. In their book *Empowerment: The Art of Creating Your Life as You Want It* (1989), David Gershon and Gail Straub suggest that you use the following criteria when creating the affirmation:

- Use positive language.
- Keep it short.
- Use the present tense.
- Focus on changes in yourself, not others.
- Go outside your normal comfort zone, to your "leading edge" of growth.

On this last point: Imagine you are standing near the edge of a cliff. If you are twenty feet back from the edge, you feel safe and secure. When you move closer to the edge of the cliff, you start to feel nervous. When your toes are hanging off the edge of the cliff, you are at your leading edge. An affirmation that just restates your present reality keeps you in your comfort zone. If you make your affirmation bold enough, you will notice that an immediate protest forms in your mind and negative beliefs quickly surface. This is a leading edge affirmation.

A leading edge affirmation feels grandiose. It stretches you to a new level of thought that seems impossible. This is desirable, because this exercise is designed not only to help you learn to state and hold onto large business goals before they become your reality, but also to elicit and then eradicate negative thoughts.

Sometimes adding the right adjective or adverb will turn a comfort zone affirmation into one at your leading edge. If you make money at your practice but find it takes a lot of hard work, a comfort zone affirmation is "I make money in my practice." A leading edge affirmation would be "I make money effortlessly." If your practice always stays just a little below full, a leading edge affirmation is "My practice overflows with ideal clients."

Here are some sample affirmations that meet the criteria listed above:

- I manifest my vision for my practice.
- I generate all the business that I need.
- My practice is highly profitable.
- I balance the success of my business with the rest of my life.
- I have a practice that fills up easily so that I can do my best work.
- I easily attract an abundance of ideal clients.
- I enthusiastically let people know about my services.
- I fulfill my personal definition of success.
- Having prosperity in my life and work is easy for me.
- I have a waiting list full of clients.

STEP 2. WRITE THE AFFIRMATION

Now use a paper with two columns to write your affirmation. On the left, write the affirmation. The reason for making the statement succinct is that you will be writing it over and over. You can do it by hand or on a computer, but the key to making this work is writing it, not just thinking it.

Once you have written the affirmation, listen quietly for any internal negative thoughts. Write down the negative thought in the right-hand column, opposite the affirmation. Then repeat this process, until the page is full. Use the same affirmation each time. Resist any inclination to change it. At the end of the exercise you will have a list that looks something like this:

Affirmation	*Negative Thought*
I do what it takes to have a full, vibrant practice.	No I don't.
I do what it takes to have a full, vibrant practice.	I can't do what it takes.
I do what it takes to have a full, vibrant practice.	That's for other people not for me.
I do what it takes to have a full, vibrant practice.	I'm not smart enough to do this.
I do what it takes to have a full, vibrant practice.	My practice never stays full.
I do what it takes to have a full, vibrant practice.	I'm too lazy.
I do what it takes to have a full, vibrant practice.	That's not me.
I do what it takes to have a full, vibrant practice.	I'm scared of doing what it takes.
I do what it takes to have a full, vibrant practice.	I don't care about this enough to do it.

The negative thoughts will read like a stream of consciousness, albeit a highly critical stream. Time after time in the classes I teach, we read out these negative beliefs and everyone is amazed at how similar they sound, regardless of who is reading them and or what the affirmation states. As long as you are at your leading edge, it will tend to bring up a long list of your fears and anxieties. This means you are doing the exercise correctly.

STEP 3. CLEAR AWAY YOUR NEGATIVE BELIEFS

Here are the Three Rs of countering your negative beliefs: run through them, refute them, or replace them. Pick one method to use.

1. *Run through them.* Exhaust them by using your affirmation to drain away their charge. Write the affirmation over and over again, day after day. Over time you will notice that your mind quiets, tires of protesting, and agrees with the statement. When this happens, begin to notice any changes in your behavior and your thinking about this issue. This may take a day, a week, or a month, depending on the affirmation you have created.

2. *Refute them.* Make a third column on your paper and use your intellect to answer back to the negative belief. Let's say your affirmation is "I generate all the money into my practice that I need" and the negative thought you first notice is "I am no good with money." Think this through. Is it always the case, or can you think of times when you've managed money well? Even if you haven't managed money well in the past, you, like others, can educate yourself and learn. Write all this down in the margin next to the negative belief. It might look like this:

Affirmation	*Negative Thought*	*Refutation*
I attract ideal clients.	I never get that lucky.	Attracting ideal clients is not about luck. I have had some good clients in the past and I'll attract more.

A good resource for refutation is Martin Seligman's book, *Learned Optimism.* He gives many examples of how to use reason to overcome pessimism. Engage your neocortex to examine your negative reactions and eliminate unnecessary negative self-talk.

3. *Replace them.* Use visualization to give yourself a different picture, a message that counters the negative belief. For example, imagine a clear mental image of the affirmation and hold that picture in mind, as the builder I quoted earlier did with the entrance to his planned hotel. Create a piece of artwork, or make a collage from magazine photos, or draw a symbol that represents the affirmation. Look at it often. Meditate on the image. Again, the point is to help your mind create a new sense of what is possible.

Exercise
USE AN AFFIRMATION DAILY FOR ONE MONTH

Here is a blank chart you can photocopy so that you have thirty blank copies. Each day, fill in one page. Write the affirmation and then write any negative thought that surfaces in response. Write the affirmation again, and repeat the process, filling up both sides of the chart. The object is to keep writing the affirmation until you clear away negative thoughts, so that at the end of thirty days you have no negative response when you write or think your affirmation. At that point, your mind has exhausted all objections and basically says, "O.K."

Affirmation   *Negative Thought*

_____   _____

_____   _____

_____   _____

_____   _____

_____   _____

_____   _____

_____   _____

_____   _____

_____   _____

_____   _____

_____   _____

_____   _____

_____   _____

_____   _____

_____   _____

_____   _____

Joanne, the cancer survivor who was ready to resume her practice, used this business affirmation: "I enthusiastically let people know I am back at work." The first week she wrote this affirmation each day for ten minutes and reported that she had loads of negative beliefs surface during the writing process, but after completing the exercise she felt internally calmer. The second week, using the same affirmation, she shared that she was having fewer negative responses and feeling a sense of eagerness, as opposed to anxiety about building her practice. She felt excited to get back to work, even though she still had no clients and had not taken any external action toward that goal. The third week she came into our session surprised and delighted. She had met with a colleague and discussed her practice with him. He was in charge of a large family agency that had more potential clients than they could accommodate. He asked Joanne if she had any space in her practice for referrals. Of course she said yes. She was very pleased to be considered, and asked him why he had chosen her. He looked at her and said, "I think it was your enthusiasm in talking about your work that really appealed to me." She had already received her first referral from his agency.

This affirmation technique can help you become congruent, in mind and action, with whatever you state. Choose the wording of your affirmation with care and creativity. Stick with it long enough for it to have an effect. Then watch what happens.

Advisory Circles

Calming your internal anxiety is one important step to take in becoming optimistic and motivated about building your practice. It also helps to have the support of others. You need to surround yourself with people who will encourage your professional growth and success. You need to have support that energizes you, instead of discourages you. One therapist told me recently that a peer group he started to provide business support degenerated each week into a complaint session about the difficulties of private practice, which only served to further his feelings of victimization.

Much of my effectiveness as a business coach is based on the support and endorsement that I offer each person during coaching sessions. I hope you will feel that support from me as you read this book. I also want to show you how to relate to your peers from a mindset of abundance and partnership, by creating an advisory circle.

If you've spent any time within a large corporation or nonprofit organization, you're probably aware of the important role of the board of directors. Ideally, a board functions as the brain trust of an organization. The CEO selects the best and brightest people he or she knows from a variety of fields, from within and outside the organization to provide oversight and direction. In a perfect world, the board operates without any personal or political agenda, save one: They want what is best for the organization.

Advisory circles are the sole proprietor's remedy for the lack of a board of directors. You may have several people you turn to for advice, but I am going to propose that you set up a formal circle of professional, highly positive support, operating on the principles of mutuality and partnership. Your advisory circle will operate as a rotating board of directors, allowing each person in it to guard against insular thinking and gain the benefit of the advice of others whom you respect.

Create an advisory group of no more than six people, no fewer than four. Who should be a member of the group? It will help if everyone is in private practice. You might include some therapists, but also consider having a lawyer, an accountant, or a management consultant. Each person should be someone you respect, whose advice and experience will be relevant and someone you would like to give your support to, in turn.

If the group has six members, everyone agrees to meet for a minimum of six weeks. Each meeting will take an hour. The format of each meeting is simple—a different person takes center stage, each time. This person takes twenty minutes to present his or her professional story and answers any questions other members may have; then the group gives their best advice. Here's a set of guidelines that work well:

STEP 1: THE CENTER-STAGE PERSON'S PRESENTATION

Take no more than one-third of the allotted time to talk about these points:

- a statement of your vision and goals for your practice (more on this in the next chapter)
- your current challenges
- opportunities you are not currently taking advantage of
- what other people should know about you, in order to best advise you (including how you like to be coached by others)

STEP 2: A TIME FOR QUESTIONS

The questions are for the clarification of your board and should take another third of the time at most. Don't let the question-and-answer time become the advice-giving time. Keep the two separate. Questions are just to help your circle understand the above points.

STEP 3. DISCUSSION, ADVICE, AND SUGGESTIONS

During this last third of the hour, the center-stage person must sit quietly. The key word here is quietly. The members of your circle will now give you advice, direction, and suggestions, based on wanting the best for you personally and professionally. They will talk about your situation, while you listen. You will hear many ideas that you may want to downplay or resist. Listen with an open mind and reject nothing at this time. Take notes. You are free to accept or reject whatever you like later, but first consider all the possibilities without excuses or explanations. When the time is over, thank your circle for their efforts. The next time you meet, it's somebody else's turn and you become part of their advisory circle.

Remember, collaboration and mutuality are the keys to this effort. Everyone agrees to play by the rules and everyone agrees to take a turn at advising and being advised. When advising, everyone agrees to speak from a place of the highest good, without personal agenda. (For this reason, you may not want to have your spouse or close friends sit in on this professional support circle, unless you are sure you can both remain loving and objective for each other professionally.) This support group can become a tremendously important, enriching asset for your business.

Now you have an understanding of the nature of private practice, know how to create a collaborative board of directors, and how to use a powerful affirmation technique to calm your anxieties. These tools will allow you to function on a more solid emotional ground, while you take the next steps to build your ideal practice.

4

The Aligned Vision Process

Whether you are new to private practice or a twenty-year veteran, I encourage you to develop a business vision for one simple reason: it makes everything else you'll need to do to become highly profitable much, much easier. Any business works best when it is guided by vision, instead of by the owner's anxiety, reactivity, or fears of survival. Although many business owners credit having a formal vision process as central to their success, few therapists have one in place, because they don't consider their practices enough of a business to need a vision. As a result, therapists often miss the wealth of benefits that having an articulated vision can bring.

If you have never taken the time to create a business vision, it doesn't mean that your practice functions without direction. All businesses follow a path of some kind. You can use several markers to see the current path of your practice. Common ones to chart include revenue, profit, services offered, client retention, or rate of referrals. However, the marker I would ask you to chart is the level of your personal satisfaction, as the business owner.

Your level of satisfaction is key to analyzing the path your practice is following. Your business needs your best efforts and enthusiasm, at all times. Your business may be making progress in many areas, but if you are not feeling satisfied, something needs attention. The hard truth is that if you don't consciously make choices for your business, circumstances will. Without giving much thought to the direction of your practice, you will follow the path that's most expedient.

Contrast the path of two practices: In the first one, the therapist has clear ideas about what she wants for her business. She can picture the future of her practice in her mind, and that picture is very compelling to her. She likes the look of the vision, and spends time exploring it mentally. It draws her forward and helps her take action. Based on this vision, she makes choices about location, advertising, marketing, networking, training, and time management. Opportunities to grow her business abound. Her only problem is which of the many opportunities to choose. All of her choices reflect her best thinking and her passion about her work.

The second therapist gives little thought to the future. She simply wants to see enough clients to pay her bills. She takes what comes, in terms of location and clients, with no real plan. She trains in whatever techniques are current, networks halfheartedly where she hopes it will do some good, advertises when she gets anxious, and looks to others for examples of what to do next. Both practices survive, but which one thrives?

The signs of a practice operating without a vision can best be seen in the symptoms of the business owner. Without a business vision, you feel unfocused, easily burned out, and unsure of what to do next. You have little energy to invest in the daily tasks a business requires. The ability to have an *ideal* practice, one that brings you both satisfaction and profitability, at the same time, is the hallmark of a practice with a vision.

Linda, a massage therapist with a full caseload, explains. "I have been a massage therapist for ten years in private practice. Somehow I got a reputation for working with women, specifically survivors of sexual abuse. Now 80 percent of my clients are in that category. I have a full practice, but I wonder how I got niched in this area. It's draining for me, because I hear a lot about their trauma as I work with them. Memories come up for them and it can be pretty upsetting for me, too, day in day out.

"For years I have wanted to balance my clientele and work with other types of people, but it never really happened. I guess I've gotten spoiled. I just take who comes in, and who comes in is survivors. They are also poorly functioning, as a rule, and don't pay well. I probably undercharge as a result. I have big accounts receivables and I hate to make phone calls, trying to collect what's owed me. So I have a full practice, but I am underpaid and overstressed."

It's not too late for Linda to correct the issues that are causing her to feel burned out. A dynamic business vision would give her work meaning and purpose, guide her naturally into preparing a yearly business plan, and provide her with the energy for completing the mundane tasks that every practice requires. In this chapter I will take you through a unique vision process that will allow you to put your specific business design in place.

RETHINKING VISION

When I ask therapists how they understand the concept of vision, most say they think of it as a future destination for their practice, something that they can build toward. The destination is in the distance, far away from their current reality. This is a linear model of vision. The problem with a linear model is that although it defines your future goals, it does not, in and of itself, energize you to reach those goals. Unless you have a reserve of willpower and motivation, a linear vision may remain a remote dream.

I want the therapists I coach to have a vision that not only directs them to their goals, but also inspires them to take action. I developed the "aligned vision model" based on the concept of vision as a *field*. In quantum physics, space is understood to consist of fields. Think of any energy field, such as gravity or electromagnetism. These are forces that can't be seen, but can be felt. We know that the field exists, based on observing its undeniable effects. I'd like you to think of vision as an energy field, rather than a linear destination. When a strong field of vision is in place for a business, it permeates and infuses the practice with the therapist's energy and ideas. You can feel its effects within the business.

Margaret Wheatley, management consultant and author of *Leadership and the New Science,* encourages businesses to take advantage of this concept of vision as a field, due to its formative properties. She says that allowing vision to permeate a business means that anyone who bumps up against the field—owner, staff, or customer, gets influenced by it. If you, as the therapist, create a field of vision that permeates your practice, it can begin to have an effect on you and your clients immediately.

This is clear to me when I visit Nordstrom, the upscale department store. As soon as I enter the store, I can sense Nordstrom's vision of customer service. It's based on a combination of several elements, some of which I can point to and some of which seem to just be in the air. Soft piano music greets me, with a formally dressed pianist seated at a baby grand. The store has an open design, with high ceilings and good lighting, similar to a fancy hotel lobby. Well-dressed, pleasant sales people notice I have entered and quickly walk over to me, asking if they can be of assistance. On a recent trip to Arizona, I shared a taxi ride to the airport with the marketing director for a new Nordstrom that had just opened in Scottsdale. She told me that the company vision includes making the customer feel highly valued at all times. This vision permeates the store and effects the customer in many small and large ways.

Your vision can have a similar impact. Your clarity about the purpose and direction of your practice can have a direct effect on your clients, from the inside out. Using the aligned vision model, you will have a plan for your practice that is in alignment with who you are when you are at your best. The model is a five-step process:

1. Find the future direction of your practice by spotting trends and "trending up."
2. Identify your professional strengths so that your vision reflects you at your best.
3. Orient your vision around your integrity.
4. Mentally picture your vision and align it with your heart.
5. Articulate all of the above with a written vision, purpose, and mission statement.

I will explain the process completely and give you clear directions so that you can complete each step. Throughout the chapter you will find worksheets to use, to help you organize and record your impressions.

SPOTTING TRENDS

Having vision means you can see beyond your immediate reality to what happens next, with unusual foresight. Your business vision needs to inform you in the present while it leads you into the future. What you can (or can't) determine about the future of your profession, the local region in which you practice, or society at large, will directly affect your ability to create a viable business.

Everyday, I know you spend time thinking futuristically. I'm not talking about psychic abilities. I'm talking about worrying. When you worry, you are trying to think ahead in time and plan defensively. I want you to bring some of that futuristic thinking to your business, but use a more constructive method. Instead of predicting the future by worrying, I am going to show you how to spot trends.

Spotting trends has been likened to flying above the landscape in a plane, according to consultant Faith Popcorn in her book, *Clicking*. As you lift off, you see the familiar airport and nearby homes. Then you go higher, and see the outlying suburbs and city passing beneath you. Finally at ten thousand feet, you can see the big picture. You see how things relate to each other in a broad way. Popcorn says that trends are the landscape of the future.

Trends are not wishes about reality. Trends are an extension of current reality. Look at what is already happening around you and mentally follow it to a logical conclusion. How will this present reality look in six months or one year from now? Trends are not fads. A fad is a momentary interest in something new, a flash in the pan that won't last. Trends are broad movements, sometimes subtle at first, but eventually they pick up momentum and shape our daily life.

The question for you is: which of the millions of details you observe as you go through life constitute a trend, and which of those trends will have an impact on the future of your practice?

TRENDING UP

Trending up is a way of expanding existing trends to see the biggest picture possible. Think about the difference between looking down on the landscape at ten thousand feet and then flying higher, to thirty thousand feet. At ten thousand feet you see how the small hills lead to the larger mountains and you can speculate about what lies behind the mountains. At thirty thousand feet you see, at a glance, that the mountains are part of a great divide, separating an entire continent.

Trending up is an attempt to see a pattern, a large cultural movement, by detaching from the emotions of the present and looking ahead. It's similar to the detachment you feel when looking back at history. Historians say we need fifty to one hundred years to pass before we can look back on events and put them in perspective. Over long periods of time, emotion and opinion recede so we can notice the relevant patterns. When my coaching classes are discussing trends that carry a lot of emotion, I often tell them to trend up until the trend no longer feels personal. For example, when we begin to look at trends affecting the field of mental health, some people always bring up the trend of managed care and all the resulting problems that therapists and clients face within that system. I ask them to "fly up" to a better perspective and look at the trend without upset, so that they can see the broader movement. At thirty thousand feet, they can begin to see that the shifts in insurance coverage are part of a large restructuring of an industry, which is still going through major changes. At that vantage point, we can discuss the futility of railing against the ongoing restructuring and simply look at how each therapist wants to position his or her small practice, inside or outside of the managed care landscape. Look for the landscape, don't get caught in the details.

By broadening the implications of any trend, you can have a stronger vantage point for positioning your vision more accurately today or next year. You then can use the information you gather about the larger landscape by scaling down and personalizing the trend. Here's an example of spotting an existing trend, trending up, and then personalizing the trend.

Ted, a licensed counselor, goes to a local health food store to post a flyer advertising a workshop he hopes to run. The workshop is for older adults, and is titled "Coping with Growing Older." The owner of the store comes over, eager to chat. Ted says, "How's business?" and the owner tells Ted that he has noticed a trend at the store—middle aged, unmarried customers are buying large quantities of Chinese herbs, thought to have properties of longevity.

Ted leaves the store, thinking about this trend. He tries to understand the larger picture, to trend up. He goes to the Internet and begins to search. He reads that as the millennium draws near, middle-aged people are the fastest-growing segment of the population. Many of these baby boomers have chosen to remain single or childless. Now they have a dilemma. By the turn of the century, half of the adult population will be single, without a family structure in place, taking care of themselves into old age. This translates into a proactive desire to remain healthy and self-reliant for as long as possible. Ted understands, in a new light, the increased drive toward longevity and preventative measures for single, aging adults.

Ted personalizes his understanding for his practice. He rethinks the seminar and calls his new workshop "Optimal Aging: How Older, Single Adults Can Take Great Care of Themselves." Ted finds that he is quite interested in this new topic and his workshop fills up easily.

Just as Ted did some research to understand a trend at a larger level, you may want to enhance your ability to trend up by reading or research-ing the on the Internet. During my Private Practice Success Program™ classes, we hold lively "trending up" sessions, using the brain power of the group. Learning to trend up takes time. You can make it more fun by trend-ing up with others in your advisory circle.

TRENDS ABOUT THE PROFESSION

Here are some further examples of trending up that relate to trends about the health and therapy professions.

Trend: Janet, a social worker, notices that her internist is now offering acupuncture treatments.

Trending up: Health professionals are blending their specialty areas with other disciplines. Practitioners broaden their services, sensing a new freedom about how health care can look in the next decade. Specialization is out, adding value is in. Psychologists teach meditation; social workers get certified in methods of bodywork; physical therapists suggest nutri-tional counseling; chiropractors offer personal coaching. As therapists have access to more information, they want to incorporate more, not less into their practices.

Personalizing the trend: Janet wants to offer more, too. She explores

several ways to do this: getting training in a field outside her area of specialty, expanding her services to include product sales, bringing in outside
therapists for consultations, or adding additional classes or groups to her
list of services. Since she specializes in eating disorders, she adds a
product line of books and audiotapes that she often recommends to clients.
Her receptionist sells them at the front desk. Her clients appreciate this
service. Janet finds that she gets some new business from people calling to
order products. These people are added to her mailing list and become
potential clients.

Trend: Tim, a psychologist, prefers to practice long-term therapy, but
knows that short-term therapy is attractive for both insurers and clients.

Trending up: Short-term therapy is attractive for those who want to
save time, especially when time equals money. Time is a precious commodity. Real or perceived lack of time is cited as a serious concern for
most working adults. Fast food, quick fixes, and multi-tasking are examples
of solutions for those people who are pressed for time. As time concerns
persist, some backlash results in a movement to simplify life and slow
down, but most of the population continues to try to do more, consume
more, and more into a limited schedules.

Personalizing the trend: Tim has run weekend couples workshops for
years, but now he begins to promote the workshops as a form of short-term
therapy. Attending four workshops a year will constitute fifty hours of
therapy per couple in only eight visits. He has each workshop participant
create a clear set of measurable goals and helps them to chart their results.

Here are some additional trends I have noticed about the helping professions, offered in no particular order. I invite you to read each example,
trend up, and then personalize it for your practice. Expand this list to
include the trends you notice about your specific profession.

- Family doctors are no longer primary referral sources for therapists,
  since under managed care they have little incentive to refer patients for
  any extra services, including therapy.
- With billions of dollars available for training and consulting, therapists
  move into the corporate environment, offering "executive coaching."

- Twenty percent of all psychotherapists leave the field each year. The higher the license the better, in terms of therapist job security.
- In 1995, one third of all Americans make use of alternative treatments, spending fourteen billion dollars out-of-pocket. Thanks to media focus, the mind/body connection is becoming an accepted concept.
- Due to malpractice claims, clergy have started to shy away from counseling, even though one study finds that 40 percent of Americans go to their clergy first as a referral for mental health problems.
- Two-worker families create more stress at home, and divorce rates are up. Research studies show that the most common methods of marital therapy are less effective than previously hoped.
- The preference for centralization and one-stop shopping has led to the "mall mentality" of group practice, as divergent practitioners band together to offer all possible health needs at one location.
- As public programs close and insurance refuses to fund therapy, therapy again becomes a luxury pursuit for the educated wealthy and upper middle class. Lower-income populations are not well-served.

TRENDS ABOUT SOCIETY

John Seiffer is a business coach who writes frequently about societal trends. He writes a free e-mail newsletter that contains many creative ideas about life and work (you can find his e-mail listing in the Resources section of the Appendix). This is an excerpt from his 1996 newsletter.

Society has undergone severe demographic shifts. Not only is the population living longer, there's a different mix in the numbers of people working vs. those who are retired and experiencing longer life. Add to that a widening gap between rich and poor and educational levels at a time when more and more jobs require more and more skills.

There's a spiritual awakening for lack of a better word. The sustained prosperity and improvement in living standards has allowed people to ask, "What's next?" Examples:

Life expectancy has improved in quantity and quality. We're living longer and becoming more fit to enjoy those extra years. More people are accepting this as a given and asking about a deeper purpose for those extra years.

Marriage and family used to be, in large part, an economic institution. Now that a person can not just survive but thrive on their own, people are looking for different things from relationships.

People are seeing our planet as more than just something to take from, but something to give to or at least build a sustainable relationship with.

What is the solution? Well, actually I'm not sure there's a problem as much as an opportunity. The solution, if you will, is in knowing how to ride the waves of change and not be drowned by them.

The focus of work is moving away from what you do toward what you accomplish. The key to riding this wave is to see that what will be increasingly important is to focus on results, accomplishment and value added.

Examining societal trends has at least two benefits for you as a therapist. First, they can help you to understand your clients better. Second, if you understand the bigger picture about cultural situations, it can help you to make better choices.

Sid, a psychologist in Washington, D.C., supervises a large group of trainees. He came to a business coaching session frustrated about the lack of response he had when marketing a seminar. He had sent out flyers to a group of trainees for a seminar on a topic they had requested. The flyers had been sent the month before and the seminar was scheduled to begin in two weeks. So far Sid had received only one re-sponse. Normally he would have felt terribly discouraged at the low response. Because he had spent time learning to trend up the week before, he decided to apply that process to his problem and to think of this as a societal trend. This helped him to understand the problem and find a working solution. He shared his thinking process:

Trend: I sent out two dozen flyers to interested trainees and got one response. I talked with two other therapists who had similar experiences with direct-mail marketing. The trend I see is low response rates to mailings.

Trending up: I get dozens of pieces of mail each day. I feel overloaded by information. I know this is part of a larger trend. Information overload means that everyone has less time to attend to mail daily and follow through. More and more is being offered through the mail. The gap between what people intend to do and what they do is getting wider. People react to the overload by shutting down or forgetting even those things that are important. Maybe this is what is happening to those people to whom I sent my flyers.

Personalizing the trend: I will call and remind people about the workshop and ask if they want to sign up, based on my belief that they may want to come and are overloaded by information.

After twenty phone calls, Sid had twelve clients signed up, enough to run the seminar profitably. Several said, "Thank you for reminding me. I really want to come. I just got so busy, I completely forgot." Sid told the coaching group that he never would have made the calls, had he not been thinking in terms of trends. It took all of the personal sting out of the low response rate. Now he could see that the failure to respond was not a personal statement about him as a trainer; people just forgot.

The first step in creating your aligned vision is to place your vision into the context of a predictable future, by becoming aware of trends and how they impact your practice. To correctly position your vision, you need to consider the trends in three areas:

- your profession
- your regional area of practice
- society at large

Think of trends in each of these three areas and then write down a trend you notice, trend up and personalize the trend in regard to your situation or your practice. Use the worksheet on page 52 to record your ideas.

Exercise
TRENDING UP

Trends about your profession:

    Trend:

    Trend up:

    Personalize the trend:

Trends about your regional area:

    Trend:

    Trend up:

    Personalize the trend:

Trends about society at large:

    Trend:

    Trend up:

    Personalize the trend:

IDENTIFYING YOUR STRENGTHS

Your business vision needs to reflect your strengths and talents as a therapist. By strengths, I don't mean a resume of the places you have worked, the types of clients you work with, or even the methods of therapy in which you are trained to practice. Your strengths and talents are not so much about what you do as about *who you are* while you are doing it. What is special about you as a therapist? What makes you happy in your work? What do you love about your craft? What are you best at?

In my experience, therapists are initially shy about defining themselves this way saying there's nothing special about what they do. I persist and ask them to answer these questions anyway. Not surprisingly, when I do this exercise in a room of therapists, each person talks about their strengths in different ways. No two therapists have identical strengths. I want you to learn to language your unique gifts. Here's some examples of how other therapists identify their most important strengths:

> *"I have an analytical mind, mixed with a large dose of compassion. I'm very good at showing clients how to solve difficult situations, using a pragmatic attitude, all the while staying empathic with their feelings."*

> *"I sense what is needed. As a massage therapist, I'm able to know what area of the body needs attention next, without even asking the question. I'm at my best bringing people back into their bodies and helping them deeply relax."*

> *"I'm a jack-of-all-trades and master of none, a generalist in this era of specialization. I know a little about a lot, which is fun for me. It gives me a sense of freedom to address many topics, and to refer freely to others for more specialized advice. I'm a clearing-house of knowledge."*

> *"I am extremely intuitive and spiritual in my approach. I make difficult moments tolerable by using a lighthearted touch and creating a meditative environment where my clients can be reflective and self-aware."*

Now that you have some examples, it's time for you to focus on yourself. What do you love about your craft? Those aspects of your work need to be included in any vision you create of your practice for the future. Even if you are new to practice, you probably have an idea of your strengths and talents from your school experience.

Exercise

IDENTIFYING YOUR STRENGTHS

Complete the following statements.

My strengths and talents:

What I believe is special or distinct about me as a therapist:

What I love most about my work:

ORIENTING AROUND YOUR INTEGRITY

Place your points of integrity, those principles and values you hold most dear, at the core of your business vision. Points of integrity are not the principles you think you *should* hold; instead, they are the principles you *already* stand for, that give your life and work meaning.

For example, if honesty is one of your points of integrity, you are honest, regardless of whether anyone else notices or cares. You are naturally drawn to speak the truth. Your honesty is reflected in all your relationships and the way you try to live your life. No one has to tell you to be truthful; you already are.

The happiest, most effective business owners I know are those whose businesses are centered around their principles and, as a result, they are filled with integrity. Sometimes simply defining your points of integrity can help you see where you have gone wrong in your practice and how to get back on track.

Robert, a psychologist, was unhappy about the lack of direction in his practice. He had been in practice for twenty years and built a specialty in couples therapy. He complained that he didn't have the energy or enthusiasm he once had and was seriously considering leaving the profession.

I asked him to complete the points of integrity index. He circled *adventure, risk, invention,* and *creativity.* In his free time, Robert loved to ski, rock climb, and travel to remote destinations for backpacking. He had a fascination with computer programming and invented new ways to streamline his billing software. These activities gave his life meaning and passion.

He couldn't wait for the weekends, to be off climbing or working on his computer.

I asked him how much his current practice reflected these principles. He shook his head, indicating not at all. He said that his current work with couples had a "been there, done that" feel. He saw the same problems over and over again, and responded in the same way. When I challenged him to add adventure and invention into his work, he was at a loss. Robert's task was to bring integrity into his practice.

Six months later I heard from Robert. He had started a new premarital program for couples, using a novel approach. He took the couples on an adventure weekend in the mountains that included an obstacle course. As the couples struggled to climb a rocky hillside or build a bridge out of fallen tree limbs and cross a swift stream, they learned the importance of partnership and teamwork. Robert was having a lot of fun and his words spilled out on the phone. He had more ideas about other adventure workshops to offer. He was writing a paper and giving presentations. By letting his integrity infuse his practice, he found a new energy and commitment for his work.

I developed the points of integrity index to help therapists prioritize their principles after seeing firsthand the effectivesness of this approach during my training at Coach University, a coaching institution that employs many such indices and exercises. Here is a list of words developed by the therapists in my classes that signify points of integrity:

health	fairness	respect	rules
strength	compassion	power	persuasion
fun	freedom	influence	encouragement
sexuality	spirituality	honor	mastering
sensuality	service	trust	winning
love	sacredness	creativity	accomplishment
kindness	security	invention	peace
grace	home	openness	quiet
understanding	family	imagination	calm
beauty	community	planning	inner strength
adventure	partnership	building	intuition
courage	growth	challenge	intellect
risk	enlightenment	discovery	play
leadership	happiness	learning	truth
inspiration	joy	self-expression	nurture
change	support	feelings	wholeness
honesty	contribution	nature	safety
patience	advocacy	action	vitality

Exercise
POINTS OF INTEGRITY

Look at the points of integrity index. Pick your top three. If you have one that is not listed, write it in. Picking only three will force you to become very clear about your essential values in life.

My top three points of integrity:
1.
2.
3.

Questions to answer:

What would a practice based on these points of integrity look like?

What would need to change about me or about the way I operate my practice?

How would I benefit from making these changes?

USING YOUR IMAGINATION

The next resource that you need in order to create your vision is one that is often forgotten in business—your creative imagination. Although we are building a practical vision, I want you to first examine it and have a mental dress rehearsal, by using a process of guided imagery. The great benefit of bringing in your imagination at this point is that it lets your creative mind begin to fill in the missing pieces. Your intuition will be the true architect of the vision. As a result, when your vision takes form, its details and actual appearance may surprise you.

The following exercise is designed to stimulate your creativity and expand your awareness of what may be possible for you in your practice. I suggest that you follow the exercise exactly as it is written. You may ask someone to read it to you, while you close your eyes, or tape record your own voice reading the instructions. Give yourself enough time to relax before you begin the exercise. Breathe easily. Then close your eyes and let your senses take over. You may see a clear picture of the vision, or you may have a felt sense of it. You may experience auditory clues or emotions as you construct the vision. Be nonjudgmental. Simply allow the vision to form in your mind. This is a natural thought process. Once you have finished the exercise, take some time and write your impressions on the worksheet. Try not to edit or critique what you experienced. Any time you want to return to the vision for more information, just close your eyes and go through the exercise again. It is helpful to revisit this exercise vision from time to time, to see how it may be shifting to adapt to your personal changes.

Exercise
MENTALLY SEE YOUR VISION

Record this into a tape recorder or ask someone to read it to you slowly. Sit with your eyes closed.

Let yourself begin to imagine a picture of your ideal practice. If you don't see a picture, allow a felt sense of your practice to come to mind. Start by imagining your practice in the future, a year or two from today. To create a picture of the future, think of the trends that you see today, and carry them forward in time. Place your practice in a future that makes sense, according to what you think is highly probable. Position your practice well, so that you can see it flourish within that future setting. As this vision evolves, let it take its own shape and form. What you see may surprise you. It is fine if this happens. Let your imagination work for you here.

See or sense your practice as an observer, looking at it from the outside. You may see specifics or just have an overall impression. Either one is fine. Take the time to allow a clear awareness of your future practice to occur to you.

In this vision of your practice, see that your practice flourishes because your true strengths and talents are evident, to yourself and others. Your practice allows your strengths and passions to shine through your work. As a result, your practice attracts those clients you most want to work with.

See that your practice is based on the most important points of your personal and professional integrity. Allow those points of integrity to be at the core of your vision.

Your practice fits within your best understanding of the future, reflects your unique strengths and talents, and is oriented around your points of integrity. As you imagine this vision, let it be big and compelling enough so that you feel very drawn to it. Let your vision encompass all of this, imagining a practice that is profitable and extremely energizing for you.

Now I want you to experiment seeing or sensing this vision with your eyes open. Open your eyes and still retain a strong awareness of this vision. Now close your eyes and take a better look. This time I want you to walk into the vision and notice how it feels to be inside it. Adapt and adjust anything necessary so that you resonate with the look, feel, and sound of being inside your practice.

Notice where you have located this vision in your imagination. Is it out in space, far away from you? To the right or to the left? Is it in your mind's eye? Imagine relocating it and placing it close to your heart. Notice how it feels to have it at the center of your chest. Hold the vision in your heart. Now open your eyes, still holding it in your heart. This is how it feels to have a vision aligned with your own heart.

Answer the following questions:

1. What did you see or sense?

2. What pleases you about this vision?

3. What disturbs you about this vision?

4. What surprises you about this vision?

Louise, a high-powered lawyer and mediator, had returned to graduate school to get a masters in social work. She complained that she "couldn't see" how to start her practice, because she needed to earn a certain amount of money. Leaving law and her status as a partner to start over in a small practice was not appealing. The dilemma she faced was that she loved being a therapist; all of her core values reinforced her decision to change professions.

She went through the guided imagery exercise and reported that she was stunned by the results. She saw a clear, detailed vision of herself purchasing an existing, very busy therapy practice that was for sale in her city. Although she knew that the practice was for sale, it had never occurred to her that she should make an offer. She wasn't even out of school, she protested. But there was the picture, in her vision, of her owning a practice and bringing all of her legal and professional skills to the new venture. She could start at the top, as the owner of an ongoing concern, instead of beginning at the bottom. She was delighted that her imagination presented such a sensible solution. The vision brought her great excitement and energy. She immediately began preparing to make an offer for the practice, which she later bought. Louise used her vision to stretch her ability to see a better future for herself and then followed through to make her vision a reality.

ARTICULATING YOUR VISION, PURPOSE, AND MISSION STATEMENT

Having a written vision, purpose, and mission statement can keep your business focused. The first part of the statement, the vision statement, is a brief sentence or two at most that sums up what you see as being possible. Bill Gates of Microsoft had a powerful vision in the early stages of building his company: *A computer on every desk running Microsoft software.* This clear, simple vision seemed possible to him, based on what he knew about the trends in computer technology as well as his passion and drive. At the time he envisioned it, it was little more than a personal dream, steeped in his imagination. Now we think of his vision as part of our everyday reality.

Martha teaches movement classes. She has developed a strong reputation in her local area of California and has self-published a book on her methods. When she mentally constructed her vision, she reported seeing a picture of herself on TV! She was selling videotapes of her classes on an infomercial. She had several emotions in immediate response to the vision—pleasure, surprise, and fear. I asked her to take the next step and write her three statements. For her vision statement, she wrote: *I help thousands of people learn to move more easily and gracefully with my movement tapes.* She identified her strengths to include teaching and enrolling others in her classes, so the idea of working with more people pleased her. One of her top three points of integrity was *contributing;* selling videotapes would make a much bigger contribution than teaching small local classes, so that appealed to her as well.

But Martha was disturbed. Being a naturally shy person, she would now have to overcome her shyness. The idea of being seen on a large scale, nationally, was scary. She loved the vision and felt energized by it, but she wasn't sure how she would be able to fulfill it, due to her shyness.

Martha realized that she would have to do a lot of work on herself. The purpose statement is a few sentences that speak to who you will need to become to fulfill your vision. Martha wrote: *I will need to be able to speak to large groups of people and stop being so scared and shy.* After she wrote her purpose statement, she began to back away from her vision. This is a normal reaction to having an expanded vision for your practice. If you see a large vision, you will be required to go beyond your normal boundaries. You may need to learn some new skills and stretch beyond your comfort zone. The purpose statement is the personal-growth component inherent in the vision process. A powerful vision will call you to become more than you are right now.

The mission statement is a list of the practical, strategic steps that will take your vision from dream to reality. Martha's list included: review written materials, develop a script, find a producer, rent studio time, find a distributor, and contact infomercial companies. She also needed to address her weakness in terms of public speaking. She added: sign up for a public speaking class, go back into therapy, and take an acting class to help overcome performance anxiety.

Although she had a long list, Martha felt challenged and excited. She would need the support of coaching to help her accomplish the steps on her list. But because the vision was a product of her deeply held values and strengths, it was uniquely suited to fascinate and appeal to her.

Exercise
WRITE YOUR VISION, PURPOSE, AND MISSION STATEMENT

Complete these three statements using short, simple sentences.

Vision: The vision I see for my future practise is

Purpose: The changes I will make within myself to fulfill this vision are

Mission: The specific steps I will take to maek this vision a reality are

---

The aligned vision process will reveal a lot about you and what is possible for you to achieve. I hope that your vision calls to you, pulling you forward to make positive, wonderful changes in your practice and your life. Making your vision a reality will depend on your ability to follow through on the steps and actions you listed in your mission statement. To do this more easily, you need to develop the dynamic mindset of a successful entrepreneur, so you can make your vision real. We will now look at what that mindset involves.

5

Entrepreneurial Mindset

The key to successful practice today is to become as proficient in the business of therapy as you are in your healing craft. In essence, you must consider yourself an entrepreneur. "Raise your hand if you are an entrepreneur," I often say to a group of therapists in a workshop. One or two people shyly raise their hands. Yet if you own a business (and your practice is a business, even if it doesn't feel like one) you qualify as an entrepreneur. For most of us, however, identifying ourselves as entrepreneurs implies more, such as having a natural drive toward business. In the words of one therapist who was bemoaning her lack of business ability to me, "It's everything I'm not." This therapist is not alone in her realization that she lacks an entrepreneurial spirit.

When Tom, a marriage and family counselor, started his practice twenty years ago, he didn't identify himself as an entrepreneur either. He followed a predictable model. First, he got his degree and license. Second, he alerted senior professionals and colleagues that he was opening a small office. He sent out announcements. Then he waited, and referrals slowly came. If he did a good job with people, he got more referrals. Tom didn't need any particular business sense to be successful. He hated marketing and felt no need to meet the public in an organized way. Even so, he soon had a viable practice.

Flash forward twenty years. Today, with a high level of competition within the counseling market, Tom finds he must be more proactive in maintaining his practice. Like it or not, Tom has decided that to be successful, he has to be a better businessperson. Being in business is *not* why Tom went to graduate school, spent countless hours in internships, and then started his practice. But it is a reality of making it in private practice today.

If you feel that being an entrepreneur is everything that you are not, you have a lot of company among your peers. I find that most therapists are lacking in the mindset and personality that is common to most successful entrepreneurs. Instead, we therapists tend to share personality traits and energetic responses to situations that are actually opposite to those shared by most entrepreneurs. By training or inclination, we are steeped in what I call "archetypal feminine energy." By feminine, please understand that I'm not talking about gender; I'm talking about a type of energy that is universal and prototypical. You can have an abundance of this energy regardless of whether you are male or female. I'll draw a distinction between feminine and masculine archetypal energy to help you understand the different personality traits of a therapist versus an entrepreneur. Once you understand the difference, I will show you how to build a bridge between the two and develop more range in your business abilities.

The feminine archetype that most therapists have in abundance is an idealistic, larger-than-life amalgam of nuturing and healing qualities. Think of the best qualities of compassion, mothering, and empathy, and you have a good idea of the archetype I am describing. Being able to access this archetype is useful when you are creating a safe holding environment for therapy. As therapists, we do this by paying attention to silence and non-verbal cues. We are trained to be sensitive and deliberate, not impulsive. We are often introverts, comfortable with the notion of "going inside ourselves" to quiet ourselves down in order to listen carefully to others, at a deep level. The feminine archetype is insight-oriented and self-aware. To be any good as a therapist, it's essential that you have enough of this feminine energy to identify emotionally with your clients.

This is just the opposite energy from what is effective in business. In business, you need a ready supply of "archetypal masculine energy." This is what I call the energetic response that helps a person move forward into the world without fear, take action effortlessly, welcome challenge and seek opportunity. The masculine archetype is a natural extrovert, relentlessly persistent, the quintessential entrepreneur. Most therapists I coach need to adopt a large dose of masculine energy to balance their surplus of feminine energy.

If this is true for you, you will want to develop a way to easily tap into this fearless masculine energy, especially when you need to be out in the world building your practice. In this chapter I will teach you a direct, easy method so that you can do this, anyplace and anytime you want. But first, let's explore the mindset of a successful entrepreneur so you can begin to consciously think and act more like a savvy businessperson.

ENTREPRENEURIAL ATTRIBUTES

The most successful entrepreneurs I know personally or read about share similar qualities in how they perceive themselves and the world. Although entrepreneurs are most often born and not made, I have found that therapists can learn to embrace the best of these mental qualities. Successful entrepreneurs have these six attributes:

1. Given an obstacle, they look for an opportunity.
2. Faced with a problem, they are both optimistic and pragmatic.
3. They count on a lot from themselves and others.
4. Persistence is their middle name.
5. They are profit-driven and enjoy making money.
6. They operate from a mindset of abundance.

I invite you to think about the above qualities. Which do you already possess and which do you need to take on? If you were to adopt all of these attributes, how would your practice and your life change as a result?

GIVEN AN OBSTACLE, THEY LOOK FOR AN OPPORTUNITY

Good chess players welcome a challenging situation on the chessboard. Faced with difficulty, they begin to scan for all the possibilities, all the combinations of moves that could turn things their way. Successful entrepreneurs often create the idea for a business by looking for a problem and finding a unique solution. If you can be alert to obstacles, you can sense when there is a need in the marketplace. Every problem holds the seeds of some business opportunity.

When a wellness center moved in next door to Michelle's solo acupuncture practice, she worried that the competition would cut into her business. They had an acupuncturist on staff and were a large practice with an advertising budget she couldn't match. She was frightened and her first impulse was to try to get out of her lease and move to a different location.

I encouraged her to stay calm, instead of running, and look for the business opportunity. The first thing I suggested was that she make contact with the owner of the wellness center to explore possibilities for collaboration. She balked, insisting that the center didn't need another acupuncturist. With some misgivings, she attended the wellness center's open house. The owner was glad to meet her. As she had suspected, he didn't need her services, but he introduced her to Sarah, the center's acupuncturist.

My next suggestion was that Michelle follow through and initiate more contact with Sarah. Again Michelle stalled, saying that she couldn't see the point, but she called Sarah and asked her to lunch. At lunch, Sarah mentioned that she was cutting back her hours at the center to have a baby, and she was worried the center might replace her. Michelle saw an opening for collaboration. A month later, the two approached the center owner and negotiated an arrangement to allow Michelle to subcontract with the center, filling in for Sarah's absence. Michelle gave the center a percentage of the fee from any referrals sent to her. The center saw this as a win-win situation. They could service their clients, and continue to employ Sarah. Michelle appreciated the extra business and the opportunity to be a part of a larger organization without sacrificing her autonomy. Michelle came to see the wellness center as the source of occasional referrals and future business, rather than as competition.

THEY ARE BOTH OPTIMISTIC AND PRAGMATIC

Successful entrepreneurs have a dual ability to hope for the best, while planning for the worst. It is often helpful to think with two minds. If you aren't able to split your attention and consider one side and then the other, find a coach, colleague, or mentor who can help.

Jack came to see me in crisis. His physical therapy practice employed three therapists and in the space of one month, all announced that they were leaving for one reason or another. He was steeped in the pragmatics—thinking up solutions for how to handle the flow of clients and cover the loss of income.

Since he was great at planning for the worst, I took on the voice of optimism. I encouraged him to see this as a good thing, a chance to upgrade his business by finding a better quality of therapist. He had been unhappy with his staff for a long time, feeling that they were not team players. With my coaching, he wrote an ad that emphasized loyalty, one of his core values, seeking young therapists who would grow with the practice. He found several wonderful therapists to replace those who left, and they brought with them a new quality he hadn't expected: ambition. Not only did they want to grow with the practice, they also had lots of ideas about how to grow the practice and help him expand, which he welcomed. When he looks back on this time, he speaks of it as his business "turnaround," when he went from a traditional hierarchical practice to a dynamic, team-built effort.

THEY COUNT ON A LOT FROM THEMSELVES AND OTHERS

It's not enough to have good ideas for your practice; you must also have the willpower to put them into action. All successful entrepreneurs are hard-working and use their drive to prevail; many entrepreneurs have the ability to bring others along the path with them. The best entrepreneurs do this by requiring a lot, and then giving back in equal measure.

One of the best examples of this I have witnessed is outside of the therapy business. Six years ago Reza, an immigrant to the United States, started a small architectural firm. The building economy was in a recession, so the new start-up business could only support one full-time employee, the owner. Reza worked in the business all day, every day.

Reza, who in fractured English describes himself as a "one-man person," did everything—computer drafting, design, sales, marketing, administration, and also stayed nights to paint the office, wire phone lines, and install carpeting.

By the second year he had enough work to hire a part-time draftsperson. I began to notice his unique pattern of hiring and training. He hired a young woman who had questionable work habits, because she was willing to work within his limited budget. I watched as he pushed and prodded her to give more passion to her work, demanding as much from her as he did from himself. He instructed her painstakingly in how to deliver a first-rate package of construction documents. She produced far beyond what she had in her previous job experience and became a highly profitable employee. His next employee followed a similar pattern. This was a young, intelligent yet unskilled man. Again, I watched Reza give him excellent training and insist that he have high work standards and ethics. Once trained, he also became enormously profitable for Reza's firm.

As his business grew, I noticed he consistently attracted employees, consultants, and associates who were immigrants, like himself, in the early stages of establishing themselves. For employees, Reza was more than an employer. He was their trainer and coach, helping them to build technical skills, learn to communicate with the public, and take on immediate responsibility. For consultants, he was a mentor, showing them how to attract clients and run a profitable business. For associates, he was a tireless resource and a friend. As he gave, they gave back. Employees worked hard for the training they received. Consultants returned Reza's generosity by bringing in new jobs, access to new networks, and much-needed skills.

By year five the small firm reached the half-million dollar mark in fees and had a reputation for excellent service with several national clients. Whenever I asked him what was most important to him in his work, he always immediately targeted two things: delivering an excellent product and giving others (his staff and consultants) a chance to grow along with him.

This is a powerful attribute for every business owner's mindset—expecting a lot from others and wanting a lot for others. For therapists it translates into having very high standards about the way you run your practice and setting guidelines that let you do your finest work. It also means that you inspire those around you, colleagues and clients alike, to join you in reaching for their personal best.

PERSISTENCE IS THEIR MIDDLE NAME

So often, success is a factor of simply showing up. And showing up. And showing up. The entrepreneurial spirit is marked by the ability to persist at a goal, regardless of adversity. In my coaching classes, I hear therapists tell me about many failures they have had. "I tried to network. I called area churches and met with several ministers. They seemed to like me, but I didn't get a referral. I've decided networking doesn't work for me." Or "I set up meetings with two other associates to work together on a project. It never jelled. I got discouraged and decided to let it go."

Good ideas require persistence to succeed. In my experience, therapists give up too easily. I hear about many great ideas that ended as failures; the therapists abandoned their good ideas because they didn't get immediate results or the effort required was greater than the therapist thought it *should* be.

The best models of persistence are salespeople. Its easy to coach salespeople. If you help them to set meaningful goals, hold them accountable for their daily progress, and encourage them to structure a system of intrinsic rewards, they produce endlessly, persisting in the face of multiple rejections. I find that therapists also flourish when coached this way. Mike wanted to expand his referral network and asked for some coaching from me to do this. Each week I asked him to e-mail me a list of people he was going to contact and then report back to me on his results. He rewarded himself by scheduling something he loved to do, a long walk in the park, on Friday evening, after he made his weekly calls. Every eight weeks I had him make follow-up calls to previous contacts. He kept notes and found that it required *four* contacts with any individual source before he would get an actual referral. He was surprised and at times frustrated at the effort required, but that was simply what it took. With sufficient structure in place to keep him on track, his networking efforts paid off.

Each month I lead a one-hour motivation group for therapists in my local area. Even one hour a month is enough for therapists to make steady, solid progress on their goals. Participants tell me that the week prior to the motivation group is often their most productive, knowing they will have to account to me and the group. They redouble their efforts to meet that month's goal. Create a motivation and accountability system for yourself, so that you can persist with all of your good ideas until you reach success.

THEY ARE PROFIT-DRIVEN AND ENJOY MAKING MONEY

When I teach the eight-week Private Practice Success Program, the topic of money is covered during week six. At the end of week five, I say,

"Next week we discuss everything you ever wanted to know about making money in private practice. Money is one of my favorite topics." I deliver this with a genuine smile. Most often, the class looks back at me with amazement. A therapist with a good relationship to money?

In my twenties, I used to listen to a charismatic preacher broadcast on the radio from California. Every Sunday, he hosted a show on the subject of prosperity, broadcast directly from his church. He would start the show with a call-and-response chant with his parishioners. The call was always the same: *Money is my friend,* he would sing out. *Money is my friend,* the congregation responded. Back and forth they went, affirming an affinity to money. This was my introduction to the concept of relating positively to money, the way that I would relate to a good friend.

Later, my father showed me how to build a relationship with profit. Prior to becoming a therapist, I worked for six years as general manager in the family business. My father, a refined man with a degree in business administration, owned and operated a scrap metal business that was unusually profitable within the industry. In a historically rough-and-tumble business, he employed a classic, textbook model of making a profit honorably. He carefully watched his expenses, took moderate risks, and followed a clear formula regarding buying and selling. When I questioned him once as to why he wanted to own a scrap business, which held little status and no glamour, he told me that early on he realized he could make a good profit. He was teaching me the relevance of profit to business.

Every day that I worked for him I understood one thing: in order to keep the business intact, all of my actions at work needed to show a profit. I was impressed that everyone in the company, from laborers to management, understood that profit was the currency that allowed the business to exist. When we made a profit, everyone benefited. More profit meant new equipment, better bonuses, a cushion through the slow market times, and a more relaxed work environment. The stronger the business, the more money circulated within and throughout the company.

In the therapy business, being profit-driven means wanting *everyone* connected with your practice to do well financially. The stronger your practice, the happier you will be, the more welcoming your office can look, the more training you can afford, the more you will have to offer your clients. The profit you make defines the ability of your business to stay strong and help others. It's hard to be an advocate for your clients' physical and mental well-being, when your business is financially ill. Chapter 10 will answer your questions about money and profit, giving you a tool kit of strategies to help you build a highly profitable practice.

THEY OPERATE FROM A MINDSET OF ABUNDANCE

The most successful therapists I interview feel no competition with other therapists. Granted, they are usually at a level of mastery of their craft and have a well-deserved reputation in place, but they often have something more: a belief in abundance. They believe there are enough clients, money, and business out there for themselves and others. It's not that they ignore market saturation. It's that they see so much opportunity, they rarely feel worried or anxious about the market being large enough to support their small share.

Ask people who love being in business what motivates them. Money will be on the list, but it is rarely the sole answer. More often, you will hear how much they love producing, creating, developing, serving, or making a difference. This is abundance.

I coach therapists to make a distinction between abundance and money. Abundance as a concept is about a way of life and speaks to the ability to have everything circulate. It means making things happen, having a pool of energy, time, friends, business, clients, and, yes, money. Money is a subset in the larger field of abundance. Money is currency with a storage value. In and of itself, it is only legal tender, paper or metal.

When you focus only on money, you are putting all your energy and attention on stockpiling legal tender. A business coach I know refers to this as "dead energy." It's like meditating on a golden cup, rich but empty. When you focus on abundance, you concentrate on "live energy"—connections, opportunity, potential. This is akin to meditating on the same cup, this time seeing it filled to overflowing with sparkling spring water that never runs out, no matter how much you consume. When you focus on abundance, you often end up with money and much more.

Suzanna, a psychotherapist, announced at our first coaching session that she was in crisis. Her divorce was now final and she was broke, with a young child to support. The divorce had been very traumatic. During that time she fell ill and cut back her hours as a therapist so that now her private practice was small. She needed money badly and wondered if I could help her fast enough.

I requested that she complete a needs assessment. I asked her to look at a list of fifty physical and emotional needs and pick those that were in short supply for her. She selected money, security, work, friends, support, respect, and inner peace. I then asked her to design one project that would, in some way, begin to address these needs. She was uncomfortable that I wasn't narrowly focusing on helping her make more money, but she agreed to try the exercise.

The next week she brought in her project. During the week she had been to a networking meeting where a group of colleagues raised the subject of stress in their lives. They casually discussed how they would like to have some form of relaxation on a regular basis. Suzanna, who had strong skills in this area, asked what I thought about creating a free peer stress-reduction group as her project. She would invite the colleagues she had met at the meeting, which would address her need to make more friends and possibly gather emotional support. Running the group would fill some hours in her empty schedule and meet her need to feel more productive, as though she were working more. Since the group emphasized relaxation, she would do the exercises along with the group, meeting her need for inner peace. She might gain some self-respect, if not respect from others, by taking a leadership role to start the group.

The only need her project did not address was money. Suzanna had some vague ideas of how the free group might eventually lead to running a group for a fee, but she felt that was in the future. She was annoyed that her project had not addressed her immediate need for money. After all, this was what she needed most and why she had come to see me. "It's just like me to forget about the money in designing a project," she complained. "I'm hopeless when it comes to making money."

I disagreed, sensing that her involvement in a positive project without the stress of money might help her shift her mindset to abundance. My belief was that money would follow abundance, not the other way around.

Suzanna began the group the next week. She enjoyed the experience of leadership. Running the group gave her confidence in her abilities. I encouraged her to enhance the effects of the group by beginning to use a daily business affirmation, "I create an abundance of work and support for myself." This helped to keep her focused on the rewards of her actions, rather than on what was lacking.

At the end of the fourth stress-reduction group, one colleague asked Suzanna if she was interested in creating a stress-reduction program for executives in her company. Suzanna was thrilled. She used some coaching time with me to develop a proposal and within a month she had secured a part-time contract for a year, generating a small but steady source of income. She also found that the exposure to executives resulted in some clients who wanted additional individual sessions. Looking back on the experience, Suzanna told me that although her skills were attractive to her colleague and helped her get the contract, she felt that the mindset of abundance was equally important to her success.

Exercise
CREATING ABUNDANCE

1. Identify a short list of your physical and emotional needs that are not being met in your business or in your personal life.
2. Design a project for yourself that begins to meet many of the needs, even in small ways.
3. Begin the project immediately. Moving forward is essential to manifesting abundance.
4. Use a business affirmation (see chapter 3) daily to help you maintain a mindset of abundance by focusing on any small rewards.
5. Don't judge your immediate results. Stick with the project and keep going.

OVERCOMING BARRIERS

When I was retooling my private practice to work with adults instead of children, I augmented my clinical hours by doing some organizational development. Working with a colleague, I delivered daylong training sessions to groups of managers in government organizations. Usually the director of human resources would start the day by introducing us to the group as "psychotherapists who work in Maryland." At the close of each session, it was very common for many of the managers, both men and women, to approach us and say, "I want you to know you are the first therapists I have ever met in person. I didn't know therapists looked and talked like you. You seem so friendly and *normal*."

Where have all the therapists been hiding? Part of our poor public image is due to the unfortunate media portrayal of therapists that ranges from the comedic to the criminal. But we must also take responsibility for how little we have done in our professions to help the public overcome the multiple barriers to understanding who we are and what therapy has to offer.

As therapists, we spend so much time in and around our profession that it begins to define our world. For us, going to therapy is a normal part of a life. We forget how many people see therapy as mysterious, frightening, or taboo. This is not helped by the depiction of therapy in popular culture, which tends to portray therapists as ineffective at best, or dangerous at worst. One exception is the daytime talk shows, which often feature therapists in a positive light, as experts who are asked to comment on the emotional problems exhibited by the guests on the show. And just in case you think that the media doesn't have an effect on the public regarding the way people view therapy, consider this: A mental health clinic director I spoke to said his clinic regularly tracked referral sources of new clients. To his surprise, *Oprah* was one of the major referral sources. Whenever Oprah hosted a show on family problems or addictions featuring a therapist who offered advice, his clinic was flooded with new intakes.

You need to become aware of the barriers the public has to overcome, in order to use your services. A successful business owner understands the role of public perception. If you are in the business of therapy, here are the barriers you may be up against and what to do about them.

THERAPY SIGNALS WEAKNESS

Our culture is based on the notion of personal independence. People seeking therapy are seen by others as dependent and weak. Many people hate to ask for help, and prefer to be self-reliant, at all costs. This stops people in our society from seeking counseling or other forms of health care. If you go to therapy, you put the therapist in the position of expert, taking away your "independence."

What you can do about it:

- Reframe your role as one of mentoring or assisting.
- Adopt a collaborative position.
- Show respect for your clients in your promotional materials.
- Be willing to offer yourself as a resource, not an expert.

THERAPY IS TOO EXPENSIVE

The cost of therapy stops many people, especially without insurance. Many people who need therapy define it as a luxury item. Luxury items are dispensable when finances are tight.

What you can do about it:

Offer a menu of therapy services for clients, from most expensive to less expensive, and encourage them to design a therapy program with you that they can afford.

For example, I offer individual sessions, evening group therapy, daylong workshops, and half-day workshops. My clients can mix and match from this list, with my recommendations to guide them. We will look further at how to develop a menu of services in chapter 8, which may be an unorthodox approach to therapy within a medical model, but within a personal-growth model it makes perfect sense. We will examine how you can set up a personal-growth model in chapter 12.

THERAPY IS MYSTERIOUS

It's difficult to explain exactly how therapy works, even for those who practice it. Most health care falls somewhere between art and science. If you practice methods of alternative therapy that are unknown to the public, such as Rolfing, Reiki, or energy healing, you have an added job in terms of explaining your craft.

What you can do about it:

Educate others. You will need to have a concise way to explain what you are doing and why. It helps to have lots of printed materials to give clients, in the form of brochures, articles, books, or pamphlets. Have a way for the public to preview your work. In future chapters I will outline several ideas about how to educate the public effectively about your work.

THERAPY IS TABOO

Portions of our society actively discourage the use of therapy. Religious and cultural concerns about therapy include a belief that therapy is bad and are mingled with the desire to keep emotional problems private, within the purview of the family or the church. Clients come to sessions secretly, not telling family members, friends, or ministers for fear of censure. Forms of therapy that rely on physical touch (massage), needles (acupuncture), guided imagery, or meditation can face an even larger barrier than talk therapy, based on the lack of public acceptance.

What you can do about it:

- Be sensitive about cultural differences.
- Educate potential clients about the process.
- Suggest additional reading.

THERAPY IS NOT CONVENIENT

Many people have trouble physically getting to therapy. The barrier may be your location, the hours you work, or that you are hard to reach and don't return calls.

What you can do about it:

- Be reachable.
- Be flexible.
- Use technology—e-mail, voice mail, fax lines—to let your clients connect with you.
- Consider working from several offices or locating your office near public transportation.

ENTREPRENEURIAL SPIRIT

When you think of the quintessential entrepreneur, who comes to mind? Maybe it's Bill Gates of Microsoft, or Mrs. Fields of chocolate-chip cookie fame, or someone closer to home, a friend or relative you admire who has built a great business. Do you ever wish you had some of their entrepreneurial spirit inside of you to tap into when you need to be out in the world building your practice? I have come to believe we all have the ability to tap into just such an internal resource. This entrepreneurial spirit is one that can be accessed by every therapist, using a process of guided imagery. Marilyn Ellis, a psychotherapist in Virginia, originally taught me this process, and I have adapted it as a business resource. You will notice that certain phrases are repeated several times for extra emphasis.

Exercise
MEETING YOUR INNER ENTREPRENEUR

Tape record the following instructions and listen to them, or ask someone to read them to you in a slow voice, giving you plenty of time to complete each step.

Sit in a comfortable chair that has a firm back.

Close your eyes and relax your body, using your breath as a focal point. Imagine directing your breath into any areas of stress or tension in your body, breathing into them. Breathe in and out easily and effortlessly, letting your breath help you to relax and be comfortable.

Now imagine a person whom you actually know, have seen, read about, watched in a movie, or create in fantasy, who might be a man or a woman, but represents the archetype of masculine energy to you—the energy that moves into the world without fear. This person has a high comfort level of self, takes action effortlessly, with pleasure, has enormous vitality, and moves forward into the world without fear. This is a person who takes risks, is expansive, welcomes public interaction, enjoys competition and challenge, radiates strength, and moves forward into the world without fear.

See this person in front of you. Note the color of his/her eyes, hear the sound of his/her breath, feel the heat from his/her body energy. Now imagine placing this person directly behind you, right at your back. Literally lean back into your chair, leaning back into him/her. Lean back and sense his/her strength, vitality, and energy. Lean back and see how it feels to move into the world without fear. Lean back and feel that level of effortless energy. Lean back and take in strength.

From this place of leaning back, think about any challenge you currently have in your private practice. Notice any new thoughts or ideas that come from thinking about this challenge, from this position.

Open your eyes and write down what you remember.

You can revisit your inner entrepreneur at any time, to get a new perspective on a business problem or to help you to stay motivated When you feel the need, just close your eyes, imagine your inner entrepreneur at your back, and lean into him or her.

Here is the experience of Sam, a social worker, after completing the exercise and meeting his inner entrepreneur during a practice-building class.

"Sam, what can you share about your experience with this exercise?"

"It was really surprising for me. My inner entrepreneur is a blend of two people that I haven't thought of for years. They just popped into my mind and became a team, supporting me. The quality that they each share is that they're really fearless in terms of being verbal and articulate about themselves and their work. They're enthusiastic and they say what they're thinking."

"What did it feel like to lean back into their energy?"

"It was really an eye opener for me because I struggle with a sense of not wanting to show off. I believe if I tell people about my successes as a therapist, I am showing off. I often want to say something positive about myself to a colleague, but then I immediately censure myself. So I don't say anything."

"What business challenge did you think about during the exercise?"

"I thought about a talk I need to give at my agency job, to present a method for helping couples cope with the death of a child. I am really good at helping couples stay strong, not letting the tragedy tear apart their marriages. I have written a paper on this and want to share it with others. I think I am doing something new and different in the way that I counsel, and I'm excited about it. In fact, I'm more than excited. I'm proud of what I am developing!"

"You have just elegantly demonstrated 'showing off' to us. How comfortable does it feel right now, to tell us about your success?"

"It feels fine, like I have a sense of normal self-esteem. I feel confident telling you what I do well. I think I can use this exercise to make my presentation go much better."

Now that you know how to develop an entrepreneurial mindset, it's time to start the hands-on work required to build an ideal practice. The next chapter will help you to achieve the first of several building blocks by showing you a key step in knowing how to generate a flow of quality referrals into your practice.

Part II

Building Blocks

6
Your Basic Message

Put me in a room with a group of successful therapists who are talking about their work and I know I will be intrigued. No matter what their therapeutic methods, there is one thing I can count on when I listen to successful therapists talk—I will hear voices rich with passion, energy, and conviction. Being passionate about your work is the best way to become a great therapist. Knowing how to convey that passion through the spoken word is the best way to become successful in the business of therapy.

When I became a business coach, the one skill that I most wanted to teach therapists was how to speak about their work with passion and clarity. I spent months trying to formulate the best way to help my colleagues do this seemingly simple task—talk about themselves in a lucid, positive, and energetic manner. I finally found a formula that helps a lot of therapists do this well. I call this strategy *articulating your basic message.*

Learning to state your *basic message*—a clear, concise, sentence that describes the essence of who you are and what you do as a therapist—sounds simple, but most therapists don't do it well. It can be painful to watch and listen to a therapist as she tries to explain what she does. The jargon or technical terms that creep into the explanation are often incomprehensible to the average person. Ask the same therapist to elaborate on how her service benefits others, and she becomes even more ill at ease. This problem is endemic. How many times have you found yourself tongue-tied at a social gathering when the inevitable question comes up?

"So, Lynn, what do you do?"
"I'm a psychotherapist. I do therapy with adults who feel depressed or anxious. I specialize in a type of group therapy that is very expe-

*riential. [Deep sigh, eyes rolling upward.] I guess you could call it
neo-Reichian, or maybe it's more post-Gestalt, although I add in elements that are clearly psychodynamic. I am eclectic, so I integrate
the emotive aspects of the field with a cognitive approach, no wait,
I see I've lost you."*

You get the picture. Explaining the work of therapy can seem difficult,
because so much of what we do is complicated, nonverbal, or technical. It's
hard to sum up your training, philosophy, and life's work in a sentence or
two, and still keep the conversation going. Your unconscious sighs and eye
rolling may reflect how difficult it is to talk about your work succinctly, but
it sends a mixed message: I am not comfortable explaining what I do. This
is not the message to send to others, especially if you would like to build
your business based on attraction—encouraging those clients who most
need your services to be able to find you and perceive a favorable impression of you.

Instead of feeling tongue-tied, imagine if the next time someone asked
what you do for a living, you could make direct eye contact, smile, and,
using one or two clear sentences, convey just the right mixture of information and positive conviction:

*"I am a psychotherapist. I specialize in showing adults, like your-
self, how to reach their full potential. I help people go from feeling
stuck in some area of their lives to achieving their own definition of
success using an innovative, powerful method of group therapy."*

When you find the words you love to say, your basic message comes
through loud and clear: I am passionate about what I get to do each day. I
love my work. I help others in an important way.

Learning to write and deliver your basic message may be the most effective step you ever take in attracting quality clients to your practice. To
date, of all the practice-building strategies I teach, articulating your basic
message has proven to have the most immediate results for therapists. One
therapist recently wrote me to say:

*Persistence pays off. I am filling my practice with quality referrals
only. I use the "basic message" you taught to introduce myself*

almost every day, in social gatherings, networking meetings, or even at the grocery store. You would not believe how well it works for me. I even got a radio interview because a reporter I met casually was so fascinated by my introduction.

During every eight-week class I teach, I hear dozens of stories about the effects of this strategy. It's so deceptively simple to speak about your work with a combination of authority and love. One of the most interesting benefits of this exercise I have observed is how the discipline of compressing your message into a sentence or two creates a new level of professional focus and clarity within each therapist. If you work your way through this exercise to its completion, I guarantee you will have to think about yourself and your services in a new way. With an articulated basic message, you will finally know how to talk about your work publicly. Instead of getting the usual bored or puzzled looks, you may hear your listeners say: *Tell me more.* This is the first step to effortlessly generating a referral every time you say hello.

CREATING YOUR MESSAGE

I want you to create a fifteen-second verbal introduction that sums up the essence of who you are as a therapist in an engaging and attractive manner. Think of this as an elevator introduction. You get on an elevator with someone who turns to you and asks who you are and what you do. You have a brief time, ten or fifteen seconds between floors, to introduce yourself. Can you do it in a way that generates authentic interest, so that your listener requests your business card? Here's the criteria of a well-crafted basic message:

- *No more than three short sentences.* This is an introduction you are going to memorize, so keep it brief and easy to remember and hold it in your mind at all times.
- *No jargon words or technical terms.* If you use a technical term in your introduction, your listener will tend to stop at that term and not hear the rest of the introduction. If you must use a technical term, anticipate

that your introduction will do little more than explain the term. My advice is that you drop all jargon and let the introduction be about who you are and what you do, rather than the techniques you use.

- *Keep your language upbeat and positive.* This is an opportunity to attract others, not discourage them. I want you to project what excites you about your work, not what you find difficult or depressing.

- *Target only one aspect of your work.* You may have a diverse set of skills, but this is a short introduction. You simply can't say it all. I suggest you target the aspect of your practice that you want to build—an area where you want to generate referrals. Are you trying to fill a new group, reach a specific clientele, attract an ideal client type? You will have more impact if you let this introduction speak to just one component of what you do.

- *Learn to love to say this introduction.* The most important part of this introduction is learning to love to say it. The sole purpose of the basic message is to become a container for your passion about your craft. The words are just a vehicle to express your underlying feelings and enthusiasm. When you can speak about your work with love, people will naturally want to move closer to you. Passion is attractive.

STYLES

I have found four styles that can help structure your basic message. Pick one to work with. Under each style I have given you several examples that come from my classes. Don't just borrow one of these, because it won't carry your particular essence. Do the hard work and compose your own.

All styles begin with this first sentence:

"My name is _____ and I am a _____."

The first blank is your name. The second is your professional title. Some therapists have trouble deciding which title to use. Use the simplest and easiest for the public to understand. Make sure to use the one you most like to say. One psychologist introduced herself as a "behavioral psychologist." I noticed that each time she said it she frowned a little. When I reflected this back to her, she said she preferred to simply say psychologist, but had been told by a professor that it was too vague a term. I coached her to stop using the word behavioral; her negative nonverbals defeated the purpose of having an attractive introduction. She now says, "I am a psychologist" with a smile.

STYLE 1

"I specialize in _____; I really enjoy _____."

Grief and bereavement counselor: "I specialize in helping parents who have lost a child move through their feelings of pain to find meaning and purpose in their lives."

Assertiveness trainer: "I specialize in teaching adults how to communicate their heartfelt needs and wants to others."

Pastoral counselor: "I specialize in working with members of the clergy who have a burning passion to live in harmony within God's light."

Yoga teacher: "I show my students how to achieve more physical comfort and renewed confidence in their ability to move their bodies."

Family therapist: "I specialize in helping families shift from discord to harmony, to go from fighting to enjoying each other."

Energy healer: "I specialize in showing men and women how to experience total health, by connecting mind, body, and spirit."

STYLE 2

"I support _____ in their desire to _____ by the means of _____."

Acupuncturist: "I support my patients to feel at peace within their own bodies and I do this by using a traditional, effective, Chinese method of healing."

Family therapist: "I support adolescents in their desire to become independent, and I do this by helping them identify their true potential."

Psychotherapist: "I help people in their desire to close the gap between where they are right now and where they want to be in the future, with the support of individual therapy sessions."

Addictions counselor: "I support alcoholics in their desire to stop drinking forever. I do this in group counseling sessions. Even if you don't know how you will ever stop drinking, I've been there and I know how to help you."

STYLE 3

"You know how _____ ? Well, I _____."

Behavioral psychologist: "You know how a sports coach helps you train your body for peak performance? Well, I am a behavioral psychologist and I can help you train your mind for mental excellence."

Movement specialist: "I do a very unique type of body therapy. You know how you can go to a favorite place in nature and just being there makes you feel more alive and peaceful? The movement techniques I teach can help you achieve that same sense of aliveness and peace within your body, on a daily basis."

Couples counselor: "You know how 50 percent of all marriages end up in divorce? Well, I work with couples to reverse this trend, by giving them skills and tools that can immediately make a marriage work better."

STYLE 4

"If you _____, I'm the kind of (therapist) who can help you to _____."

Personal coach: "If you feel without direction in your life, I'm the kind of personal coach who can help you design and then implement a road map to success."

Psychotherapist: "If you are a person who has been in therapy before and is ready to try it again in order to make lasting change, I am the kind of therapist who will keep you working deeply so that you reach the goals you want."

Transpersonal psychologist: "If you long for a life that is based on purpose and meaning, I'm the kind of therapist that can keep you focused on making choices that reflect your highest values."

Get the idea? Your fieldwork is to pick a style and compose your own introduction, get feedback, and practice saying it until you are very comfortable with the way you look and sound. The feedback is important. Ask people you trust to tell you how you come across. In the classes I teach, my clients spend several weeks refining their introductions and getting feedback from others. My goal is that everyone leaves the course with a sparkling introduction that they love to say.

You will know you have done your job well with your introduction if you get one of the two following responses from a listener: *"Tell me more"* or *"I know someone who needs your card."* Either one of these responses are "wins." To get the first response, you must have more to tell, so don't say it all in your introduction. Keep it brief and make it provocative. Remember, you are inviting a listener into the beginning process of a relationship, the first step in generating referrals. You have to make space for them in the process, including a space for their questions and comments. Say a sentence or two, then pause and take a breath before continuing.

Exercise
CREATE YOUR BASIC MESSAGE

Write your basic message, using the above criteria and selecting one of the following styles. Start with: "My name is _____ and I am a _____." Then choose from one of the following styles:

Style 1: "I specialize in _____; I really enjoy _____."

Style 2: "I support _____ in their desire to _____ by the means of _____."

Style 3: "You know how _____? Well, I _____."

Style 4: "If you _____, I'm the kind of (therapist) who can help you to _____."

Get feedback from at least five other people you trust. Rehearse saying it out loud until you can deliver it calmly, conversationally, and with a natural smile.

EXPANDING YOUR MESSAGE

Once you have written your basic message in the form of an introduction, you can expand it. Here are some steps you can take so that your message reaches others:

SPEAK TO ORGANIZATIONS—ON MESSAGE

The easiest way to expand your reach is to speak to more people about your message. One low-cost way to speak in public is to let organizations sponsor you. You may not be paid for your talk, but you also will not have to carry the cost of direct mail or advertising. You will have access to many more people than you might reach on your own.

If you have tried to go this route already, you may have learned that public speaking does not always result in referrals. I was very curious as to why some therapists find public speaking to be their best way to generate referrals, and others find it absolutely useless. After interviewing those therapists for whom it does offer good results, I believe the decisive factor in attracting referrals from speaking is whether or not you are speaking on your basic message, in other words, speaking with passion. Those therapists who stick to their basic message give the same talk each time, although they often use different titles. They know their commitment and passion about their message will reach like-minded others, and referrals will naturally occur. They relax and let their message carry them.

Louise, a licensed counselor in private practice, has a passion for working with couples. She got invited to give talks at "brown bag" lunches inside small corporations and larger government agencies. During these on-site lunches, employees attend a free hour talk. Louise gave a lot of talks, but the result was the same: no referrals. She picked topics about the workplace that she thought would make sense to her audience. Louise continued to offer the talks because she had heard it was a good way to get more clients, even though it wasn't working for her.

Then the director from a women's center asked her to speak to her staff on the topic of relationships. Bingo! Now she was speaking about her passion. At the first talk, Louise got excited, and it showed. She laughed a lot and engaged with the audience. She immediately got a referral from a woman in the audience who became a wonderful client and referred a few friends. Each time Louise talks on relationships and allows her passion to show, she gets referrals.

If you think about it, this makes common sense. Certain emotions are very attractive, and passion and enthusiasm are two of them. This is why it is so important for you to first define your basic message—what you love, what is unique about you and the work you do. Orient both your practice and your public speaking around your message.

WRITE A NEWSLETTER—ON MESSAGE

Many therapists I coach generate a steady flow of referrals through their practice newsletters when they are *on message*. A good practice newsletter is one that you author, not one that you purchase prewritten from another company. It lets clients know more about who you are and includes your best thinking. It's written from your heart and contains something of value for your readers.

Are you unsure about what to include in your newsletter? Keeping it simple can be effective. Have you read an important book or taken some training that is inspiring you in your work? Write about that. Are you finding a new technique or a thematic topic that occurs in sessions that fascinates you? That would be a good thing to include. Your newsletter can be as simple as one typewritten page. Just make it of value to others, instead of promotional. This is not a flyer, advertising your services. Your newsletter is another way to extend your reach and express the essence of your work.

Here are ten good reasons for writing a newsletter:

1. *You're published!* Publishing a newsletter requires only your computer or a copying machine for you to become a writer. After editing several newsletters for profit and nonprofit organizations, I realized that newsletters are the most effective, low-cost, and easy way to get your ideas into print and in front of a wider audience.
2. *It's educational for your clients.* I suggest that all my coaching clients start their newsletter distribution right in their offices, making them available to their existing clients. If you take time and make your

newsletter interesting and informative, it can educate your clients in two ways: first, it lets your clients know more about your services and your philosophy; second, it lets them know how to explain you to others.

3. *It soft sells your services.* Newsletters are not quite advertising, although you may well have a portion devoted to explaining your services or upcoming events. The bulk of what is written needs to be of value, that is, your best thinking.

4. *It will force you to stay in touch with your mailing list on a regular basis.* If you have a mailing list that you ignore, a newsletter with a quarterly publication date will force you to stay current. The rule of referrals is that people come to therapy when they are ready. That can be a long wait. There is nothing you can do to rush another person's process to get ready. It helps to simply stay in touch. I have had many people contact me after several years of hearing my name or getting a mailing. They waited until they were ready. Staying in touch with them via my newsletter is one way to help them feel connected to me and makes it easier for them to call, when the time is right.

5. *It gives your clients something to hold onto.* A marketing executive I talked with told me that the major value of a brochure or a newsletter is the security value that attaches to a tangible item. People like to hold something in their hands. It's nice to have a newsletter, instead of a brochure, to send out when people ask for more information about what you do, because it offers you the opportunity to say more about your practice.

6. *It will make you think about and articulate your thoughts about your work.* I publish three newsletters twice each year. This sounds like a lot, but it is actually very manageable. Two are sent by direct mail and one by e-mail. Every six months, when I am faced with writing three short articles, I get re-invigorated about my work.

7. *It can be passed around to others.* One group practice of six therapists pools their separate mailing lists to compile a list of twelve hundred names. Every therapist writes a small, nonpromotional article that would be of interest to the public, and all the articles are combined for a multipage newsletter. Their newsletters are low-tech— no graphics, typed on plain paper. The articles are well written and the

newsletter has legs—it gets passed around from clients to friends, generating new business for the whole practice.

8. *It generates spin-off.* My newsletters go out to a relatively small mailing list, yet they have yielded radio interviews, speaking engagements, and a part-time teaching position. I have also had my articles excerpted and placed onto a popular Internet site, and as a result received calls and e-mails from around the globe.

9. *It will help you feel like an expert.* Building a reputation starts with having something to say or share and going public with it. Here is a forum for you to begin to promote your expertise. Writing will help you define your philosophy and identify your professional goals.

10. *They are inexpensive to produce.* Your newsletter can be one page, front and back. I produce mine on my PC. I write a short article, include a boxed quote, and a top-ten list. I add a small bio and a list of services. I have the finished product photocopied or professionally printed on a glossy paper for a more professional look. Total cost for seven hundred copies of a folded, one-page newsletter with two colors of ink is usually three hundred dollars at my local printer. The return in business always covers this expense.

Even a one-sided newsy "letter" sent to your mailing list and existing clients is a good first step. You can grow into the process and let yourself have a learning curve. E-mail newsletters may be the lowest cost of all to produce and send, allowing you to reach large groups of people without mailing costs of any kind. If you are producing an e-mail newsletter, ask your web server to set you up for "listserve." Listserve automates subscription to your e-mail newsletter, so that you can post your newsletter on the "list of lists" (a general listing service) or have people subscribe automatically from your website. Your web server will also show you how to compose and send a newsletter to your entire list with the push of a button. You will need to edit your e-mail articles thoroughly and strive for brevity. People at a computer lose patience with anything that is too long, since it has to be scrolled through and can be more difficult to read than a printed paper. You may not have the benefit of graphics, so make sure that your content reflects a lot of valuable ideas and some helpful information.

WRITE FOR PUBLICATION

Anna, a counselor who specializes in helping single people find loving relationships, wrote a one-hundred-page manual she called *Fix Your Bad Habits and Find a Good Mate.* Since she was on a very limited budget, she hired a freelance editor to polish her writing and had the manuscript copied and bound for ten dollars a copy. Book in hand, she began to teach a workshop by the same name for singles; the book was included as part of the cost of the workshop. With this experience behind her, Anna felt confident to approach a small, local newspaper with an article based on the first chapter. She added anecdotes from her workshops to make the article more lively and relevant. The newspaper printed her article. She wrote another the next month and submitted it. After printing three articles the editor offered her a regular column. In the space of eighteen months, Anna developed a niche as a relationship therapist, a reputation as a columnist, and a steady source of new readers. An easy flow of clients into her practice followed.

Getting an article published can be the first step in developing your confidence about your writing. Your long-term goal may be to write a book, find a publisher, and build a reputation for your work. Since major publishers receive hundreds of book proposals each week, you will want to have strong credentials, a prior publishing history, or a very well-produced book proposal. If you end up with a handful of rejection letters, don't despair; you can still get your book in print.

Another option is to consider self-publishing your book. Many people like to go the route of self-publishing because it can help avoid the waiting time of a year or more to get a book into people's hands. To self-publish, take your edited material directly to a self-publishing company and underwrite the costs of printing. You will be responsible for everything involving the book, although self-publishing companies can steer you to an independent distributor. Among the benefits you receive are having complete control over your product, including control over editing and cover design. You will also receive all the profits, once you have sold enough to cover your costs.

If you have a larger budget to play with, consider this strategy used by a motivational speaker. He self-published his first book for a total cost of forty thousand dollars. This price included twelve thousand copies of a bound soft-cover book, typesetting, printing, production, and basic marketing support. He then hired a distribution company to place his book in major stores, including Borders, Waldenbooks, Barnes and Noble, as well as on-line bookstores. He promoted the book with his frequent speaking engagements. With a proven track record of sales and self-promotion, his second book was picked up by a major publisher.

BECOME THE "WALKING BOOK"

If you don't like to write, you can become the "walking book"—educating those you meet without writing down a word. I know several wonderful therapists who take this approach. Each one of them qualifies as an original, often brilliant thinker and has developed fascinating new techniques, based on their many years of experience. They are all senior therapists who spend some time supervising other therapists. None of them want to take the considerable time and effort to write a book; they would rather see clients.

These therapists embody their work. They walk their talk. They are master teachers and trainers who educate in the course of each session; it's inspiring to be with them, because you know you will learn a lot. If you choose this path, you need to attend to your career with care and seriousness. Focus on teaching others what you know. You will need to carry your message through your workshops, classes, individual sessions, and supervision. You may do all of the preparation and study that an author would undertake, without the end product of a book. Instead, you will change lives by your immediate, direct experience with others.

PUBLISH A WEB PAGE

Another way to expand your message is to put it on the Internet. To publish a web page you will need your site to be designed and then "hosted" by a website provider. There are many providers to choose from. I have included two in the Resources section that have done a good job for me. They offer Internet hosting, website design, interactive website features, e-mail broadcasts, and even teleconferencing (rental of telephone "bridge" lines, so that you can offer low-cost conference calls).

What can you expect in terms of return on your investment with a web page? It depends on the type of clients you are trying to attract. I hear a variety of reports from therapists about the referrals from the Internet. Some have found it to be a great way to connect with clients who are computer savvy and prefer to shop on-line, even for therapists. For myself, I have had very good success attracting business coaching clients from my web page.

Your site is a way for potential clients to learn more about you, so take the time and effort to make sure your message comes through. Here are some tips to think about when you create your own website.

- *Offer value.* Make the site valuable to others. Include useful articles and information. More is more—offer a lot. Update your material every few months. Your website might offer articles reprinted from past newsletters, a self-assessment test that can be downloaded, information about your services, a photo of you, your bio, several "top ten" lists, a book list, and links to other sites. Consider having an email newsletter as well.

- *Link with others.* The best sites are linked to others, increasing traffic for all. If you find a great site that you think would be a good link to yours, don't be shy to suggest it by e-mail to the owner of the site. Most people using the Internet like linking their sites. You also need to list your web page with the major Internet search engines, so that people who are surfing the net can find you. Your website host can point you in the direction of finding the internet-based companies that will do this for a fee or you can do the listing for free yourself.

- *Advertise your website.* Your website is similar to a brochure, but bigger and longer. It's out there on the Internet, competing with millions of other sites. You have to advertise your website, so that people will visit. The more you advertise your site in other mediums, the better. Join the large Internet referral sites that have been created to promote your profession (see the Resources). Include your site information on your print advertising, your business card, and your print brochures.

With your basic message at the heart of your presentation about your work, you will be on your way to attracting the clients you most want to see. In the next chapter, we'll explore more strategies that successful therapists use to generate a flow of referrals.

7

Generating Referrals

The heartbeat of any successful practice is the therapist's ability to generate a steady flow of referrals, keeping the practice strong and healthy. A practice with good referral sources can withstand a lot of changes and continue to stay profitable. But without a consistent way to bring in referrals your practice may limp along, gasping for breath. If you are new to practice, generating referrals will be your first order of business. If you have an existing practice, referrals may only be a priority from time to time. This chapter will help newer therapists get a strong start in finding referrals and will offer new perspectives on securing a larger client base for more experienced therapists.

Referrals are a special type of client, typically the best clients for a therapy business. My definition of a referral is: *a person who has already started the introductory phase of the therapeutic relationship.*

Remember when we discussed the many barriers to therapy? A referral is a person who is past the initial hurdle of deciding to enter therapy. A referral is ready to hear what you have to offer or, even better, eager to start work right away with you. With a solid referral system in place you can relax in your practice, knowing that the right clients are finding you with a minimal effort on your part. Since a referral system offers so much to the health of a therapy practice, it makes good business sense to develop a solid referral system for your business.

At this point, you may think I am going to lecture you about marketing for your practice. But, believe it or not, I don't want you to market your practice, at least not in the way you might think. Instead, I want you to generate referrals. Let me draw a distinction between the two.

MARKETING BY PROMOTION

Most therapists tell me that they hate marketing their practices. For them, marketing involves some form of advertising, overpromising, self-promotion, or seduction. If this reflects your definition of what it takes to market your practice, then marketing will *not* be your most effective strategy for bringing in good clients. The price you pay for pushing so hard for clients will be too high for you, on a personal and energetic level. Even though *push marketing* can be a means to get the word out about your practice, consider what it costs you personally, in terms of increasing your level of anxiety. How much does push marketing cause you to distance yourself emotionally from your business? Any amount of distance from your business is too much, in my estimation. I want you to love your business and spend time in your business, not recoil from it.

Push marketing or marketing by promotion can signal a concern to others about your survival. You appear desperate. Most of us have had some experience being on the other end of promotional marketing and know what it feels like to be someone else's prospect. Push marketing ignores the complexity of the therapeutic relationship and focuses on the end goal—making the sale. Since it's linear in process, it always looks and sounds like you are selling yourself. Just the act of pushing for the sale can create a feeling inside you that you don't have enough or are not good enough. For a profession like therapy, push marketing rarely attracts ideal clients because you are compromising your integrity when you push too hard for clients and ignore the all-important aspect of therapy, which is about building relationships. Marketing by promotion is rarely about building relationships; more often it feels like pushing yourself at people to get their attention.

GENERATING BY ATTRACTION

I make a distinction between push marketing and generating referrals. Generating referrals is a way of attracting clients to your practice instead of pushing them. Attracting clients means *honoring the best of yourself as you build relationships within a larger community.* Generating by attraction feels like a magnetic pull, highlighting the best elements of your work that allow the right clients to naturally gravitate toward you. Generating by attraction is a process of coming into alignment with *yourself* as a business owner. It is nonlinear and carries no personal, human cost.

Notice the difference between the two verbs—generate versus market. Think of generating as building an engine. The engine requires some work to build properly and put in place, and it needs continual injections of high-quality fuel, but once it begins to run, it keeps going. I want you to build a referral engine that you can depend on, fuel every now and then, and forget about the rest of the time. Once you do this properly, the engine will have a life of its own.

On the other hand, marketing is basically selling; each sales call requires considerable effort from you. This is why so many therapists get tired even thinking about marketing—it's an exhausting process. Generating can be energy *producing,* once the engine gets set and going. The small actions that build the engine can have steady, lasting results. Instead of getting up each day and *digging* for referrals, I am going to teach you a strategy so that you learn how to seed relationships in your community.

When I interviewed successful colleagues to understand how they filled their practices, I found that those therapists with waiting lists all spoke about the following three steps to generate referrals.

1. Articulate your basic message (covered in chapter 6).
2. Create enthusiasm in others so that they carry your message.
3. Ask for the referral.

When the three steps are used together they form a straightforward, highly effective strategy. With this strategy in place, getting good referrals will no longer seem like such a mysterious, difficult issue. The first step, articulating your basic message, was covered in the last chapter. In this chapter we will examine the next two steps so that you can implement this three-step approach to generating quality referrals.

CREATING ENTHUSIASM IN OTHERS

How do referrals happen? What motivates other people to refer their friends, colleagues, and relatives to you? Once people feel excited about who you are and what you have done for them, it is natural for them to want to tell others about you. If you consistently do good work as a therapist, your clients will tell others and, over time, you will build a practice of referrals. But building a client base of referrals from your existing clients takes time. You may want to speed up the process, or reach out to a wider pool of people than your existing or previous clients. If so, you need a way to share who you are with others on a wider scale, and you need a way to do it that evokes a positive emotional response from the public. In the last chapter, you crafted a basic message. Now you need others to carry your message for you, to expand your reach. To put it simply: You need to be out in front of more people, so that they can feel enthusiastic and excited about you and your message.

Creating enthusiasm is an art. It works best when people can get a sense of who you are easily, without too many barriers in the way. You can be in charge of making it easy for people to get their first look and experience of you. As we discussed in chapter 5, one barrier that makes it hard for people to know about you, or even meet you briefly, is the expense of a therapy session. The fastest way to create enthusiasm in others about your work is to bypass the money barrier and offer something of value to the public, for free, so people can see who you are in a positive, constructive setting. The important goal here is to greatly expand the number of people who have a direct, extremely positive experience of you. Here are several action steps that can help you to create enthusiasm in others.

GIVE A FREE "HIGH TOUCH" PREVIEW

"High touch" means that like the old commercials for the phone company, you reach out and touch someone, but in this case you touch someone *emotionally.* Don't just give a dry lecture and say what you do. Show it. High touch introductions can be a wonderful way to build enthusiasm.

Peter, a sports psychologist, specializes in peak performance coaching. One evening each month he hosts a two-hour introductory session, where he gives others a small sample of his work. He invites existing clients and their friends and family. He holds the talks regularly, each month, in his office (having these free talks in your office creates a sense of familiarity with your space and is one less barrier for new clients to overcome). He distributes flyers about the upcoming previews in his office and drops a few off at his health club. That is his total marketing plan. About ten people attend each preview—a mix of old or existing clients who want to hear him speak and some new people. The content of the talks is always the same—he begins with a brief go-round; people say their names and share a little about an area of their lives where they would like to perform better. He gives a fifteen-minute, entertaining talk about peak performance. For example, at one preview he explained the secret of how Houdini mastered a famous escape from a straightjacket inside a water chamber. (Houdini practiced mental relaxation techniques to help him stay calm while he was submerged upside-down in a sealed box of water. As he slowed down his breathing and heart rate, he could complete the trick and escape without peril.)

Then Peter guides the group through a similar relaxation exercise. He shows how to take that state of calm to mentally rehearse a difficult challenge. This is the "high touch" part—he uses an experiential exercise to let people see what it's like to work with him. He tells the group, "This is one exercise we will do in my office, when you come to see me for a session. Over time, you will get very good at staying relaxed and performing at your peak." Then he lets people share briefly whatever they learned during the exercise that is of value. The sharing time is often fascinating and fun for the participants, as they relate what they experienced during the relaxation exercise. Peter builds on the comments, encouraging people to think how their experience might help them in daily tasks. This relaxed, informal introduction nets him a small stream of quality referrals. The people who come for therapy after attending a preview feel that they already know him and, more importantly, know what to expect.

Here's the key to making a successful preview: You have to detach from the outcome. Select a topic you enjoy and would gladly offer to one person or one hundred, so that the results of who actually shows up don't matter to you. If you are tied to the results, the preview will feel like a roller coaster. You will be up when you have a lot of people in the room and down when there are fewer. You will be discouraged if no one immediately signs up for ongoing sessions. Instead, offer the previews as a way of playing and having fun, in a professional sense. You will become more attractive and positive results will come more naturally.

I hold a free "meditation and spirituality" group, one hour each month. I picked this topic because I wanted my therapy and coaching clients to have a spiritual practice that would enhance the work we do together. I am also a big fan of the adage that "you teach what you most need to learn." I need to learn to deepen my meditative practice, and this group keeps me on my toes. I asked a colleague who has a solid meditation practice to co-lead this group with me. We limit attendance to fifteen people because that is all my office can hold. I run this group because it adds to the quality of my life and my practice, yet it generates several referrals into my practice each year.

I have also offered previews with a group of therapists. I formed an association of therapists who are trained, as I am, in a method of group therapy that is highly experiential and difficult to explain to new clients. The group holds a two-hour preview every other month, and uses it as both a way to educate potential clients and a screening process. We give a standard lecture the first hour (each time we rotate who will give the lecture) and then guide the attendees through a series of experiential exercises the second hour. Each therapist invites potential clients to attend. We hold it in a large group space that holds up to thirty people. This has proven to be a wonderful format for bringing people into our ongoing groups. It's a good bridge between an initial phone call from an interested client and the client making a six-month commitment to join a group. We offer a full-day workshop (for a fee) the day following each preview, so that interested clients have something to attend immediately.

The preview and workshop give our association of therapists a chance to promote our model of therapy, evaluate potential clients for group as they go through the preview and/or the workshop, and work together professionally on a regular basis. We usually have a mix of new and old clients attending both the preview and the following day-long workshop, so that new clients come into a welcoming community, where some "old-timers" know the ropes and help newer clients acclimate to the therapy process.

Determine the goals you want to achieve with your preview or introductory talk, and then set up your free offerings so that you feel supported and relaxed as the leader. Make the preview easy and fun for you. Your attitude will be infectious, helping to build enthusiasm within others about your work. Frequently, when I talk about this action step of giving free introductions, I will hear a therapist say, "I tried to give a free talk (or talks), and it didn't get me any clients. That strategy doesn't work." Let's look at three elements that need to be in place to convert people in an audience into clients.

Be Highly Attractive in Your Presentation

By attractive, I don't mean that you need to look better. I mean you need to be more attractive as a person and make sure that you "walk your talk." You need to be a model of what you present. For example, if you are speaking about the importance of care-giving, you need to model that. Care about the audience. Demonstrate your message congruently. One therapist who came to see me for coaching gave talks regularly, but never got referrals. Her evaluations read, "Good information, but presentation feels rushed." She talked fast because she was nervous, but it sent a message to the audience that was negative. We worked on ways to let go of the information in favor of building a relationship with the audience. She learned how to put herself (and her audience) at ease. She had previously launched immediately into the information and shown slides. Now she started by telling an amusing anecdote and then asking the audience some leading, fascinating questions to get them thinking. She had more fun with the presentation. Her results spoke volumes. She began to get referrals every time she spoke. Her evaluations read, "Speaker is informed, and *I really enjoyed the talk.*"

Identify the Gap

You generate referrals by clarifying a person's desire for change. Define the gap between where your audience is right now and where they want to be. Then show them (don't just tell them) how you can help close the gap. I attended the keynote speech at a conference. The presenter, a well-known therapist, chose to speak about our vulnerability as human beings. She gave example after example of how life sends us unexpected, sometimes heart-wrenching situations. One story concerned a couple she worked with who had to deal with the tragic, unexpected death of an only child, which led to their divorce and unending grief. Another story was about her parents' loss of their business during the Depression, and how it broke her father's spirit and health. The stories she offered were sad, and she told them directly, without drama. Then she talked about how to take these challenges and transform each experience, to grow through it.

She offered a story about this too—a story about a couple she worked with whose child was kidnapped and subsequently murdered, and the different way they dealt with the situation. The child had been on an outing with one parent when the incident occurred. While the statistics show that few couples can survive this type of an ordeal, unable to overcome feelings of guilt and blame, she helped this couple use techniques of forgiveness for each other. They went through a "dark night of the soul" where they chose to continue life with each other, rather than separately. They grieved together and over time formed a foundation to help other parents, which helps to direct some of their anger and energy. They became a model for the community of love for each other and that it is possible to overcome life's tragedies. Everyone in the audience was moved. The first step, she said, was helping the couple release feelings of judgment, blame, and guilt and replace them with a sense of calm. This was an intriguing idea. She offered an exercise so that the audience could experience one of the methods she used with the couple. The exercise, a simple meditation, was powerful. Now the audience felt inspired. In the space of two hours, she moved the audience from concern to curiosity to inspiration. This therapist has a long waiting list. It's clear why she generates so much interest and so many referrals every time she speaks.

You may not be a professional presenter, but you can improve your referrals from presentations. Get some feedback from a peer about your level of attraction and congruence (see chapter 12 for some helpful hints). Let go of the amount of information you deliver in favor of facilitating a positive experience for those present. Remember, you're a therapist, not a consultant; your goal is to build relationships with the audience, not just provide data.

Give It Sufficient Time

This action, like many others, needs to be in place for a while to show results. Some people are cautious consumers and want to check you out several times before they will be ready to commit. These are often good, serious clients, but you must give them time to have more than one exposure to you. I always set up previews or talks in a series of six before I evaluate their effectiveness. If I am offering a monthly preview, I plan to repeat it for six months before I judge its value. It takes time for word of mouth to build about a free event. Don't stop too soon. Set up your preview so that it's easy and fun, so that you are happy to put it in place, and let it run for a enough time. This is an engine you are building, not a one-shot sales pitch. Build the preview engine, let it run, and reap the rewards over time.

HOST GATHERINGS OF YOUR COLLEAGUES

Want more referrals from your colleagues? Maybe you need to show them what you do, as well. It's hard for colleagues to refer to you unless they have direct experience of your skills. Invite a small group of colleagues to join you for a chance to learn something new and teach them something that you do well.

What do you know that you could teach to your colleagues? Sam, a licensed counselor, had good skills helping teenagers to manage their anger. To build his peer referral network, he invited a circle of colleagues for coffee and bagels on a Saturday morning and taught them two effective techniques that help angry teens calm themselves. The group discussed the techniques, brainstormed about ways to adapt them for broader clinical use, and socialized. This boosted his reputation and referrals from those who attended.

Pamela, a body therapist, taught colleagues a lovely, gentle meditation. Jay, a social worker, facilitated a formal book club with a reading list of clinical texts. Arnold, a massage therapist, showed his peers how he combined deep breathing exercises with muscle relaxation. You don't have to be brilliant or have a revolutionary new method to make this strategy effective—just be willing to give away your best ideas for free. Some therapists think they need to fiercely guard their hard-won knowledge. I find that creativity works best when it's free-flowing. The more good ideas you give away, the more good ideas will occur to you to replace them.

OFFER A FREE TWENTY-MINUTE "LIVING BROCHURE"

This is an alternative to a printed brochure, taught to me by a talented marketing expert named Robert Alderman, from California, which I have adapted for the therapy profession. Robert analyzed the inherent weaknesses in a printed brochure and set about correcting this with a living brochure—one that you deliver in person.

In a printed brochure, you try to accomplish four goals:

1. Create an initial relationship with a potential client.
2. Help the potential client determine his/her need.
3. Articulate the ideal resolution of that need.
4. Define the services you offer.

Unfortunately, most printed brochures fall short of this ideal. It's hard to establish a relationship and determine the needs of a potential client whom you have not actually met. To overcome this problem, some therapists try to include everything on a printed brochure, covering all their bases. These are the brochures that contain too many words and ideas. Both readability and visual impact suffer. Some therapists go to the other extreme and produce brochures that look good, but say too little. They miss addressing the needs of certain clients.

Most therapists would agree that a face-to-face meeting or even a phone call accomplishes the four brochure goals more effectively than a single piece of paper folded in thirds. The living brochure structures a mini-session to meet the goals of a printed brochure.

Use a living brochure for those potential clients who need something following the initial phone call before they can commit to a first therapy session. Some people who could use your services need to be gently led into the process of therapy. This is a way to build a relationship with them at a slower pace.

Here's how to set up a living brochure.

Create an Initial Relationship with the Client

When a potential client calls to ask about your services and you sense that he or she might be interested but not ready to purchase a first session, you can say, "Some therapists might send you a printed brochure to look over at this point, to help you make a decision about therapy. I would like to offer you something I call a living brochure. It's my alternative to a printed brochure. It's a twenty-minute gift of my time, at no charge, when we can meet and have a chance to talk. It will let me understand what you are looking for and see if I am the right therapist for you and if I can be of help." You can successfully do this brochure by phone or in person. It's a nice technique for those who need an intermediate step in their decision-making process.

Help the Potential Client Determine His/Her Need

Your first step is to select a few questions to ask the potential client from the following list. You talk 20 percent of the time and the client talks 80 percent of the time. Notice that these are not diagnostic questions. This is not an assessment interview. These are more general, again in keeping with the tone of a brochure. You don't need to ask all of these questions. Just pick a few, to get the conversation going in the right direction.

- What problems are you having in your life right now?
- What are you most irresponsible about in your life?
- What do you most want to change about yourself?
- What do I need to know about you to work successfully with you?
- How could you best use therapy?
- What are the three most important things you want to accomplish in your life right now?
- What's the biggest opportunity you are currently not taking full advantage of? What stops you?
- How long since you were engaged in activities that make you happy?

After hearing the answers, resist your desire to diagnose. You will be doing something else with the information you have heard by integrating what you have just seen, heard, and sensed about the person.

Articulate the Ideal Resolution of that Need

Once someone identifies a need, the next step is to put into words how you envision him resolving that need. In a living brochure, you articulate a mini-vision for the person, a picture of what you see that is possible. This is similar to the vision statement process you went through yourself in chapter 4. In that process you stated what was possible for yourself. Here you are doing this for another person, drawing on your therapeutic skills and your position as an objective observer. It sounds like:

"I hear you are having problems and feeling hopeless. I'd like to see you feeling happier, more hopeful, and at peace within yourself."

"You tell me that you are having trouble knowing if your marriage will last, although you very much want it to work. What I want for you is that you have some real, tangible communication skills that can help you shift from fighting to talking things over calmly."

"I can see how much physical pain you are in on the right side of your body. I'd choose for you to have more mobility and general comfort within your arms and legs."

If you do this well, the person will respond to your statement by saying, "Yes I'd like that for me, too" or "That sounds good to me." Once you have a general agreement on a direction to take, it's time to state how your services fit into the resolution of the need.

Define the Services You Offer

You have just articulated a mini-vision. Resist your inclination to over-promise. Be clear and ethical about your services. Say:

"The therapy services I offer that can help you to take the first step in that direction would be weekly individual sessions (or couples sessions or group therapy, etc.). When you are ready to work with me, we simply need to schedule a first session."

Have a policy sheet to give the person. (We discuss the policy sheet in chapter 10.) End the living brochure on time. Don't feel disappointed if the person isn't ready to schedule a session immediately. Detach from the outcome. Learn to enjoy the process of offering the living brochure—it can be quite satisfying to sit with a person for a short time to hear about his or her concerns and needs, and then creatively construct a mini-vision that speaks to the resolution of the needs. Going from need to vision in minutes, thinking on-the-spot, is great practice for you in developing a positive, hopeful outlook in life.

ASKING FOR THE REFERRAL

This is the hardest step in the strategy for most therapists to adopt. When I graduated with a masters in social work, I was very shy about doing any type of self-promotion for my practice. Although I had started a small practice, I still felt unsure about my skills. I had lunch with a colleague who graduated a year ahead of me. He worked full-time and had a small practice of ten clients he saw in the evenings. I was extremely jealous. I thought that ten clients would be heaven. I boldly asked him how he had been able to find so much business. He gave me a lesson I never forgot. "How many people have you told that you are looking for clients?" he asked.

"Counting my husband and my parents?" I answered. "Three."

"Here is the difference between you and me. When I meet someone, I always mention that I am building a private practice, and I say that I have some openings in my new practice that I am looking to fill."

What a revelation. You just say what is true. I am grateful to him for teaching me an honest and comfortable way to express a business need. "I have some openings in my new practice that I am looking to fill" was a magic phrase to me, because it expressed my need so perfectly. Since that time I have discovered many other steps that also fall under the heading of asking for the referral. Some of the steps are variations on a theme; some will take you out into the community in ways that challenge your isolation, requiring you to strengthen your network; one is designed to keep you spiritually open and ask the universe. Lets start with the basics.

PRACTICE ASKING FOR REFERRALS

Try practicing the following statement: "I have some openings in my practice I am looking to fill." I encourage you to use this simple phrase at least once a day when you are in active practice-building mode. Add it at the end of your fifteen-second basic message. You will be surprised at the power of this phrase. In business, it's normal to talk about your business needs to others.

GET THE WORD OUT TO COLLEAGUES AND CLIENTS

You may be surprised to hear this, but people don't immediately think of sending you referrals if you don't express the need. Even though a desire for referrals may be a topic that is never far from your mind, it is not high on the list of those you meet. Your existing clients may be shy about referring others unless they know that this is an appropriate behavior. A short sentence in your policy sheet or on your brochure that says that you are open to new referrals can educate them. You have to educate and remind everyone that you have space for new clients.

I had two experiences this year that underscored this point. I have a colleague in my local area to whom I've sent a lot of referrals over the years. I said to her, "You know, I'm just curious. I've never gotten a referral back from you. How come?" She said, "I had no idea you would need one. I thought you were full. I'd be happy to think of you." A month later I got a good referral from her.

A woman called to ask if I would speak to her association about the group therapy work that I do. I said to her, "I would love to have members of your organization know about my therapy groups. In fact, your members are the ideal clients for me to work with. Currently, I have a few openings in my groups I'd like to fill." She immediately told me of two people in my local area who had asked her if she knew of any groups they could join. She had told them no (even though we have had contact many times over the years). As she told me, "Your groups would be great for them. I just never thought about you."

Don't assume that you stay on the mind of others. Gently remind them about your services, from time to time. Let them know about your ideal client profile, your basic message, your business vision, and the fact that you have openings in your practice.

MEET AND CULTIVATE FOUR "PRACTICE ANGELS"

"Practice Angels" are people who are well connected in their community and are already a source of referrals. Leveraging your time is important when you have a small business. It helps to find four or five people who are good sources of multiple referrals. These may or may not be professional contacts within your field. The rule of thumb is to find those key people within a community who know a lot of other people intimately, often hear about the psychological or health problems of others, and could offer your name as a referral.

The most obvious sources are doctors, ministers, human resource managers, or employee assistance program directors—often the first point of contact when someone wants to find the name of a therapist. But I have heard of other good referral sources, including: alternative health professionals (massage therapists, nutritionists, acupuncturists); self-care professionals (hair dressers, manicurists, sports trainers, personal shoppers); educators (teachers, school counselors, school secretaries, principals); organizers (committee chairs of social organizations and business organizations.) The list goes on and on. Look around for those well-connected people you see or hear about, and get to know them.

IDENTIFY YOUR CURRENT REFERRAL NETWORK

List your existing clients and who sent them to you. You might be surprised as you do this and begin to chart how clients are finding you. For example, if a high percentage of clients come through existing client referrals, that is the area to put the majority of your energy and resources into by having more mailings, newsletters, or offerings for existing clients. See if you can spot the pipelines into your practice and then focus on those channels, enriching them

EXPAND YOUR ROLODEX

This action step is a lot of fun. You can become a professional resource for your clients by finding out who is the best at everything within your community and maintaining a great Rolodex. Create fifty categories and then take a year to fill in the blanks. Get to know fifty highly qualified people who provide services your clients need, such as a really fine accountant, lawyer, financial adviser, nutritionist, body worker, internist, meditation instructor, etc.

This will require that you get to know more people in your community as you search for the best. When you are interviewing someone to add them to your list, most likely he or she will also want to know about you. Before you know it you will be well connected and know a great circle of fifty influential people in your local area.

ASK THE UNIVERSE FOR REFERRALS

The problem with focusing on referrals is that your quest for more clients can become an obsession. If you are in the early stages of practice-building, you may find yourself thinking of nothing else. Eventually this type of anxious thinking takes a toll on you, your family, and friends, and even on the mindset you would like to have about your practice. If you find yourself in this dilemma, you need to lighten up. Take the actions we have explored in this chapter, but put your mind at ease by engaging in a spiritual contemplation about business. Use a conceptual or spiritual process that supports your efforts.

You can use a business affirmation; select one from the list in chapter 4 that supports a belief in abundance. Work with it every day for two months, releasing your negative beliefs and anxieties, allowing the affirmation to quiet your mind. Prayer or contemplation is another time-honored way to engage in contemplation. Psychologist Wendy Allen, who is also my sister, helped me to translate a concept from one of Neale Donald Walsch's books that defines the "proper form of prayer." In the book, *Conversations with God,* Walsch says that conventional praying for something actually pushes it away. Saying we want a thing is a statement of lack and only furthers our reality of deprivation. In other words, saying *I want* only gets us more *wanting.*

The correct prayer, according to Walsch, is a prayer of gratitude. He suggests you thank the universe in advance for that which you choose to experience. Acknowledge it as already existing, looking for any tiny kernel that breathes within you or in your reality. "Asking the universe" is expressing gratitude for what exists already, and then opening yourself and your awareness to the fact that more of the same exists, so you have even more to be grateful for. This is another definition of abundance.

Here's the exercise Wendy and I formulated to help therapists ask the universe for referrals. I have given you an example of how to apply each step.

Exercise
ASKING THE UNIVERSE FOR REFERRALS

1. *Think of what you want in terms of what qualities your want would give you.* "I want more clients. More clients would let me be more relaxed and confident."
2. *Think of how these qualities exist already in your experience.* "I have times of being relaxed and confident with the few clients I have."
3. *Thank the universe.* "I feel and express gratitude for the relaxation and confidence I experience each week."
4. *Open yourself to more of the same.* "I notice how there are more times when I can choose to feel relaxed and confident each day, and as a result, I feel even more grateful."
5. *Do concrete actions that further your gratitude in the material world.* "I keep a journal. I write about those times each day that I am relaxed and confident and I leave pages blank, on purpose, for more examples that I can add."

   "I consciously try to be more relaxed and confident in my sessions and I look for ways to further relaxation and confidence in my existing clients."

   "I open up some files for new clients and leave them empty. I mark spaces in my calendar for 'new client time only' and don't fill the hours with anything other than new clients."

In the next chapter we will look at how you can use strategies to expand and diversify your practice. I will suggest more ways to generate referrals as you take the steps that make a small practice feel larger.

8

Making a Small Practice Feel Bigger

The greatest strength of a small business dwells in its flexibility. As the owner and operator of your small practice, you can move quickly and make immediate, on-the-spot decisions. Do you have a new idea for a class? Need to change the way you bill existing clients? Want to find a better location? You can implement solutions and make changes in the practice immediately, without needing anyone's approval. You can keep costs low, run a lean operation, and enjoy control over the profits when your caseload is full.

But sometimes being small is hard. When a client is pushing at your business boundaries or when you are feeling tired and wishing for more administrative help, you may look with longing at larger practices that have office staff and more marketing power. You may wish for the diversity, financial reserve, solid policies, firm guidelines, and layers of structure that often exist within larger organizations. Even though you are a small business, you still want to feel strong and secure.

Having the best of both worlds means retaining the advantages of being small, while adopting the key aspects of a larger business. In this chapter, I will show you how to do more of both by using a comprehensive five-step "practice upgrade plan." The plan shows you how to extend the reach of your practice and develop strong business boundaries so that you feel more substantial, even if you are a sole proprietor.

Imagine the difference between two trees—one tree has a wide, impressive stretch of branches, a solid trunk, and deep roots that project stability, breadth, and substance. The other, a young sapling, has a narrow trunk and surface roots that may bend or break in a strong wind. The mature tree can bear fruit, withstand a storm, and offer shade and shelter to others. The small sapling can do little more than hope to survive while it grows. I want to show you how to take a practice that feels like the young sapling and make it more mature. Even therapists in practice for twenty years often have some part of their practice that is like the sapling and can benefit from this upgrade plan.

To follow this plan, you'll need to evaluate the operations of your current practice. Step 1 will force you to think about your practice with more sophistication; steps 2 and 3 require that you extend your thinking to diversify; steps 4 and 5 encourage you to upgrade your clinical methods to the next level. Therapists using all five steps of this plan often report an unintended but welcome outcome—generating referrals as they make each change—a normal benefit of expanding the reach and stability of their business.

THE PRACTICE UPGRADE PLAN

Use these five steps to take your sole proprietorship or small partnership to the next level.

1. Run a business, not a hobby.
2. Diversify your services.
3. Connect to a broader network.
4. Go beyond competency.
5. See each client as a long-term relationship.

RUN A BUSINESS, NOT A HOBBY

When JoBeth, a bodyworker in private practice for six years, called to set up an appointment, she said she felt very confused about the current operation of her practice. "I struggle with the idea of whether I really want to make a commitment to my business, or continue to treat it like an expensive hobby. I need you to coach me how to take my business more seriously," she said.

JoBeth, like many therapists who have full-time jobs or are full-time parents, set up a home-based, part-time practice. She never marketed her services and happily saw only four or five clients each week. She had spent the last fifteen years raising her children; family came first and the practice came second. With the children now teenagers, her thoughts turned toward growing the practice. The desire to grow larger raised immediate feelings of fear and self-doubt. She felt a fear of competition and a lack of certainty about her own skills. She kept my business card pinned on her bulletin board for six months, before she got up the nerve to call me. As therapists, we know how hard it can be for clients to take the first step to call a therapist; the same hesitancy often lives in us, as therapists, prior to deciding to get help for our businesses. I complimented JoBeth on taking the first step to making a commitment to her practice by calling me.

The next step would be a hard one. I wanted JoBeth to let me in on all the details about the daily running of her practice. She felt embarrassed, she said. Her practice felt like a very personal, very private enterprise. In the same way that it's hard for your clients to open up their lives for your examination, it's often very uncomfortable to allow someone to really look into your business. I asked JoBeth to list all of her current practices and policies, and all her reasoning behind each one. As we went through her list, she laughed defensively about some of her weaker policies and proudly explained her rationale for others.

JoBeth and I reviewed her list to note all the ways that her practice operated as a hobby, instead of a business. Most of the "hobby" aspects involved her inconsistent practice management. I gave her my "Practice Management Checklist," a quick professional checklist for therapists, which I include here for you to use in your practice. As you look at this checklist, you will see that it focuses on management items. It does not include financial or accounting items, because I have devoted an entire chapter to money and profitability. Since each practice is different, freely adapt this list so that it works as a checklist for your particular practice, adding or subtracting items to make it right for your business.

PRACTICE MANAGEMENT CHECKLIST

Check each item that is true for you.

___ 1. I have a clear business plan I am using to guide my practice this year.

___ 2. I know my top five business goals for this year and the action steps to take in order to accomplish each one.

___ 3. I look for ways to upgrade my administration systems, including billing, record keeping, and filing.

___ 4. I have a good accountant, lawyer, and business coach who I can turn to for advice.

___ 5. My day-to-day operations run smoothly with few problems.

___ 6. Each working day I take one action designed to strengthen my business.

___ 7. I return calls promptly and follow up on information in a timely manner.

___ 8. I devote one specific time each week to handling all my business paperwork.

___ 9. My office is well organized and set up to let me do my best work.

___ 10. If I employ staff, we have good communication. They know how to please me and perform their job with minimum input from me.

___ 11. My office is a good environment for both me and my staff.

___ 12. I have a client policy sheet that states all my policies in writing. It is openly displayed in my waiting room and given to each new and prospective client. (The elements of a policy sheet are explained in chapter 10.)

___ 13. My clients know that I will hold firmly to the boundaries of my policies.

___ 14. I educate my clients about how they can get the most out of our working relationship in therapy and become my ideal clients.

___ 15. My time at work is a valuable commodity and I manage it carefully.

___ 16. At least 75 percent of my total time at work is spent doing what I do best—seeing clients and delivering service.

continued

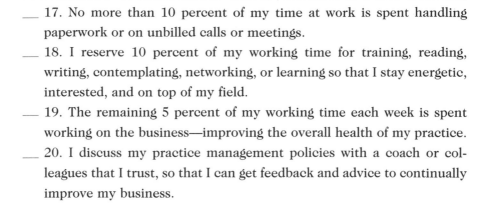

PRACTICE MANAGEMENT CHECKLIST
continued

___ 17. No more than 10 percent of my time at work is spent handling paperwork or on unbilled calls or meetings.

___ 18. I reserve 10 percent of my working time for training, reading, writing, contemplating, networking, or learning so that I stay energetic, interested, and on top of my field.

___ 19. The remaining 5 percent of my working time each week is spent working on the business—improving the overall health of my practice.

___ 20. I discuss my practice management policies with a coach or colleagues that I trust, so that I can get feedback and advice to continually improve my business.

If you examine all the practice management elements of your business and can check off every item as "true" you will have achieved a professionally managed practice. I told JoBeth to keep her practice small for now and just focus on raising her score on the checklist. She started with the fact that she had no written policies of any kind. After writing a policy sheet, she tightened her billing procedures and instituted regular, weekly bills. She looked at her low investment in administrative equipment and bought a computer and record-keeping software, to cut the time she was spending on paperwork. She instituted a missed-session policy so that her clients showed up consistently or paid for the session.

Since her caseload was small, I requested that she only work with "serious clients"—those that would use her services with a sense of commitment. I wanted her to value her decision of having a small practice by seeing the limited sessions she provided each week as a prized commodity, one that she could only offer to a select few. This was a big shift for her, and she began to feel that her work was not negligible, simply because her practice was small.

As I coached her to adopt higher professional standards, she began to ask more of herself as a therapist and of her clients. Her clinical work improved and clients appreciated the difference. Now that JoBeth felt she was running a real business, it was easier for her to decide whether or not to increase the size of her practice based on solid business criteria, rather than guilt, pressure, or emotion.

You, too, can use this checklist to take your practice from a hobby to a professionally managed business. Take a long, hard look at all of your policies. Let a trusted colleague or a business coach review your practice operations and help you correct the areas that are weak and inconsistent, so that you can have the professional feel of a larger company, even though you are a small business.

DIVERSIFY YOUR SERVICES

As a sole practitioner, your practice can have the feel of a larger business by using strategies of diversification. Diversifying does three things for your small business:

- It allows you to have more than one source of income and energy fueling your practice. A highly diversified practice can eliminate the feelings of boredom some practitioners face from doing the same thing, every day.
- A diversified practice eliminates a sense of boredom within your clients by giving them more than one choice. Each of us likes to have choice. When you go to a restaurant, you expect to be able to choose from a menu of items. Your clients may appreciate some choice within your offerings, too.
- Diversification lets you develop additional "practice muscles." Years ago, health fitness experts realized the value in "cross training"—incorporating more than one form of exercise into a workout to keep an athlete in peak condition. This is why ice skaters work out by lifting weights, not just practicing their skating. Weightlifters work out using yoga stretches, in addition to lifting weights. Just like an athlete, it's good for therapists to become cross-trainers and diversify, to become more flexible, versatile, and well-balanced, important qualities for an athlete and a small businessperson.

Here are some steps to show you how to take action in this direction.

Develop Multiple Profit Centers and Revenue Streams

Bruce, an acupuncturist, has three separate profit centers within his sole proprietorship: individual acupuncture sessions; classes in martial arts; and a selection of healing herbs for sale. Linda, a clinical social worker, has four profit centers: individual therapy sessions; audiotapes of meditations she has recorded and packaged for sale; pamphlets on psychological topics she authored; and parenting classes that she gives, sponsored by a local church.

Both therapists report that each profit center creates referrals for the others. Bruce has lots of crossover from his martial arts classes into his private sessions. Linda finds that when she promotes her audiotapes at conferences, she inevitably finds customers for her pamphlets. Some of these customers then decide to become therapy clients, as well. When Linda's client count falls, due to a seasonal low, she turns her attention to her audio sales. It reinvigorates her and gives her something to do that is productive and lucrative, while she waits for her client count to pick up.

Here is a list of profit centers you can add to your therapy practice.

- individual sessions
- workshops
- classes
- weekend retreats
- telephone consultations
- books, workbooks, or pamphlet sales
- audiotapes
- videotapes
- additional product sales
- writing for publication (for pay)
- radio or television appearances (for pay)
- public speaking (for a fee)
- business/corporate consulting or training
- program development
- licensing your programs to others
- a website with a membership fee (offer valuable information, a monthly e-mail newsletter for members, testing materials)

Consider adding an additional profit center to your practice within the next six months as a permanent feature of your business. Set aside the resources, space, and a budget to finance the profit center and treat it like a separate, yet valuable part of your existing practice. Track the income separately and the time involved. Note the cross-referrals it gives you. Then when this is well established, add another one. If you add one additional profit center each year, you will have a full, diversified practice within five years.

Package Your Services in at Least Five Different Ways

Create a menu of options for clients. Choice is a strong business selling point, and one that is severely underutilized by therapists. To offer more choice, list the services you currently offer in menu form. Then find the best combination of services for each person. This combination of services is what I call a package. Custom design an optimum therapy package for every client. Try developing some sample packages to suggest to new clients. One way to present these packages is to name them and include them along with your policy sheets.

Even if you offer only one service, I will show you how to create a menu and a package. Let's say your only service is individual therapy sessions. The variables we will use for your menu and package of services will be time and frequency.

Here are your two menu items:

- individual sessions, ninety minutes
- individual sessions, fifty minutes

Based on these two menu items, here are three packages a client can choose from. Each one has been given a name and a description:

- Package #1: *Intensive Therapy.* Ideal for someone who is in crisis and needs intense, immediate attention. Two sessions per week, each session lasts ninety minutes.
- Package #2: *Working Through.* A chance to make solid gains and achieve your therapy goals. One fifty-minute session each week.
- Package #3: *Moderate Support.* Supportive therapy to help you maintain good functioning and reinforce your gains. One fifty-minute session, every other week.

Packaging is a creative way to present therapy when you are looking for ways to offer choice and value to clients who pay out-of-pocket. A counselor in the Midwest who specializes in working with women who overeat offers this menu of services:

- short-term psychoeducational classes for women who overeat
- individual follow-up sessions for these same women
- aftercare groups (for those who have completed the psychoeducational classes)
- telephone support sessions for those out of the area

Her clients mix and match from these services to design a package that will most effectively help them to lose weight, fit their financial budgets, and make lifestyle changes.

In my practice, I have also enjoyed letting clients mix and match from a variety of services. I offer:

- individual psychotherapy sessions
- weekly ongoing group psychotherapy
- weekend therapy workshops four times per year
- individual business coaching sessions in person or by phone
- eight-week business coaching classes in person or by phone
- free monthly meditation groups
- free e-mail support for existing clients (I am responsive to quick check-in questions and updates by e-mail)

I have experimented with offering combinations of these services and found that it's possible to get very good results with packaging these items into some untraditional formats. For example, one psychotherapy client attended the four weekend therapy workshops a year and reserved a monthly individual therapy session, over the course of several years. This client lived outside of my area and wanted therapy on an intensive, yet infrequent basis. It worked for him. Another client comes for bimonthly business coaching classes and the monthly meditation groups. Another therapy client worked with me briefly in weekly individual sessions, left the area, and communicated with me occasionally by e-mail for six months and then moved back to the area and resumed weekly treatment. Since we had e-mail contact, he felt like he could continue the therapy from where we had left off.

Potential clients can view my menu of offerings in the waiting room, and during the initial session can design a program with my input and suggestions. Arrange your practice so that you offer the services you enjoy and accommodate the clients you most want to see by offering choice.

Niche Your Practice by Specific Outcomes, Not Client Type

The mantra of many marketing consultants to therapists is: *Get a niche.* This assumes that specialization is your only strategy to success. I have found this to be a poor strategy for therapists who want clinical diversity within their practice. These therapists end up feeling pressured to narrow their clinical skills and offer specialized services to a small section of the market, such as adults with Tourette's syndrome or teenagers who have school phobias. If you want to niche your practice, another way to do it is by the outcomes that you provide, instead of the types of clients you will see. Outcomes are the results you work toward with your clients. By highlighting *outcomes* as your niche, you have the option to work with all types of clients, but still develop a focus within your practice.

Here's a short list of possible outcomes. Notice that they are broad enough to allow you to work with several populations, but specific enough to allow you to develop a reputation for offering your special brand of therapy:

- Improve decision-making ability.
- Maintain a healthy balance between work and family.
- Manage difficult emotions with integrity.
- Set strong personal boundaries.
- Have loving relationships with your family.
- Overcome negative thinking.
- Turn your work into play.
- Let go of old fears and pain and enjoy your current life.

You can diversify and build a program around any well-articulated outcome. Notice that this list of outcomes uses ordinary, everyday language so that a potential client can feel drawn to the outcome. Using outcomes as a niche can help you to distinguish your work from others. I can imagine a "relationship-building" social worker, a "total relaxation" massage therapist or an "effortless sex" marital therapist. It helps to remember your sense of humor and playfulness when you think of outcomes. One family therapist I know routinely says "I teach kids how to raise good parents," instead of the other way around, which is an amusing description of his niche.

CONNECT TO A BROADER NETWORK

The old business maxim, "It's not what you know, it's who you know" might well be changed to "It's not who you know, it's how many you know" for the small businessperson today. In an article about networking in *The New Yorker* ("Six Degrees of Lois Weisberg," January 1999) writer Malcom Gladwell looks at the business and social power that is inherent in the quantity, not quality, of relationships you can develop. The power comes not from the depth of your relationships, he says, but from the sheer numbers. Using a series of studies he shows that those individuals who know the most people, *especially superficially,* have a much greater chance to gain business success.

Gladwell refers to sociologist Mark Granovetter's classic 1974 book, *Getting a Job,* regarding the "strength of weak ties." Superficial acquaintances will actually provide you with more reach and success than friends and family, because the acquaintances who operate outside of your natural social or business world are more likely to know things or other people you don't. Hence the far-reaching power of the broad network, versus the limited power of a close inner circle. The new definition of poverty is not deprivation, Gladwell concludes; it's isolation.

Therapists in a sole proprietorship are often the most isolated businesspeople I know and, in this way, impoverished. Therapists tend to be isolated by the type of work they do, which is private and confidential and isolated by the lack of networking within and between various therapy professions. Overcoming the poverty of isolation will be one of the most important strategies of expansion you can acquire, and it must become a lifelong pursuit. Here are some action steps to take in order to broaden your network:

Cultivate Diversity in Your Professional Network

Its easy to isolate yourself professionally and socially. It takes intention to have a life outside of your work. If you are isolated professionally, start with a baby step within your existing professional network. Seek out difference. Gravitate to any committee or activity that is new to you. If you are a massage therapist who specializes in working with women, and your tendency is to go to meetings of the American Massage Therapy Association and only sit with your friends, begin to network with those who you don't know, especially those who practice massage differently. If you are a social worker and always volunteering time for the legislative action committee of your local National Association of Social Workers chapter, sign up to be part of the committee that organizes the next benefit picnic. You will be meeting a wider circle of people and expanding your network from the inside out.

A bigger step is to cultivate more diversity within your professional network by connecting with those who are in other professions. Your networking efforts might include connecting with groups of businesspeople, teachers, community activists, and a variety of therapy professionals to give you access and reach within some other pockets of your local community. Take a day a week to have lunch with business owners who are clearly outside your field. After one year, you will have fifty new sources for ideas, expanded thinking, and referrals. You can also network professionally on-line, using the Internet to join the e-mail lists of professional groups. See the Resources list in the back of this book for ways to connect with a diversity of professions using the World Wide Web.

Increase the Number of Worlds You Belong To

My friend Kay (not a therapist) is an outgoing person with strong ties to her community. She seems to know everyone and is a great source of referrals for everything from the best place to get a moderately-priced haircut to a top-notch financial planner. Although she doesn't currently work outside the home (she has two young children), I asked her how many "worlds" she belongs to. She counted eight—the parents and teachers at two separate private schools her children attend, her synagogue, the neighborhood pool (she sits on the board and knows all the members), colleagues from jobs she had years ago (she stays in touch with lots of people), her husband's professional colleagues (he is a lawyer), the local democratic political organization (she is a committed participant), and the chamber of commerce (her husband is past president). This doesn't include the world of her close friends, neighbors, and family members.

How many worlds do you inhabit? Increase your spheres of operation, and broaden your ties to society.

Develop More Hobbies

You can let your network expand naturally by developing hobbies and pursuing them with the same energy you give to your work. I asked a group of therapists in a practice-building class about their outside hobbies that involved direct contact with others, and heard about horseback riding, flying small airplanes, jewelry making, local politics, painting, sculpture, skiing, white-water rafting, biking, and furniture building. If you tend to be consumed with work, add a hobby and get to know others engaged in the same pursuit. Your hobby will do many things for you professionally: It will give you rich metaphors to use with clients, challenge you in different ways than your profession currently does, and hopefully get you out of your office and out of you house, enabling you to develop more connections with others.

Read Outside Your Field

Richard Carlson, author of self-help books including *Don't Worry, Make Money,* reports that he and his wife purposefully subscribe to the most liberal and conservative political journals available, to try to open their mind to all points of view. Look at what you read and make sure it's broadly based. Read magazines that stretch you to understand a new point of view. This strategy offers several benefits: Reading outside your field is a great way to develop a broader understanding of topics to use as metaphors with your clients, so that you can illustrate therapeutic ideas using nontherapeutic words. It will also give you some topics to talk about when you are making small talk, an essential skill for effective networking.

Expand Your "Weak Ties"

As therapists and experts of deep relationships, we tend to disdain weak ties, those superficial acquaintances that Gladwell explains are powerful networking tools. The key to Gladwell's strategy is to appreciate and pursue those less than profound relationships. Cultivate acquaintances, not just friends. Appreciate weak ties, which are a welcome break from deep relationships. It's like the difference between scuba diving and snorkeling. Scuba diving is wonderful, but requires planning, gear, training, and a commitment of time, expense, and effort. Sometimes it's nice to snorkel—just slip on a mask and flippers and go splash about. Weak ties can be your way of splashing about in the oceans of people right outside your door.

GO BEYOND COMPETENCY

As of 1999, there are roughly five hundred thousand clinically trained psychotherapists (social workers, psychologists, licensed counselors, and psychiatrists) in the United States; each year, thousands more graduate from school. The number of massage therapists is skyrocketing, too. Ten years ago there were ninety schools teaching massage therapy; today you can find close to nine hundred. The field of personal coaching has exploded in the past three years, with training centers and associations forming to train and accredit thousands of new coaches. The marketplace is filled with experienced therapists, trying to stay in business, as well as newer therapists who are just getting started and willing to charge low prices. You face a lot of competition. The secret to expanding your business in a competitive market is to go beyond competency. To stay competitive, you need to be of consequence. To succeed in this market, you need to hone your skills and highlight your experience.

Gerald, a psychotherapist for over twenty years, complained to me about the difficulty of dealing with competition. With his full mane of gray hair, wire-rim glasses, and broad smile, he looks like a stereotype of a wise, approachable therapist. He teaches in a small town at a local university that graduates seventy-five masters-level psychotherapists each year, many of whom want to settle in the town. We looked at how he could stay competitive by using the following action steps. See if you can make use of these strategies, as well.

Become Truly Excellent in One Aspect of Your Practice

Find one aspect of your practice to master. The easiest way to approach mastery is to select one small part of your practice in which you will shine. Decide to devote time, energy, and money to purchase the training and development required, so that you feel great about your skills in this area.

Gerald specializes in transpersonal psychotherapy and had this step well in hand. He studied in Europe and the United States with the best in his field. In terms of his craft, he feels he is a master in his specialization and projects confidence about his skill level.

You may be well experienced in your field, but not acting as though you are. Spend some time evaluating your training and experience. One therapist I coached got stuck on this strategy and told me that she was not excellent at anything. I knew that she was expertly trained, got great results with her clients, and had been in practice for fifteen years. Yet she acted as though she was still a novice, unsure about her level of competence and her impact on her clients. We spent time evaluating her expertise and skills; she finally admitted that she was better trained than any therapist she personally knew. She understood that it would benefit her to behave in a way that more accurately reflected her considerable expertise. It helps to get some feedback from a coach, supervisor, or colleague to recognize and accept your own existing strengths and talents.

Make an Annual Investment in Your Training

In this market, you need to stay on top. New methods and ideas continue to emerge, and you need to keep pace. Training keeps you fresh, invigorated, and technically sharp. Most therapists are required to get CEUs each year, but you will want to consider training that goes beyond what is simply required. Go for mastery and excellence. Invest a lot in yourself.

Gerald, a teacher himself, realized he was not budgeting for his own continued training. When we explored this further, he said he missed the energy and excitement of learning new things, and some of this may have contributed to his feelings of anxiety. I originally suggested a figure of 5 percent of his gross income to budget each year for training. Because he had spent considerable amount of money on training for so many years, Gerald felt that 5 percent of his gross revenue (he makes $70,000 per year) was too much ($3,500 per year). However, he could agree on 2 percent or $1,400 annually, which would include his travel expenses and lodging at conferences and training sites.

Lead with Your Strengths

This is common sense, but not always self-evident to therapists. When you are putting a lot of time and money into a specific area of your training, make sure you put this area of expertise at the center of your services. This is what you want to become known for. Communicate this to others in your verbal presentation and written materials.

Gerald is well-known to the students he teaches, but these were not his ideal clients. He wanted a more mature clientele. He told me that he rarely talked about transpersonal psychology to the public, because he felt it was hard to understand, even though this was his strength as a therapist. Instead he presented himself as a family therapist, an area of skill but not his passion. I asked him to reorient his practice exclusively around his expertise. We spent time phrasing his basic message and promotional materials to make clear to the general public that he was an expert in transpersonal psychology, a therapy that combines spirituality and psychology. As a result, he began to get better known to the general public as an "alternative" therapist, and was asked to join a speakers bureau of other alternative healers. Once on the speakers bureau, he clearly stood out from the crowd based on his articulation and passion for his subject.

Develop a Respected Reputation in Your Field

Developing a reputation starts by being more of a public person by writing, speaking, and teaching. You can be considered an authority about a topic by having done one or all three of these things. Using a variety of methods of promotion and public relations to piggyback on your writing or speaking efforts can allow you to develop a stronger local or national reputation.

Gerald has been part of a national therapy association for years and wrote articles for a few professional journals. He contributed chapters for two clinical books, presented at national conferences, and taught classes at the university. Writing a book might be a logical next step, but he resisted that notion and opted for doing more public speaking. He scheduled a series of talks sponsored by a health clinic in his town and proposed to teach a short course for adults in "The Art of Subtle Communication" at a community college. By the end of the year, he had broadened his circle of referrals sources and felt on a stronger financial footing.

Match Your Professional Image to Your Level of Mastery

Some experienced, masterful therapists don't look like experts and as a result, have trouble staying financially competitive with newer, less experienced therapists. If this is your problem, you may be sending a contradictory message to others about your degree of excellence. Studies show that shoppers in a grocery store become suspicious when a supposedly better product is packaged cheaply and sells for much less than all the other products on the shelf. Packaging has meaning, like it or not.

Gerald admitted that after twenty years in practice he charged less than what some of his students commanded, straight out of school. He had set a fee when he first opened his practice and never raised it. His office was cluttered, with old furniture and had torn carpeting. His low fee and worn office contributed to the mistaken impression that he was not an expert. I coached him to immediately upgrade the look of his office and raise his rates to reflect the current marketplace. Although fearful about the effects of the fee raise, he actually went from a two-thirds full practice to full for the first time in a year. (More on why raising your fee can attract more business in chapter 10.) With these changes in place, Gerald had more energy and interest in his work, found that he had a busier practice, and made more money. He felt less worried about the competition in his area and especially enjoyed spending time in his new, spruced-up office.

DEVELOP LIFETIME CLIENTS

In business today, you are encouraged to develop "lifetime" customers—customers who will stay with your company over the long term, repeatedly purchasing your services or products. Adopting this mindset as a therapist doesn't mean that you work with a client forever, but that you take very good care of your relationship with a client over a long period of time—whether they are an active client (someone you currently see) or inactive (a past client). If they are inactive, you still regard them as a client; you find ways to keep communication open and continue to expand your services so that when they revisit your practice, you have services that match their needs.

To understand this strategy, think about a relationship you have with someone who treats you in this way, as a lifetime client. I have this relationship with my hairdresser Becky, a lovely, talented woman whom I have known for ten years. She works at a very busy hair salon and if I wait too long, I can't always get an appointment with her. When she is booked and I am frustrated, needing to get my hair cut right now she happily makes referrals to other hairdressers in the same salon. One time I liked Becky's referral a lot and stayed with the new hairdresser for a year. Becky happily greeted me each time I walked through the door, even as I marched over to someone else's chair. There is a striking lack of jealousy or professional envy in the salon, which the owner attributes to his belief in abundance (he is a very successful entrepreneur). Another time I left the salon to try another hair stylist. After a year I decided to return to Becky. She warmly greeted me as though I had been in her chair just the month before. In her mind, the relationship had never ended. She clearly considers me a lifetime client, and it feels great to be on the receiving end of this mindset. As a result, I consider her my primary hair stylist and I always return.

Here are action steps that can further your intention to have lifetime clients in your practice.

Make Every Termination a Positive Experience

Good endings are part of a good relationship. Ending well with a client makes good therapeutic and business sense, but I find it is not discussed enough within the therapeutic community. As a therapist, I was trained to view termination, especially unplanned termination, as potentially problematic. Clients act out in the process of therapy, my professors said, and will threaten to leave or actually walk out rather than confront their issues.

It is your job to interpret this acting out and retain them long enough so that they can complete their work. In my office, many clients have told me about particularly difficult experiences they had ending relationships with previous therapists, having to sneak out or leave abruptly, or feeling shamed and blamed for not continuing their therapy work. I understand the other side of this dynamic, and know how painfully frustrating it can be for a therapist when a client who is on the edge of a major therapeutic breakthrough announces "I quit." It can be hard to let go of clients gracefully, even in the best of circumstances, when each client represents a portion of your weekly income and you don't have a waiting list. But if you can contain your disappointment, fear, irritation, or exasperation and help your clients to leave you with your full support, it is easier for them to return when they are ready to proceed again.

Full support in leaving translates to educating your clients about their role in making a good ending and then doing your part—helping them to leave with an absence of guilt or shame. If you polled your therapy clients, you might be surprised that most have never left anyone or anything well and as a result don't know a lot about how to leave. I find that when clients announce they are leaving me abruptly or in anger, often it is because they don't know how else to leave.

To offer my full support means that in the first session with a new client I might say, "I want you to know that one of my policies is to support all termination, for whatever reason. When you are ready to leave, I would like to help you to leave me well. (At this point I usually hear a sigh of relief from the client.) In order to leave well, all you need to do is give me advance notice. Several weeks is sufficient, although some long-term clients let me know several months in advance. When leaving is handled this way, it often turns out to be the most productive time in therapy for my clients. Even if you are not able to give me advance notice, I will still do my best to help you leave well."

I also have words to this effect written into my client policy sheet. Of course, this does not ensure that every client leaves well. But it helps to make the majority of leavings very positive. When the client gives notice that they are ready to leave, I begin the work of creating a good ending. For some clients, a good ending means dealing with any issues that have as yet been untouched, so as to leave with completion. Clients may have profound breakthroughs at this point—it's as though their unconscious mind says, "Wait, don't leave without attending to this old problem."

For others, a good ending involves looking at the meaning inherent in choosing a particular time to end. I will make some interpretations to the client regarding this, but not with the intention of changing a client's mind. I will also usually lay out a plan for what the next piece of work would be, if he or she chooses to stay. Sometimes hearing this plan causes a client to decide to stay longer and complete a further piece of work, sometimes not. I support the decision either way.

In the last few sessions I begin to focus the therapy sessions on reviewing the course of our work together and saying good-bye. I suggest we not look for new issues to explore and just begin to wind down. We talk about how far the client has come, what he or she got from therapy, and what didn't get accomplished this time. We look at what he or she can take from our experience together, and express appreciation for working with each other. The final session has a sense of completeness and finality. The appropriate emotions of sadness and respect often surface in both of us.

If you feel anxious about your finances when a client leaves, you need to go back to chapter 3 and practice the techniques that help contain business anxieties. This is the time to use a business affirmation such as: *I attract an abundance of great clients.* Also review chapters 6 and 7, and take one action right away to generate new referrals. Taking action is a great antidote for anxiety. Remember, it's safe to let go; you will find additional clients that you like to work with and your practice will continue to grow.

Refer Clients to Others Sooner, Rather than Later

When you are a small business, one way to act like a larger practice and, as a result, take better care of your clients, is to know when to refer them to other professionals and then make the referral sooner rather than later. If you make a referral quickly and decisively, rather than waiting and hoping things will work out, you will be taking better care of your client. This strategy holds true for referrals of all kinds, including referring a client who is clearly not right for you to another therapist or referring a client you see to others for adjunctive services.

This strategy requires you to detach from a client and recognize that you are just one therapist with one approach. While your approach may be right for many clients, it certainly can't be right for everyone. Take a deep breath, let go of anxiety, and think about this client's best interests. I think you will find this strategy has long-term, positive effects, both on your relationship with clients as well as with the other therapists in your network.

In the coaching community that I belong to, it is standard procedure to ask each new client to interview two other coaches before deciding to hire you, so that the client can be sure they have found the right coach. This is a good idea for therapy clients as well, but more difficult for them to effect since most often therapy clients come in at a low point in life and are not at their most resourceful level. Knowing this, you can take on the resourceful role for clients, because you are in a better position to know if you will be a good match. If you have a sense that you are not quite right, or that they need other services in addition to seeing you in order to make this a successful relationship, make the referral.

Communicate with Lifetime Clients

Stay in contact with old clients. Keep them on your mailing list. Maintaining your communication each year by mail with inactive clients can allow them to stay current, knowing what is changing in you and in your practice. Should they return they will have a better idea of who you are and how they can use your services.

Now that you know how to expand and solidify your practice, the next chapter explores a major trend in today's marketplace: the concept of adding value to your business.

9

The Impact of Adding Value

In the United States, as we have shifted from being an industrialized society to a service-oriented one, the public has come to expect a high level of service. Since therapy is a service business, you should be aware of the current thinking about customer service. Keeping the customer *satisfied* is considered a baseline, a starting point. To retain clients in a competitive marketplace, customers need to feel more than merely satisfied. How do you go beyond client satisfaction as a therapist? What does it mean to offer a high level of service in your practice?

Traditionally, providing good client service in the therapy business meant being fair and reliable, while adhering to the ethical and therapeutic boundaries of your profession. This is still important, but delivering a high level of service requires that you do even more—you need to create a "client connection." Think of the client connection as an evolutionary process. Connection occurs organically, as you build stronger and stronger ties with your clients. During the process, your clients begin at satisfaction, the baseline, but evolve to feelings of loyalty, advocacy, and finally enthusiasm, all resulting in improved client retention.

The first stage in the connection is *client loyalty:* Clients establish a bond with you. This happens when you respond to a deep, bottom-up understanding of who your clients are and what they really want, not just what you think they need. The second stage is *client advocacy:* Clients put their trust in you. This comes as a result of doing a lot for clients, continually giving back more to them. Ultimately, you reach the third stage, *client enthusiasm:* Clients feel excited about working with you. This occurs when you create a rich environment for clients; as they pursue their goals in therapy, they enjoy the journey.

The easiest way to help the evolutionary process of increased client connection to occur is to turn your therapy practice into an *added-value* business. Added value means that every year your practice offers more value to your clients. If your practice is well-built, this will happen naturally. In this chapter we will look at how you can add value to your practice easily and regularly, so that you attract and retain great clients who appreciate the services you offer and, as a result, get to do your best work as a therapist.

Many therapists already have an added-value practice, with a strong client connection in place. If you have been in business as a therapist for more than ten years and your practice is thriving, with a continual flow of great clients, you are probably using this strategy. If so, this chapter can aid you in becoming more conscious about how you connect with your clients and give you some additional ideas. If you have been struggling in your practice and confused as to why your ties with clients seem weak, this strategy will help you see what you need to do in order to retain good clients. If you are new in practice, this chapter will give you the opportunity to build an added-value business from the start, putting you on a fast-track to long-term success.

Before starting to write this chapter, I thought about all of the successful therapists I know who have built an added-value practice and have a strong client connection. Some of these therapists are superstars—national authors or professional speakers with a large audience. They are at the top of their profession and their added-value approach is so well-honed that it's hard to follow in their footsteps. I wanted to offer you an example of an added-value business that was more approachable and easier to model. I thought about Carol Kurtz Walsh, a colleague in Bethesda, Maryland, whose thriving added-value therapy practice is also a great example of a personal-growth business. (We will take a closer look at how you can go beyond a medical model toward a personal-growth business in chapter 12.)

I have followed Carol's business development for seven years and seen that, like most therapy practices, it has some normal ups and downs. But even when her practice slows and a few clients leave, in a month it is full again and she has a waiting list. This is one of the benefits of an added-value business—it has resilience and as a result is inherently profitable. I will give you an overview of Carol's practice to show you how she turned a traditional private practice into a thriving added-value business, and then I'll spell out the client connection strategy so that you can implement it, too.

When Carol, a clinical social worker, started her private practice she offered traditional, limited psychotherapy services—individual therapy sessions and a weekly women's therapy group. Early in her practice she suffered a personal tragedy, the kind of event that causes a person to question the purpose and meaning of life. Carol, an artist and author, began to write a manuscript about spirituality as a way to make sense of her experience. As she explored the topic of spirituality for herself, she was surprised to hear many of her therapy clients also questioning the meaning of life and wanting to explore spirituality during therapy sessions.

To respond to this, Carol decided to offer a service outside the realm of clinical social work. She started an ongoing women's spirituality group, shifting her role from that of traditional psychotherapist into therapist/teacher/mentor. She did this with some trepidation, and found that when she talked about her group at professional meetings, colleagues sharply questioned her untraditional approach. Her clients in the group, on the other hand, were very pleased with her approach and worked deeply on themselves, with good results. She took another step and self-published her book on spirituality, so clients could read more about the topics they discussed in the group. She submitted several articles to a free alternative health magazine and was asked to write a regular column. The topics of the columns were issues that Carol was exploring for herself or with clients—making choices, creativity, dreams—and she began to design a workshop or class that mirrored the topics she wrote about in her column. Her existing clients read the column and came to the workshops, but so did a flow of others who got to know Carol and her point of view from the magazine. In time, her practice became a resource for a more spiritually-minded therapy client.

During the process of enlarging the scope of her practice, she also enlarged its size. She and her husband, Tom, also a therapist, leased an office with additional space for other therapists. Carol and Tom encourage collegiality and collaboration among the therapists. All of the therapists work in combination with each other, running groups, workshops, and classes, as well as contributing articles for a free newsletter, mailed to a pooled direct-mail list.

On a weekday evening it's not unusual for Carol to see her small waiting room overflowing with chatting, laughing clients, waiting for one of the many therapy groups or sessions to start. Carol heightens the aspect of enjoyment in the office by creating a lovely physical environment. Wonderful works of art (many of them created by Carol) adorn the walls. She posts funny, upbeat articles and cartoons on a large bulletin board. Carol herself runs five or six groups each week. The office feels like a bustling personal-growth center, rather than a somber, serious therapy office.

Carol's practice incorporates all four steps of the following client connection strategy. She is attracting her ideal clients, who like the direction of her spiritual practice. They are loyal, send her referrals, and openly express appreciation about her work with them. She provides a wide menu of classes, workshops, and groups and offers them in a fun, energetic environment. She encourages a warm community within her office space, with both her colleagues and her clients. As Carol goes to professional courses and explores new areas of her own personal growth, she brings back ideas and makes them relevant for her clients, increasing the value of her practice. Using her skills as a writer, she regularly articulates the added value she creates through her column and in her practice's newsletter. The flow of people, ideas, and energy circulating around and through her practice gives it an elasticity, an ability to bounce back from normal attrition. When a client leaves, others are poised to take his or her place.

Now let me show you how you can incorporate all or some of these elements, by using the client connection strategy:

1. Create client loyalty.
2. Create client advocacy.
3. Create client enthusiasm.
4. Articulate the added-value aspects of your business.

CREATE CLIENT LOYALTY

Going beyond the baseline of client satisfaction to client loyalty is accomplished by helping your clients feel a shared bond with you. Loyalty usually occurs when clients feel that you take the extra steps to understand what they want and need in their work with you. Carol explored spirituality on her own, for personal reasons; she created client loyalty by listening to her clients and hearing that they wanted to explore spiritual matters, too, even though this took her outside a traditional role for a psychotherapist. Her clients responded and went from being satisfied with her services to feeling loyal and appreciative for the extra dimension Carol brought to their therapy.

Creating client loyalty by attending to your clients' wants requires that you momentarily set aside your clinical assumptions and listen with a sense of curiosity and openness. A therapist came to see me for supervision regarding a case that was going badly, citing a lack of connection with her client. The client, a man in his early thirties, came to see her with a clearly stated goal: He wanted to find a better job for himself. After six sessions, the issue of his unhappiness at work had not been addressed. I asked the therapist to describe the content of their sessions. "I have focused on his need for empowerment and his lack of a true identity."

"What about the issue he came in for?"

"In my estimation, to explore that single issue, finding a better job, would foster dependency. It would encourage him to use me as a crutch. Once he becomes more empowered he can figure that problem out for himself."

Her client left therapy after one more session, frustrated with his lack of progress. The therapist interpreted his leaving as evidence that he wasn't ready to change. I saw the case differently. Although the therapist may well have been correct in her analysis about the underlying issues, I felt she had missed an opportunity to take a step in the direction of client connection by addressing what he wanted. Instead, she gave him what she thought he needed.

In a competitive marketplace, if you can't provide the service a person wants, the most predictable outcome is that the person will go somewhere else to find someone who can. In most businesses, finding out what your clients want is considered essential, valuable information. Entire marketing and sales staffs spend hours with top clients to do precisely that— understand their clients' wants and needs. This specific information then drives the process of product design and production.

As therapists we are trained to follow a medical model that too often places us in the position of re-interpreting our clients' words. In the process we may miss important verbal cues. Making the crucial distinction between what your clients want (and will happily pay to attain) and what you think they need can be a wake-up call for therapists. It was for me. Now that I understand this distinction, my work with clients is more productive.

Many times the difference between what clients want and your perception of what they need is just a matter of language. For example, say you have a client who gets extremely nervous in social situations. As a result, he speaks abruptly and inappropriately to people at work and, to his chagrin, even to women he casually dates. Your interpretation is that he is socially phobic and needs to learn to tolerate external stimulation and reduce his impulsive anxious responses. But during the first session when you ask him what he wants, he insists, "I just need more confidence." Unless you can bridge the language gap between "social phobia and impulsivity" and "more confidence" he will not feel understood. You will miss an opportunity to create client loyalty. Bridging this language gap between a client's stated wants and what you, in your clinical opinion, think he needs, is your next step.

When I have asked therapists to tell me what their clients want, I most often get back lists filled with clinical jargon. I understand the tendency to think this way, since I was also trained in a similar way to describe issues using therapeutic terminolgy. I want you to develop a business skill of articulating *client wants* without clinical jargon, so that you can communicate with clients as both a therapist and a smart businessperson. Listen to your client's language, which will often be less technical than yours; and then borrow his or her words to explain your perspective. Here's a short list to help you think about the bridging you may need to do in order to speak more directly to what your clients want:

What a Client Wants	*What You Think He or She Needs*
to be happy	to resolve family-of-origin issues
to stop worrying	to deal with depression
more free time	time management skills
to look better	self-discipline
confidence	to work through past trauma
success at work	to overcome negative self-devaluation
to relax	to reduce psychosocial stressors
peace of mind	to reverse negative self-statements
to be liked	assertiveness skills

CREATE CLIENT ADVOCACY

You build client advocacy as a result of giving back to your clients. Carol builds advocacy by continually expanding her already wide range of services. She offers a new workshop or class each six months, while continuing a full schedule of ongoing groups. She writes columns for the public that contain her best thinking regarding personal growth and spirituality. Her column and newsletter are available, free of charge, to active and inactive clients.

One benefit of offering an abundance of services is that you will have to anticipate your clients' future needs. You'll be one step ahead of them. Being out in front of your clients is a good position for the owner of an added-value business.

What added-value services can you offer for your clients to create client advocacy? Offer solutions, ongoing program content, resources, and optimism, for a start. All the training you take, books you read, cases you think about, supervision you purchase, and changes you make to build a better business can add value to your practice.

The key to adding value is to use a plan. Add services gradually, perhaps one new service a year or one every six months. Adding too much, too soon, will diminish the importance of any single service, overwhelm you, and confuse your clients. Keep your practice expanding slowly, yet consistently. Add value with a method, not randomly. Since adding value is an ongoing process, make it part of your overall business plan. Organize your offerings around a theme for the year. Add value that reflects your vision, purpose, and mission statement from chapter 4.

Here's a list of added-value services you might want to offer over time:

- *Teach a system instead of a class.* There is an old maxim that says: *"Give a man fish, feed him for a day. Teach him to fish, feed him for a lifetime."* It's more valuable for clients to have a program or a system they can use for life and can refer back to when needed than to take a one-day, one-shot workshop targeting a specific problem. To turn a workshop or a class into a program, include these elements: a manual, self-tests, exercises, progress reports, follow-up exercises, occasional additional sessions, a stand-alone network to connect to, or an ongoing support system you provide to keep the program in place.
- *Create methods of self-evaluation.* Your clients can benefit from any type of evaluation that they can use on their own, to help them extend the value of therapy sessions. For an example, look at the pre- and post-test in the Appendix. Create a similar checklist based on therapy outcomes that your clients can have and keep to help them chart their progress over time.
- *Publish a list of resources (be a turn-key solution).* Compile your best ideas and resources and make them available to your clients. You might create a list of inspiring books, soothing music, great self-help audio-tapes, or a "top ten" list that you have written (example: The Ten Best Ways to Stay Calm When Stressed). One talented personal coach publishes a quarterly "tool kit" of ideas for her coaching clients and sends it out by e-mail.
- *Give high value on the front end.* Offer additional services to brand-new clients, to help them get off to a strong start. Suggest specific readings, time that they spend writing in a journal each day, five-minute check-ins to you by phone between sessions, or any other services that will insure

that they get results immediately. This is an effective strategy for added value, even within long-term treatment plans. No matter whether therapy will be long-term or short-term, you can plan to have results right from the start.

- *Expose your clients to other wonderful teachers and therapists.* Host workshops of other therapists and teachers whom you admire. Allow their ideas and methods to inspire your clients to work more deeply. Use your regular therapy sessions with clients to explore the ideas that surface following their exposure to the guest teachers. You can't be an expert on everything; bringing in others with additional talents and skills you don't possess can add value to your practice and your clients' lives.

- *Write a workbook.* Have a lot to say to clients? Give them a workbook to augment their therapy. One yoga teacher is in the process of documenting and illustrating all of the exercises she uses in her classes. She gives this out to her clients, free of charge. This is an added value that lasts, and can help clients remember and review all the good work she does with them. A workbook takes time and effort, but may dramatically increase the results from traditional services. That's added value!

- *Help clients enlarge their community.* If you choose, you can help your clients expand their connections into the broader community. Offer information, resources, or suggestions of how to connect to others. Help clients build a mini-community within your classes and workshops. In my eight-week classes, each person is encouraged to find a "buddy" to talk with between classes. These buddies become important, ongoing friends. In my one-day or weekend workshops, those attending are encouraged to eat lunch each day with at least one other person. Mini-communities that occur within your classes and workshops can provide support and friendship long after the event is over.

- *Record an audiotape.* If you have a good speaking voice, your clients might like to listen to your voice outside of a session. You can make an inexpensive audiotape of your favorite stress-reduction exercise, meditation instruction, or story that you like to tell. Duplicate the tape and sell it at cost or give your clients copies for free, as part of your overall therapy package.

- *Create a practice newsletter that really inspires and educates.* When your newsletter is written with care, it becomes an added value for your clients. Don't use your newsletter solely as an advertisement; let it become educational for others. Reread chapter 6 for more ideas about how and why to write a great newsletter.

- *Open up your program design process.* The easiest way to make sure that you offer a program that clients want is to let them help you design it. Invite a group of existing or potential clients to discuss a general theme, and run an informal focus group to design a class or program. Distribute the notes from the focus group to participants, as a way to say thank you. The participants of the focus group will often become your first class members when you are ready to formally offer the program, because it's designed with them in mind.

- *Write a Q & A column.* If you find yourself getting asked the same questions repeatedly, take a hint from Ann Landers and write a question and answer column, using short questions. Questions you want to answer might include, "How does therapy work?" or "What should I do when angry feelings surface during my work day?" Incorporate the Q & A into your newsletter, offer it to a publication within your profession, or just make it available for clients on your waiting room bulletin board.

- *Anticipate client trends.* Listen carefully to the themes your clients voice and stay out in front of your clients' interests. Two years ago I heard several clients independently mention a book they were reading about relationships. I got the book, read it, found out where the author was giving a workshop and signed up. This helps me to be out in front of my clients, by quickly moving to educate myself about their interests.

- *Know the stages of personal-growth.* In chapter 12 we will look at the stages of personal growth. Have one added-value service that is appropriate for your clients for each stage of development.

CREATE CLIENT ENTHUSIASM

Client enthusiasm occurs when your clients feel positive emotions about your practice—emotions like excitement and appreciation. Fostering client enthusiasm may require a shift in your mindset about therapy. The medical model sees therapy as medicine; treatment is not supposed to be pleasurable. If you are inclined to move away from a medical model as you build your practice, you may want to take some time to explore how to make the process of therapy more pleasurable for your clients, so that they can feel enthusiastic about coming to see you. You can do this by enriching the physical environment where you offer therapy, so that it is more pleasing, or by enhancing the conceptual environment—your ideas and beliefs about delivering therapy services, and making that more pleasing, too.

Carol does some of both. She creates a physical environment for clients that is welcoming and fun to be in. She invokes a conceptual environment of high energy, by encouraging collegiality and cross-referrals between therapists and adding a lot of classes and workshops into the mix.

To promote client enthusiasm, there is one belief you need to confront. This belief is held by many of us in the therapy profession—that therapy is hard work. Many of us have been taught, trained, or somehow encouraged to believe that therapy should be hard work. We measure the success and value of our services by how hard our clients are working. As one who has been in this camp and is now a "recovering hard worker," I want to draw a distinction for you between *work* and *hard work,* the way it was done for me.

When I hired Pam Richarde, a business and personal coach, I asked her to help me achieve some specific goals, including how to better structure my life. After listening to the way that I set up my work and my life, including one long accounting of a simple potluck dinner I hosted that I had managed to turn into an exhausting (but perfect) event, Pam bluntly said, "Lynn, I want to tell you something. There is a difference between work and hard work. There is nothing wrong with work. For most people, work means effort and industry. You, however, have the uncanny ability to take all work and make it hard. Everything you do involves you working *hard.* You work hard in your personal life. You work hard running your business. You work hard at your professional training. And, from the sound of it, you work hard as a therapist. I even hear that you like your clients to work hard, too."

This was an eye-opener for me. The more I thought about it, the more I could see how much I valued *hard* work over work. I thought about the way

I conducted psychotherapy sessions. In my mind, my clients were only doing well if they were working hard. All of my many years of academic training, and my own experience as a client in therapy stressed hard work as the standard to be upheld. Could there be another way, equally effective and better for me and my clients?

I began to interview other therapists and realized that not all my colleagues shared my enthusiasm for the hard-work theory of therapy. Some therapists I admired actually enjoyed their clients, worked easily with them using a lighter touch, and still gave very fine value. Their clients got good results. The therapists seemed much happier than I. I was jealous.

So I changed. To my surprise, my clients got better results without my insistence that the work of therapy be "hard." I know that good therapy can be demanding, rigorous, serious, and emotional. But good therapy can also be pleasurable, relaxed, and full of exuberant laughter. I now offer therapy that is a combination of the two.

From a purely business sense, it is easier to satisfy clients in a fee-for-service business when you offer therapy that is balanced between hard work and pleasure, containing some of both. I encourage you to evaluate your thinking about the hard-work theory of therapy and see where you can add more pleasure, in both the tangible and intangible environment you create in your practice.

Look at the physical setting where you conduct your sessions. Do you work in an office that pleases you? Is it attractive? Does it inspire you to do your best work? If not, fix it. Look at your schedule and the way you work. Do you look forward to your day? Do you like the methods of therapy you offer, the population you work with, and the groups and classes you run? What about the intangible aspects of your practice? Do you value creativity, learning, innovation, experience, or a connection to nature? How are these intangible aspects represented in your work? What could you do to make your work reflect your true passions, values, and talents? Once you feel more pleasure in the way you work, you will transfer this pleasure to those clients you see and be a long way toward achieving client enthusiasm.

It's hard to impart enthusiasm to your clients when you are physically and emotionally exhausted from being a therapist. Is therapist burnout inevitable? David Treadway, who has written extensively on this subject, says that therapists need to prioritize and practice what we preach, so that we have balanced lifestyles and adequate self-care to prevent burnout from our stressful jobs. Maintain some form of ongoing supervision or coaching to stay fresh. Set up your practice so that it allows you to make good money and do great work—the best antidote I know for burnout. Building an ideal private practice can go a long way toward making you feel excited again about your chosen profession.

ARTICULATE THE ADDED VALUE OF YOUR BUSINESS

The easiest way to articulate the added-value aspects of your practice is for you to focus on the results you produce, as opposed to simply listing the services you provide. Here are a number of ways to help you articulate added value.

LIST THE WAYS YOU HAVE SPECIFICALLY HELPED CLIENTS

I have coached many good therapists who don't know how to clearly explain how they help people, other than to talk about the qualitative subjective changes that they (the therapists) notice during treatment sessions. "She seems happier, he has more access to his feelings, her body is less tense, he is able to speak about his issues to me with less anger."

Communicating results involves learning to speak a new language—that of outcomes. You need to shift your attention and look at client behavior outside of the therapy session. Try this: Make a list of current and past clients, and next to each name, write down the results he or she got from therapy with you, *as evidenced by* some specific change that happened in their life, outside of the therapy session. "As evidenced by" requires you to look at the real, tangible results of your services.

Here is an entry from a psychotherapist, who charted the tangible results of one client at three months and again at six months:

Initial session: The client, a middle-aged woman, says she feels sad. She looks demoralized and depressed. She has had no contact with her family for three years due to a long-term family fight, which upsets her. She has few friends and hates her job.

After three months: She made phone contact with her mother and was planning a trip to see her. She shopped and dined with two coworkers, liking the friendship that was developing.

After six months: She saw her mother and has regular phone calls with both her mother and her sister. She found a better job. She paid her bills on time for the first time in five years.

Results from therapy: In six months, this client went from feeling sad, depressed, and isolated to becoming much more functional and active in her life, as evidenced by re-establishing contact with her family, socializing with coworkers, finding a better-paying job, and becoming more financially responsible.

Notice that this therapist might also talk at length about how the client's mood shifted and lightened during the sessions or the changes she saw within the therapeutic relationship. This is the highly subjective case material that is important clinically, but not relevant to the idea of learning to identify tangible results. Focus on "what happened, what changed, what actions your client took" to define the outcomes you, as a therapist, help to produce.

HELP EXISTING CLIENTS ARTICULATE THEIR GAINS

Begin to talk more with your clients on a regular basis about the results you see. Too often therapists don't have this kind of discussion with clients until the termination process, as a way of evaluating the course of treatment. The results your clients have gained may be integrated and hard for them to recall. Waiting too long too communicate with a client about results can sound like this:

"What do you feel you have gained from your time in therapy during the past year?"

"Well, I'm not sure. I know we did a lot. Things are easier at home. I feel OK."

"Anything else?"

"No, that's all I can think of."

This doesn't signal that you did a poor job as a therapist; in fact, it may signal just the opposite. It may mean that all of the work your client did is well integrated, to the point where it feels to him that the changes in thinking, feeling, and behavior are now an accepted part of his self.

If you wait too long to identify results, you will find yourself trying to remind your clients of the outcomes they have achieved, instead of doing it together. Consider helping your clients to articulate their gains on an ongoing basis, so that they really understand the effectiveness of their therapy.

One therapist I know does this at the close of many sessions, saying, "What was most important in our work today? How specifically might you make it count in your life this week?" Another therapist has a three-month progress update with his clients, complete with a form that they both fill out, looking at results and gains from that time period. He tells me that this is a favorite time for him and his clients. Frequently, at the end of an evaluation session, they both end up feeling impressed with their work. Other therapists do this by having their clients complete a written result-survey form every month. Find a process that works for you, within your therapeutic style.

Since I work long-term with therapy clients, I tend to do this less formally, noting results as they appear. If a client mentions accomplishing an important goal in an offhand, matter-of-fact manner (which tells me that the change we have been working with has been integrated), I'll say, "You know, two months ago if I told you that you would have accomplished this, you would have laughed at me and told me it was impossible." I make a written note of this; later I can look through a long list of results for each client. It's a lot of fun and highly rewarding at the end of treatment to pull out this list and share with the client the wonderful results he or she has achieved.

This is one way that therapists begin to use one of the skills of coaching within their work, by prioritizing results and outcomes within the therapy session. Identifying results benefits your clients in two ways: It gives them a way to chart their progress and it gives them the words to use to talk about their results. It's easier for your clients to feel validation regarding their decision to be in therapy with you when they are clear about the results.

SPEAK IN OUTCOMES

Using the language of outcomes means speaking about the benefits of therapy, instead of the features. Here's the distinction between features and benefits: If you go into a store to look at a washing machine, the salesman will tell you a lot about the features of the machine—the length of the cycle, the temperature settings, the control panel, and the high-tech digital readout. This may interest you, but when you are faced with a pile of dirty clothes all you really care about are the benefits of the machine. Will it get your clothes cleaner, faster? Will it shrink your favorite shirt?

The features of your practice—your training, degree, license, certifications, places of previous employment, and where you have been published all give you credentials, but they don't tell potential clients what they most want to know. To explain the benefits of your practice, you want to be able to answer these important client questions: Can you help me make the changes I desire? What will it take?

One way to address these questions is to use anecdotes. Have a success story or two that clearly explains the benefits of your services. A success story is short synopsis of a successful case, structured so that it doesn't violate client confidentiality. The focus is on the plot, not the character in the story. To create a success story, think about your five "best" cases. Omit all personal, identifying details and highlight the outcome—what happened. You can use success stories in many ways as you build an added-value practice.

A potential client came for a first session. She wanted to learn how to stop dating men who were unavailable for a serious relationship. She asked, "Do you help people with this? How would therapy work?" To answer, I told her this success story:

"Many clients I counsel find that they learn to have good relationships as a result of their work with me in therapy. I have had success helping women learn to make healthy choices when it comes to relationships. I counseled a woman with similar issues to yours, who had some negative patterns that kept her attracted to unsuitable men. We looked at better, more constructive ways to select a partner. She found that after spending time exploring her patterns and making some changes within herself, she easily and naturally attracted and married a man who treats her with love and respect. I like doing this type of therapy and would be glad to help you work toward a similar goal."

My success story relates, in plain language, the benefits that others received from therapy with me. I didn't talk about techniques, jargon, or give any identifying client details. I drew a general map, in a short narrative form. Without overpromising results, I let this woman know that I have been down this road before and can travel the same path with her.

Sometimes it is hard to transfer clinical case material into a success story. As therapists, we are used to highlighting the difficulties of a case. To compose a success story, we must look for the wins. I asked a therapist to give me a case study and then coached him to turn it into a success story. Here is the case study, also about a client with relationship issues. In the original version, it highlights the features (techniques) of therapy:

> I saw a man in his mid-thirties, with depressive tendencies and anxiety issues. He had never had a relationship with a woman lasting longer than two months. He had been emotionally abused as a child and was frightened of intimacy. During the early months of therapy we spent time exploring his history and family of origin, using a psychodynamic approach. Then I switched modalities and put him into group therapy to learn some social skills and have a place for interaction and immediate feedback. This was a good choice and helped him reduce anxiety with women and confront his isolating tendencies. He began to date a woman. True to form, after two months he exhibited symptoms of extreme anxiety. However, he worked through his fear with group support. He made major gains, stayed in the relationship, and began to experience good sex and real intimacy with her. He asked her to marry him and they did indeed get married.

Here's the edited success story, which now focuses on the benefits of therapy:

> I worked with a client whose major goal was to be in a lasting relationship for the first time in his life. With therapy he developed better

social skills, conquered his fear of intimacy, modified a pattern of life-long anxiety, found a loving partner, and later married her. Checking back with him after two years, he is still married and deeply in love.

Here's another success story told by an acupuncturist I coached:

I saw a woman who had very bad digestive problems, untreatable with traditional medicine. She was often in a bad mood as a result of her pain and said she saw nothing good in her life. Working with me as well as a nutritionist, she reduced the pain and nausea that were always present immediately after eating. After six months of treatment she is able to eat whatever she wants with no discomfort. She gained weight, was able to exercise for the first time in four years and is now energetic and leading a normal life. One of the side benefits, which often happens in treatment like this, is that not only did she digest her food better, but she also began to digest her life better. She discovered a passion for writing poetry, and has become voracious in her desire to experience life. She travels, writes poetry, and spends time in nature.

Here's the edited version:

I treated a woman who had a problem with digestion, which left her in pain and affected both her mood and her enjoyment of life. With the help of acupuncture and nutrition, she is now able to eat whatever she wants with no discomfort. She has also learned to digest and absorb the pleasures of life more fully and spends time traveling, writing poetry, and being in nature.

Take some time and think through your successful cases. This is fun to do, because we all love to be reminded that we help others. Edit out the identifying features, clarify the benefits, and eliminate clinical jargon. Practice telling your success story out loud, so that you use a conversational tone. Now you have another choice for a response when someone says, "Tell me *more* about what you do."

You can also help your clients tell their own success stories. One movement specialist who teaches classes asks her students each week if they have any success stories to report based on their work in the class. She says that during the first few weeks of class she gets little response, but she keeps asking and as the class progresses wonderful examples get shared. Hearing success stories motivates others in the class and creates a supportive environment.

Your promotional materials should also speak the language of outcomes and identify the solutions you offer. Make sure that the written materials you send to the public articulate your "basic message," create enthusiasm in others, and focus on results. If your brochures, newsletters, advertisements, or flyers, don't satisfy these elements, it's time to rewrite your materials. Help your ideal clients find themselves in your materials. Make sure that your materials speak to the benefits of your practice as well as the features. To make your printed material excite others, offer a constructive perspective of what you can honestly guarantee. Don't over-promise. Just write in terms of what you can deliver.

10

Why Good Therapists Go Broke

I hate to see therapists fail financially in private practice. Unfortunately, many therapists have an uneven profit picture; even having a full caseload may not guarantee financial success. Therapists need a way to talk with each other about money and profitability, but it's usually a hard topic to initiate. The subject of money tends to carry the weight of old, childhood beliefs and difficult, unexamined emotions.

How you currently handle the finances of your practice is often a mirror reflecting your core beliefs about money. Maybe you believe the topic of money is tawdry or dirty; you wish you could disregard it altogether. "I don't like to discuss money. I just love being a therapist, Lynn. I wish money didn't enter into it," you tell me. As a result, you rarely initiate discussions regarding your fee with your clients, don't bill them on time, carry the debt of uncollected accounts when you do bill them, and can't figure out why you are so broke.

Maybe you grew up with money deprivation. There was never enough money for your basic needs as a child. You still believe money is in short supply and watch every penny, reluctant to spend on anything "unnecessary." You won't attend major conferences, because they cost too much. You irritate the colleagues who share office space with you, because you refuse to pay for simple amenities like magazines, flowers, or even bottled water to add ambiance to the waiting room. You don't join associations, because it's not cost effective. As a result, you fail to give your business the resources it needs to flourish. You miss networking opportunities, skimp on training that would benefit your work, and don't see the collegial resentment building up due to your lack of sharing.

Maybe you grew up in awe of money; in your family, money came first. You think a lot about money, and how to make as much money as possible. You'll see clients you don't like, as long as they will pay your full fee. You'll work an exhausting caseload of fifty hours a week, as long as you are making good money. After a while, money becomes the driving force; you feel pressure to keep earning more each year, giving rise to complaints about the exacting nature of your practice. As a result you feel burned out too soon, and you want to quit and find something less demanding to do.

Maybe you grew up believing that money was mysterious. In your family it magically appeared and then, just as randomly, was gone. Your family spent wildly when money was present, then panicked when they got into debt. You ride an emotional money rollercoaster. When you make money, you are up, feeling great. When your practice goes through a slow time, you are down and self-critical. You alternately feel blessed or panicked based on your financial bottom line and clueless about how to bring the situation under control. As a result, your practice swings from positive to negative cash flow. You feel exhausted from the ups and downs, unable to take the steps necessary to keep your practice on an even financial keel.

Maybe money scares you. You watched anxiety on your parents' faces when they talked about money, so you feel anxious when you have to deal with it, too. You are too frightened to raise your fees, negotiate a better rent, or hold your boundaries about your established policies. Clients bully you into charging less. Landlords easily get you to pay too much. You find all aspects regarding money painful and difficult. As a result, you attract clients who pay too little and demand too much, or work for others for a split-fee arrangement, letting someone else handle your billing so that you don't have to confront money issues with clients. You end up wishing you could have more autonomous control over your practice but feel too fearful to handle the business finances yourself.

We all grew up with different beliefs and attitudes toward money. To be successful in business, you will need to recognize any childhood beliefs you hold and not act them out within your practice. Develop an adult relationship with money. You can learn about your money, in the same way you learn about other important things in your life. Hire a reliable accountant and financial advisor, and read about money management. Your accountant can advise you about the best status for your business—whether or not to incorporate and other tax strategies. Check the Appendix for books that can help you manage your money in an adult manner.

Because money is a topic many therapists shy away from, in this chapter I want to engage you in a relaxed conversation about the basics of money management and profitability. Let's start with the first thing you need to know about making money in private practice.

PROFIT AND SERVICE

To be a therapist in private practice, you need to decide to really be in business. This starts by finding a way to reconcile two seemingly opposite concepts, *profit* and *service.* Here's a simple definition of both:

- profit = financial gain, an advantage, moneymaking
- service = assistance, helping others, benefiting the public

A business is an enterprise that makes a profit through financial gain. Yet as a therapist, your focus is on service and helping others. You need to resolve these concepts for yourself or you will falter when it comes to making the necessary, sometimes hard business decisions that will keep your practice financially healthy. There is no one right way to unite these two concepts—I just want you to have a way that makes sense to you, in your own mind. As you think about reconciling profit and service, add in a third concept: autonomy. I want you to be in control of the profitability of your business. For that to happen, you need to have the final say on all of your decisions and policies about money. You can't control the finances of your business if you work for someone else, are part of a managed-care arrangement, or participate in any other shared-fee situation.

If you currently are involved with managed care, decide to have one part of your practice that operates as a fee-for-service business. Do this on paper, so you see two separate profit centers and the expenses that apply to each. Over time, enlarge the fee-for-service aspect of your practice, that side of your business that gives you optimal financial control. As we talk about money and pricing, I will be addressing the part of your practice that operates as a fee-for-service business.

YOUR BUSINESS PLAN

If you have been following the exercises in the book you have already completed two thirds of your business plan: You have a vision, purpose, and mission statement, a strategy to generate referrals (similar to a marketing plan), as well as steps to help you expand, diversify, and add value. Now you need the financial part of your plan. This looks similar to a financial budget, but a budget that tracks your current year and then helps you to project into the future. Having a financial plan is empowering and can help you understand a lot about your business—what you have made, what you will make, how much to spend, and what you can accomplish in the future. Turn to the Business Budget form in the Appendix and use it as a guide. Record and track all of your income and expenses for this year. Based on the goals you now have for your practice, allocate funds to each goal, so that each has a budget. Once you have filled out the financial budget, here are some questions you can ask yourself:

- How much money can I anticipate to make this year?
- What will I spend?
- What services produce the most profit for me?
- Which are least profitable?
- What cycles does my practice go through each year?
- If I wanted to increase my profit by 15 percent how could I do it?
- What expenses could I cut?
- What extra income could I make?
- When was the last time I raised my fees?
- What was the best month for me last year?
- What was the worst month?
- When should I plan to take my vacation time based on my business plan?
- How much profit did I make during the past year?

Here is a brief definition of the financial terms I use:

1. *Gross income or revenue:* all of the money that you earn in your practice
2. *Expenses:* the costs you incur from doing business. There are two types of expenses I will look at with you: *direct expenses*—the essentials that must be in place to allow you to run your business (office space rental, utilities, telephone, licensing, supervision, billing, accounting, postage, supplies, malpractice insurance, self-employment tax, etc.); and *indirect expenses*—those expenses that you may write off to the business that are nonessential, but helpful (travel, publications, office decoration, meetings, conferences, etc.).
3. *Net income or profit:* what's left of your revenue after you pay your direct and indirect expenses

Some therapists have low direct expenses (they work out of their home, employ no staff, don't advertise, have few equipment needs) and others have more overhead (high rent and utilities for multiple offices, advertising budget, direct-mail campaign, staff, a billing service, subcontractors to pay, equipment).

Here is an important point to understand: Whether you are a sole proprietor or part of a group practice, whether you work from home or out of a fancy downtown office, a therapy business is considered an *expensive* business to operate; your expenses will always be a substantial percentage of your gross income. It may not seem that way when you have a small practice, because there is relatively little start-up expense, especially with a home office, but when you look at your expenses as a *percentage of gross income,* you see the true picture. Let me contrast a therapy business with other kinds of business, for you to understand this better.

A manufacturing company makes and sells a product, like t-shirts, that can be duplicated in unlimited quantities. The more t-shirts that are made and sold at a profit, the lower the overall expenses of machinery and labor become, as a percentage of the gross income. The sheer volume of production and income offsets the cost of the fixed expenses. Having a lot of product to sell is one way to bring down the costs of a business.

This same rule applies even when we take a look at a business that is closer in nature to a therapy practice, such as a consulting company. If the consulting company sells a combination of services, it can also have a lot of product to offset expenses. Some of the product, in this case the services, are consulting sessions, similar to therapy sessions and billed by the hour. But other services are projects—programs delivered to a company, written reports, data that are compiled and analyzed. Billing by the project allows a consulting company more flexibility to bring costs down, and can be more profitable than consulting sessions, since lesser-paid staff may be able to complete a project.

As a sole proprietor of a therapy business, your product is likely to be your therapy services and you may only bill based only your contact hours with clients. You can't send in a lower-paid "substitute therapist" to deliver therapy. You also can't mass produce your sessions. Your time and energy is limited—there are only so many client sessions you can conduct each week. Based on this limitation of time and delivery of service, a private practice can't easily match the high profit ratios of a manufacturing or consulting business. You simply can't produce as much product.

Even though I suggest ways that you can boost your income by leveraging your time or selling ancillary products, if your primary revenue stream is generated by delivering hourly sessions, your profit potential will always be capped. Since you have some set expenses that must be in place in order to operate, your ratio of expenses to profit will always be relatively substantial. In order to be as highly profitable as possible, you need to carefully consider how to charge for your time and how to control your expenses.

MAKING A PROFIT

How much profit can a therapy business make? Each practice is different, but there are some general guidelines that can help you see how you measure up. Let's look at a sample profitability formula for a one-person therapy business:

100%	gross income
−40%	direct and indirect expenses, *including self-employment taxes*
−5%	maintenance of operations (systems and facility)
−5%	business reserve (cash reserve for emergencies)
50%	profit (includes your "salary")

Now 50 percent profit looks incredible, until you remember that you haven't taken your compensation, or a salary, yet. Your compensation comes out of this profit. This profit amount will also be subject for additional federal, state, and local taxes. Since your salary comes out of profits, if you want a "salary" of $40,000 a year and your expenses run 40 percent, you need to bring in a gross income of $66,000. If you want to follow the above profitability formula and allocate funds for an annual systems update and a cash reserve, you will need a gross income of $80,000. Your hourly fee must be set in such a way as to cover your total expense of doing business.

Therapists in private practice traditionally follow a medical model when billing clients for therapy sessions, charging for contact hours (therapy sessions) and some secondary services (such as phone consultations, court testimony, testing, or writing reports). Unlike lawyers, who bill clients in increments for every expense that is involved (filing, reading e-mails, making phone calls, typing), therapists rarely bill for administrative time. If you bill according to a medical model, your fee will need to cover the actual time you spend with clients, as well as the unbilled services you perform. You need to understand that your hourly fee must reflect your total business expense.

Let's look at the annual billable hours one therapist can generate based on a formula offered in Linda Stern's book *Money-Smart Secrets for the Self-Employed* (1997).

Hours you can work in a year

2080 hours	40 hours a week, 52 weeks a year
−120 hours	3 weeks vacation and/or training time
−80 hours	10 popular holidays
−40 hours	a week of sick leave
1840 hours	
−184 hours	marketing time—unbilled time to network and generate referrals (10%)

−184 hours	administrative tasks—unbilled office operations (10%)
−184 hours	downtime—those hours that don't fill (10%)
1288 hours	26 hours per week, 49 weeks per year

This formula concurs with national surveys showing that therapists in full-time private practice see an average of 25 to 30 individual clients per week. Part time therapists average 10 to 12 client hours per week.

Remember how we discussed that if you want to net $40,000 per year, and your expenses are 40 percent, you need to make $66,000 per year? If you work an average of 25 hours per week, that means you need to charge a minimum of $55 per hour, every hour you work, for 49 weeks per year.

What if you take four weeks off for vacation or work-related training, instead of three? What if your client count drops to fewer than 25 hours? Maybe your administrative time runs more than 10 percent. What if you get sick for two weeks instead of one? What if you decide to attend a training that costs $2,000 dollars, pushing your expenses up? You still have additional taxes to pay. You will want to have a cushion built into your fee to absorb these and other things that come up in the normal course of doing business. Since your hourly fee is your only source of income, it has to contain all of your many expenses and be able to buffer your practice against the normal ups and downs of a small business.

This is why the private pay fee for therapy sessions generally falls in the range of $70 to $250 per hour for therapists. According to recent surveys in several national association newsletters, psychiatrists, executive coaches and therapists working in consulting positions command the highest range ($150 to $350 per hour and up); mental health therapists such as psychologists, social workers, and licensed counselors are in the middle ($75 to $175 per hour); alternative healers, including acupuncturists, massage therapists, and energy healers tend to charge at the lower levels ($45 to $90 per hour).

SETTING YOUR FEE

The right way to set your fee is to consider your overall business plan and keep in mind the following six criteria:

1. *Your vision for the practice:* Your fee needs to reflect your philosophy of service. If you want to work with senior citizens with fixed incomes, your fee must be low to reflect that market. If your service is extremely specialized and of very high value, your fee needs to be high. If your vision is to create a practice that stays full with a big flow of clients, your fee needs to be priced in the middle of the market to keep you competitive.

2. *A desire to adhere to your business goals:* Look at your business plan. What did you want to earn this year and why? What do you need to cover your expenses and insure a profit? What are your goals for the year? If you are in the expansion phase of your business and need some cash reserves to purchase a new office, you will consider raising your fees. If you are scaling back your workload and concerned about retaining your existing clients, you may prefer to keep your fees flat.

3. *Market forces:* It's important to know what others charge in your local area, as well as what your market can pay. For example, therapists in a rural area generally charge less than those in a major metropolitan city, based on market forces. Therapists with corporate clients need to stay current with other training companies and charge enough to be taken seriously. (Corporate consultants and trainers generally charge between $175 and $500 per hour, or $1,000 to $5,000 per day.)

4. *Perceived value:* The unwritten rule of business pricing is that you can charge what the market will pay, based on your real or perceived value. Perceived value is a felt or intuitive sense of what something is worth, based on the benefits offered. Two therapists in the same city can offer the same type of therapy, but one will be able to charge twice what the other one does. The one who charges a lot has clients who perceive that his or her skill and talent is top quality and therefore they are willing to pay top dollar.

5. *Your time line to fill your practice:* At one point in my career, my husband was laid off from his job. I was leisurely building my practice and immediately rethought the timing of my business plan. I needed to move quickly and decided to start several groups at a low fee so that they would fill without a long wait. Over time, I raised the fee of the groups to bring them into line with the going rate of therapy groups in my local area. If you need to fill hours fast, you will probably set a lower

fee. If you have no money pressures and are in no hurry to add extra clients, you can wait for those clients who can pay full fee.

6. *Professional courtesy:* Sometimes you will set your fee as a courtesy to another therapist. I had a colleague who was seeing a wife and asked me to see the husband. She also asked if I would match her fee, which I agreed to do out of professional courtesy. This includes setting your fee to work with a referring organization or a sponsoring group. One therapist worked out a relationship with a local church, where she offered church members a discounted rate for the first three sessions, another example of professional courtesy.

Now that you know six *right* criteria to use when setting your fee, here is a list of *wrong* ones:

1. *Anxiety:* Emotion doesn't have a place in deciding how much to charge. Decide on a fee that is fair, meets the right criteria, and reflects your business objectives. Don't raise or lower it based on your worries or fears of keeping or losing a client. Use the other techniques I have suggested in the book to deal with your anxiety. Your fee must be based on logic.

2. *Guilt:* Some therapists feel guilty about charging what they are worth. Feelings of fear regarding success or confusion about reconciling profit and service are often the source of guilt. Get therapy, coaching, or supervision to help you resolve your feelings about money.

3. *Zero-sum game mentality:* This mindset says that there is only a fixed amount of money in the world. If I take more, you get less. If I win, you lose. This is both illogical and demeaning to your clients. Instead, see your decision to set a fair fee as a win/win scenario. With the right fee, you can become a better therapist and better serve those clients you choose to see.

4. *Love:* Some clients confuse the caring or affection with which therapy is often delivered with love, and feel offended at having to pay for love. You are not selling love. I heard a senior therapist in New York explain it to a client this way, "You pay me for my skill. The love I choose to give is free."

5. *Anger:* Sometimes therapists will set a fee based on anger or resentment

with a specific client or a certain type of clients. For example, therapists say, "I don't like to work with that type of diagnosis. It's too difficult. If a person comes in with that diagnosis, I'll see him or her but charge double." This is not a good way to set a fee. You will do better to refer clients you don't want to others and let your practice contain only those clients that help you to work at your best.

6. *Identity questions:* I have witnessed new therapists, fresh out of graduate school, decide to charge a high fee as a way to validate themselves. "I have a lot of life experience, I know everything I need to about psychology, I'll charge $150 an hour," a new graduate might say. This often speaks more to an issue of professional identity than to good business sense. I have also seen this go the other way, where a therapist with thirty years of experience, who works wonders with clients and has a waiting list, seriously undercharges and suffers as a result. She feels she isn't worth more.

You will know that you have set your fee well if you can state it out loud with ease, as naturally as you might say your name. I would suggest you practice stating your fee in front of a mirror and then observe your nonverbal behaviors. If you can't say your fee without grimacing, rolling your eyes, an embarrassed laugh, or looking down at the floor, go back and review the criteria to make sure you have set a fee that makes good business sense for you.

RAISING YOUR FEE

Here are six good indicators that it's time to raise your fee:

1. *You're impoverished:* It does no good for you to be broke and sacrificing within your business. If you are in debt or facing poverty, look to see if you are undercharging.
2. *You increased your expenses:* If you have upgraded your business with a new location, expanded phone service, bigger staff, or more services, you may need to raise your fee to cover these added values.

3. *You want a cost of living raise:* Be a good boss to yourself. Give yourself a raise to cover the cost of living. Raise your prices, raise your self-esteem, and lower your resentment.

4. *You received additional training:* Most therapists invest heavily in their ongoing training. If this is true for you, know that this investment will serve you well and benefit your clients. Raise your rates to match your level of experience and certification.

5. *You want existing clients to work with a deeper commitment:* When you raise your rates, it forces your clients to take their therapy more seriously. Raising your fees can be a gain for your clients, helping them to approach therapy with more diligence. Raising your fee models self-care and may help clients take steps to ask for a raise themselves at work. Often, when I ask therapists who are undercharging to raise their fees, they report a positive result with clients. I hear many stories of clients who took this as a signal to become more empowered.

6. *You have a waiting list:* Sometimes raising your fee can be a response to having too much business. Raising your rates may help slow down referrals a bit and ease up the pressures of a long waiting list. Of course, if you are really tops in your field, clients will expect to pay more to see you. In this case a high fee will not discourage them from seeking your services. In fact, it may just add to the perceived value of your skills.

When you are ready to raise your fee you can do the following steps to preserve your ongoing relationship with existing clients.

GIVE ADVANCE NOTICE

Give advance notice of at least thirty days prior to instituting a fee change. For example, if you want your fee raise to coincide with the calendar year, at the beginning of December you might alert your clients that you will be charging an increased rate as of the first of January. Give this notice both in writing and verbally at the beginning of a session. In general, all business matters and boundary changes that affect your clients are best delivered verbally and/or in writing, at the beginning, not end, of a session. Usually, our anxiety makes us want to procrastinate and not talk about money until the end of the session, as though that will let us off the hook.

We can dump the bad news and let our clients deal with it on their own. Calm your anxieties and learn to make space for all issues, including the business of therapy, within the session. Allow your clients to have their reactions within the session, instead of on the way out the door. It's important that you give your clients time to process business matters with you directly, and bringing them up at the start of a session makes time for this to happen.

By doing this, you can model how to talk about difficult issues. For example, a therapist I supervise told me about a client who announced in the last thirty seconds of a session, "I forgot to say that I'm having a problem with money. I need to cut back to every other week and I have to start immediately, beginning next week." With another client waiting in the corridor, there was no time to talk about other options, much less explore any deeper meaning within the announcement. If you educate clients to bring up their business matters with you early in a session, it will help them better resolve difficult issues.

ANTICIPATE A REACTION

Whenever I make any change within the therapeutic boundaries, such as raising my fees, taking time off, or changing the hours of a session, I anticipate that clients may have an emotional response to the change. Most of us don't like change of any kind. I do two things to make changes that I institute therapeutic: I tell each client about changes early in a session to allow enough time for him or her to process the change in my presence. I also present it cleanly, so that he or she can have a full reaction. I don't offer an overly long explanation or rationale, which will only serve to dilute my client's response. A long explanation may soothe your anxiety when you tell your client that you are raising your fee, but it tends to diffuse your client's reaction, weakening a therapeutic opportunity for growth.

Instead, clearly state the fee increase and make a space, with your silence, for your client to express his or her feelings, if any. Try to interpret what your client is trying to communicate. Very often important information is embedded in a client's emotional reaction. Usually it concerns feelings about money, abandonment, fear, anxiety, or deprivation.

Although you may worry that clients will leave as a result of raising your fee, in my experience of presenting boundary changes in this way, few do. Rather, this becomes a session where we can discuss money, including how the client handles money, if they feel deprived, if they are blocked from earning what they need, etc. By not getting defensive or anxious in the face of a client's reaction to your business decisions and policies, you can make this type of session a valuable one that strengthens the relationship between you and your client.

If you are charging below the market rate in your area, and have not raised your fee in years, you might consider raising your fee in two increments. To effect a thirty percent raise, increase your fee by 15 percent within thirty days and another 15 percent after six months. I suggest you tell your clients about both raises so that they know this is a planned strategy. You might say, "I will be raising my fees from $60 per hour to $80 per hour in two stages during the next year. The first increase will take place at the beginning of the next month. Starting January 1, my charge will be $70 per hour. Then, on June 1, my rate will go up to $80 per hour. It will stay at the new rate for the next twelve months."

DISCOUNTING YOUR FEE

If you decide to raise your fee, what do you do when someone says that you are too expensive? Many therapists have a sliding scale. But before you jump to the conclusion that you must have one as well in order to retain clients who can't pay your full fee, consider these questions: How does a sliding scale fit into your business plan and business vision? What purpose will it serve? How will you determine the rates? A sliding scale presents some inherent problems for you, placing you in a role for which you have no formal training—that of a financial analyst/evaluator. If you offer a sliding scale pegged to a client's income, you assume the task of evaluating what your client earns, spends, and therefore can afford to pay for therapy. I believe that a client who asks if you have a sliding scale is really asking if he or she can pay you less, not to have his or her financial life examined. However, if you want to use a sliding scale, make sure it is clearly formulated and well defined. Put your sliding scale in writing. Give a copy to clients, and don't vary from your formula.

Let's look at some other options you can have, other than a sliding scale, for clients who can't pay your full fee.

RUN GROUPS

Offer ongoing groups at a rate lower than your individual fee. Groups let you leverage your time and still offer quality service. An ongoing group might start with one person; add others as you can. Group therapy is a great way to deliver therapy services. I recommend that every therapist learn to run groups and then offer at least one group as part of his or her menu of services.

Marilyn Ellis, a veteran clinical social worker, has managed to lead large, weekly ongoing psychotherapy groups successfully for over twenty years. I once asked her how she defines a group. I was thinking of starting a new group at the time and wondered how many people she thought I would need to get started. Her answer surprised me and freed me from my limiting perception. She told me that she defines a group not by the number of people that attend, but by the type of work that takes place. For her, the therapy that happens in a group is distinct and different from what she does with a client in an individual session.

Think about your experience with groups and define what makes your groups different from individual sessions. For example, in my groups I use peer feedback, highlight the group psychodynamics, encourage methods of emotive therapy that I don't employ in individual sessions, teach conflict resolution techniques, set up role-plays between group members, design community-building interactions, and use gestalt exercises that can only be done within a circle of people.

When you are clear that group therapy is distinct and different from what you do with a client during individual sessions, you could conceivably start a group with one client, as long as he or she understood that in time, the group would fill with others. I coached a therapist who had a group of two people that ran for a year. Both clients felt that they benefited tremendously from the experience. The work was different than an individual session, with much more time for feedback and a focus on social and group dynamics. Neither client felt that the group lacked anything; it felt "full" enough to them. Redefine your perception of a group and run more groups to offer value and simultaneously leverage your time.

PRO-RATE YOUR TIME SLOTS

Offer hard-to-fill times at reduced rates. This gives you a way to fill your hours and have some discounted sessions. Give each session a rate. For example, early morning sessions are $80 per hour, midday are $70, evening sessions (prime time) are $90.

OFFER SHORTER SESSIONS

Some clients might prefer thirty-minute sessions at half your rate, instead of full-hour sessions at a full rate. This is especially helpful for clients who want frequency rather than intensity. Instead of seeing a client for two hour-long sessions a month, you could schedule that same person for thirty minutes twice a month. For well-motivated clients who need to pay less, this can be a helpful treatment option.

DISCOUNT PREPAID PACKAGES

Prepaid packages reward those who pay up front and make a solid commitment. You save on billing time and retain serious clients who have reduced financial circumstances. If your going rate is $80 per hour for individual sessions, offer a special package: ten sessions over a three-month time frame for $750, prepaid. Define all your packages and discounts in writing.

Review the packaging ideas and menu pricing in chapter 8, so you have many options to offer for those who think you are too expensive. When someone questions your fee, or the fact that you don't accept managed care payments, you can let him or her know that you have many options that make therapy affordable: groups, discounts on prepayment, less intensive packages that allow someone to see you fewer times but still receive high value and make progress, time-of-day slots that are discounted, and shorter sessions for a lower price.

STAYING HIGHLY PROFITABLE

To stay highly profitable you need to increase your earnings and decrease your expenses. The first step to increasing your earnings is to bill at your full fee the majority of the time. Plan to bring all your sliding scale clients up to full fee over twelve months and, at the same time, remove yourself from managed care panels. Devote more time to generating referrals. Meet the other therapists in your area that have full fee-for-service practices. Borrow their model of business and follow it until you get the same results. Be sure you consider everything that they do to build their practices. Maybe you need more supervision to raise your skill level, or you need to relocate to a better office. Use the strategies given to you in the last three chapters. Determine what others are doing that works well, add your own ideas to the mix, and move forward. I have coached many therapists to transition to a full fee-for-service business. It's not impossible, it just takes vision, determination, and follow-through.

One therapist took my eight-week program and then immediately resigned from all managed care panels. She kept a careful record of her time and told me that the time she saved having to make phone calls to insurance companies and write long treatment reports represented an astonishing 20 percent of her time each week. She decided to devote the same amount of time to networking. At first she lost money, but by the end of the year her income had almost doubled. Here's why: Every new client was at full fee. She had a much larger network than before. As a result of the larger network, she had diversified her practice and was even giving some training sessions for a local business, at twice her hourly rate.

Besides raising your fees or working more hours, you can increase your earnings in other ways:

- Leverage your time by running groups or teaching classes.
- Sell ancillary products (books, tapes, merchandise) that represent passive income (does not rely on client hours).
- Employ others and make a profit from their services.
- Diversify by securing contracts where your fee is higher, such as corporate consulting, expert testimony, or training and development contracts.

To reduce expenses, chart everything you spend and cut it by 20 percent. Look carefully at what expenses help you to be a good therapist and those that are less essential. However, *don't* cut back on:

- *Networking:* You need a strong, active network.
- *Your business identity:* Put in the time and effort to articulate your services.
- *Training:* Go for mastery in at least one area of practice.
- *Supervision:* Give yourself abundant professional support.
- *Self care:* Stay in good mental and physical shape.
- *Small, meaningful touches in your office:* Provide your office with small things that heighten your enjoyment in your environment.

Do cut back on these items:

- *Your menial work:* Hire others to do menial work and free yourself for the important aspects of delivering service or networking.
- *Expensive equipment:* Buy what you can afford now, not what you think you will be able to afford next year. Computer costs drop over time. Waiting to purchase certain types of equipment is a smart business move. Make sure that the equipment you buy will generate profits immediately.
- *Major office furnishings:* A leather couch is nice, but your clients come to see you, not the couch. Resist your impulses to outfit your office when you need to cut your expenses. Make do with less.
- *Advertising:* Advertising is expensive, needs repetition to be effective, and yields results sporadically. Instead, network in low-cost ways. Go to lunch with a different potential referral source every week.
- *Printing:* Black-and-white printing works fine when you are on a budget. Save money by using your home computer and a copier, instead of hiring a printer to produce a four-color brochure.
- *Image:* You don't need an expensive wardrobe to be an impressive therapist. You can serve your clients equally well from a modest office as a luxury suite.

Direct and indirect expenses in a streamlined therapy practice generally run between 30 and 40 percent (including self-employment taxes). Some of the expenses you incur with a therapy business are less obvious, but still real. One is the psychic cost of working with the psychology or physiology of others. Since you need to be emotionally open and empathic with clients, you may take in some of their feelings. You need to psychically clean out from time to time. Get a weekly massage, good professional supervision, some spa time, your own therapy, take meditation breaks or a daily walk in nature to clear away the emotional stress you take in. You may also face a hidden expense as you deal with feelings of professional isolation. Get sufficient positive peer support. You may contend with physical ailments if you are a psychotherapist, based on sitting still for hours at a time. If you are a physical therapist or other type of body worker, you may find your own body aches from the efforts of massaging or manipulating others six hours a day. Again, make sure you budget for the self-care you need to stay in good shape.

To cut expenses, eliminate your debt. Debt is costly, based in part on the interest you lose by not having collected monies owed to you, but also in the time you spend trying to collect unpaid fees and the psychic energy or feelings of frustration you carry in association to the debt. Avoid carrying large amounts of receivables, the payments owed to you by clients, by instituting a policy of getting paid at the time of delivering service. If you have existing receivables, contact all the people who owe you money by phone or letter. Be firm and try to clear up the accounts. If that doesn't work, consider using a collection agency to collect large amounts. If some of your accounts receivables are the result of therapy that ended poorly, and a dissatisfied client refuses to pay, a better business decision may be to simply write off the account as a "bad debt" and take the loss. Sometimes the energy you will need to expend to recover payment from a dissatisfied client is counterproductive. If the amount is under $1,000, you may find it is best to walk away from the situation and put your energy toward generating new, and better, referrals. Talk with your accountant about the tax advantage of writing off all your bad debts at the end of the fiscal year.

When a coaching client is in serious financial trouble, I instruct him or her to immediately consider a business "turnaround" plan. One client, not a therapist, came in feeling desperate. She was a wonderful jeweler, but her business was going bankrupt. She earned $3,000 a month, but her

expenses ran $4,000. She had a lot of expenses for such a small business—
a long list of accounts receivable, an expensive inventory of jewelry supplies, a showplace space rental that cost more than she could afford, and
expensive phonebook advertising. The elements of a turnaround plan are
always the same: cut expenses, boost revenue. The jeweler turned her
business around in one year. Now she earns $12,000 per month with
$2,500 in expenses. Here's the turnaround plan I designed for her, which
you can adapt for your own business:

Cut expenses by 50 percent immediately.
- She found less expensive space, not a showplace but functional, at half
  the price.
- She stopped all advertising and relied on face-to-face connections to get
  commissions.
- She used the practice management checklist from chapter 8 to establish
  quality control.
- She collected all unpaid money she could from customers and wrote off
  the rest as bad debt.

Double your income.
- She increased her working time for three months, working 65 hours per
  week. This included networking and marketing time.
- She designed and followed a marketing plan.
- She established duplication of her successful income strategies.

Duplication of income strategies means that you look for what is currently working to bring in income, and do more of the same. For example,
a therapist I coached was close to bankruptcy. As we explored his referral
network I saw that he had one income stream that had low costs, a good
area for duplication. This income stream was referrals from a divorce
mediator who sent him clients for brief psychological consultations. The
consultations consisted of meeting with a couple to educate them on how
to safeguard their children psychologically during the process of divorce.
This was a minor part of his practice. He usually got only one client from
this referral every few months. I asked him to immediately find and meet
eight more divorce mediators. He did this within two weeks. (Remember,

desperate times call for desperate measures.) Four seemed willing to refer. Instead of one couple every few months, he began to average three. In our next coaching session, I asked him to find eight more mediators to talk to. He couldn't find that many in his local area, so he got on the phone and called mediators within a fifty-mile radius, offering to do consultations by phone. He got more referrals. You may think that his willingness to comply with my requests was unusual, but when your business is failing, you often feel motivated to take strong actions.

When you need quick results, be ready to put profitability ahead of your comfort. Review the "Meeting Your Inner Entrepreneur" exercise from chapter 5 and use it daily to give you drive and energy. Be an exacting manager of your practice—know precisely where your money goes. Cut expenses unsparingly. Spend 90 percent of your working time delivering services and generating referrals, and the remaining 10 percent of your working time doing everything else.

SETTING STRONG BOUNDARIES

Part of becoming highly profitable is having strong financial boundaries in place. You need a written policy statement that outlines all of your practice policies, including all your financial ones. This should be given to clients during the initial session and be available in your waiting room. The policy sheet will strengthen your resolve and keep your boundaries clear. It lets you behave more like a larger business. You can stand behind a policy, even when you personally don't feel strong. I have seen therapists operate with a one-page policy sheet and those that hand out a small booklet of ten pages. Your guide in creating the right policy sheet is to have one that allows you to do your best work as a therapist, one that lets you feel secure. Here are some suggestions about what to include in your policy statement:

- your fees for all services, clearly listed and explained
- your menu of services and any packages you offer
- your missed session policy
- your cancellation policy

- any insurance agreements
- when you work and when you don't
- what clients can do in an emergency
- issues of confidentiality
- your statement of support for all termination (see chapter 8)
- any legal requirements you follow (such as when you report to authorities)

Having strong policies and boundaries makes for a solid, sturdy therapy practice that will stay strong over time, in case you want to have a business that you can sell. I suggest that you build a business to sell, not just to run. Building a business to sell serves two purposes. You give extra attention to your practice now, which provides you with a strong business and a steady source of income during your working years, and you reap additional rewards when you sell it later, as part of your plan for financial independence.

Is it possible to sell a therapy business? Yes, but you will need to start positioning it *today*. In order for your therapy business to be attractive to buyers, it needs to have multiple assets. Too often, a therapy business has only one asset and it's a nontransferable one—the therapist. Even though you are the star attraction of your business, your cachet can't be easily transferred to a potential buyer. To sell your business, think through what other tangible assets you can build into your practice.

Create tangible value that is transferable. Turn your ideas into programs, document those programs and establish your methods of therapy in writing and on video. Create as much product as possible. Write, research, and publish to validate your methods. Begin to train others in your methods, so that you have a pool of potential buyers when you are ready to retire. Here's a list of tangible assets that can add to the selling price of your practice:

- *Brand name:* If you can name your type of services in a recognizable way as separate from your identity, you have a salable asset. You can more easily sell your methods than sell yourself. Look at your professional field for examples of this. You will find programs and methods that are trademarked. In the field of marital therapy, two brand names that come to mind are: Imago Therapy, the form of couples therapy designed by Harville Hendrix, and the PAIRS program, designed by Lori Gordon. Both Hendrix and Gordon train and certify others to teach their programs. The brand names carry value, since they have a separate identity, apart from their developers.

- *Direct-mail list:* Build a large direct-mail list for your practice. Use your advertising and speaking engagements to build your mailing list, not only to generate referrals. A practice with a direct-mail list of 5,000 current names can significantly add to the value of a business.
- *Promotional materials:* Develop brand-name recognition via your promotional materials now, with brochures that highlight the method or the program name more than the therapist. Keep a portfolio of winning advertisements, brochures, or flyers that have generated good results, along with the details of those results. This is part of the package you can offer someone who wants to reproduce your results.
- *Measures:* Have a system of tracking your effectiveness. For example, if you develop a great survey for clients that measures their satisfaction and you have used this not only to boost client satisfaction, but also as part of your promotion, this transferable measure is a definite asset for a potential buyer.
- *Ancillary products:* Have products to sell. Even if you have not promoted your product line, it doesn't lessen their potential value to someone else. You might have developed a wonderful set of meditation tapes, for example, but perhaps you didn't market them aggressively. If these tapes are part of the business you sell, the potential buyer may see this as a valuable asset to be exploited. Get legal advice regarding licensing agreements for all written and recorded products.
- *Practice management:* If you have created a thriving practice with easy-to-understand administrative systems in place, you have an additional asset. Start to do this now. Find a billing system that is user friendly. Document your office resources in a written manual—staffing procedures, outside contractors, maintenance services, written agreements you use. Present a potential buyer with a clear, complete practice management program.

What price can you expect to get for your business? While a manufac-turing company might be sold for five times annual earnings because it has a product, plant, staff, and system in place, a therapy business without the above elements in place might typically sell at one time annual earnings. You can double or triple this ratio by deciding to build a business to sell as soon as possible and integrating this strategy into your business s plan, so that you have many additional assets to include in order to boost the selling price. You can have a licensing agreement on top of the sales price for the programs you have developed and another additional price for products you created.

Now that you understand how to become more profitable, it's time to think about the finishing touches that can set your practice apart from others.

PART III

Finishing Touches

11

Loving the Business

When I was a young child, my family often spent summer vacations at the beach. Toward the end of the second week of a two-week vacation, I would notice that my father was edgy, eager to get home. He enjoyed vacationing with the family, but he missed his business. For him, business was always part work, part fun; he didn't like being away from it for too long. He loved running his business, which naturally translated into his considerable business success.

This is true for you as well. If your business feels pleasurable to operate, you will want to spend more time working on it. This naturally leads to success—your business flourishes from having your care and attention, as does any other area of your life. Not surprisingly, I always find a direct relationship between those who love running their businesses and those who make a lot of money. Since our goal is for you to be highly successful, I want you to consider how you can make running your business more pleasurable. What can you do to make the business of therapy feel easier and more fun?

I recently coached a social worker from the Midwest who counseled a number of men facing layoffs from their jobs at a manufacturing plant in his city. He wanted to start a series of classes to teach men how to proactively find new jobs. He rarely taught classes, so the idea of creating the curriculum, marketing the classes, and deciding on the logistical details felt overwhelming to him. I urged him to get started on his plan, but he procrastinated. He was too busy with his existing caseload, and bringing in more business felt too hard. It just wasn't worth it to pursue this idea. Still he voiced a real longing to teach the class.

He didn't know that the preparation for teaching a class could be fun. Finally, he agreed that this goal was important and he was ready to get started. Together, we designed a road map, a step-by-step path for him to follow. I wanted to make each step small enough so that he felt it would be easy to accomplish. To tell if a step was the right size, I simply requested he take action and listened for his response. When he felt the step was doable, he always immediately said, "No problem." For example, I asked him to write a class curriculum. "It's going to be hard to do that," he sighed. I gave him a smaller step: Give me a one-sentence goal for each of your eight classes. "No problem," he said and did it in a week. He needed to decide on the logistics—location, fees, and class size. "There's so much to consider, I really get stuck thinking about it all," he said. I asked him to devote one weekly coaching session to determining each logistic, with my help. "No problem," he said. In the space of three weeks he had his class logistics planned.

Step by step he proceeded to complete the plan. The first class filled easily, and he found that he loved teaching it. The fact that he had diversified his practice with teaching pleased him greatly. Later, when we debriefed on a coaching call, he told me how empowering it was to have taken a vague idea to fruition. "Using this format to achieve my goals for my business, there is nothing I can't do. It's just a question of finding the right steps to take. Working on my business this way actually feels fun," he said.

In business, if you can define what you want, there is often a linear strategy to get you there. Look for strategies that make business easier. Learn to work smarter and remove the struggle and suffering in regards to your practice. Develop systems that help you to work with more relaxation. Organize your business so that you give it the resources, maintenance, and attention it requires to run smoothly. Find stress-free ways to achieve your goals. Favor strategies that have a generative nature, so that once put in place, they take on a life of their own.

BUSINESS AS PLEASURE

Here are a number of ways to proceed to make running your business more of a pleasure:

1. Take action based on love, not fear.
2. Send love to your practice.
3. Stop suffering.
4. Optimize your time.
5. Focus on the "how" instead of the "what."
6. Model success.

TAKE ACTION BASED ON LOVE, NOT FEAR

I attended a class about small business development several years ago where the teacher talked about a very un-businesslike concept: the two basic emotions. The teacher said that human actions are driven by one of two emotions—fear or love. He asked us to think about our recent business decisions and determine whether they were based on fear (of survival) or love (of the business, our services, our profession, and ourselves.) This was eye-opening for me and, since that time, I regularly ask my clients to think about their business actions and plans in terms of these two powerful emotions. Is your plan based on love or fear, I want to know. If my client says fear, we examine how he or she can think beyond survival and create a business plan based on love. Although this may sound like a new-age premise, I have found this mindset to be both practical and profitable. Taking action in your business based on fear often carries a high personal and financial cost. You rarely make good decisions based on fear. Whenever we take action based on love, we feel energized. As a small business owner, your level of energy is one of your most important resources. Taking action based on love costs little, frees up creative thinking, and often yields a bonus in terms of energy and profit.

Curt is a psychotherapist with fifteen years in private practice in

Chicago. He specializes in working with couples. His practice was going quite well for many years, but then life handed him a hard challenge. His wife became seriously ill, and he cut back on his work to take care of her. As he pulled his attention away from his practice to concentrate on helping his wife, he got fewer referrals. About this time the health insurance situation changed across the country. He decided not to be a part of managed care. Referrals dropped off again. As his income dropped, he began to feel desperate. Finally he took a part-time position with a county mental health center. When he called me for coaching, the first thing he told me was that the treatment center was closing. All he had left was a part-time practice, and it wasn't much of a business.

I asked him what ideas he had. "I could go to work for a state-run hospital, except I hate the setting and don't want to work there. I'd be miserable. I could stop my practice and look for a job in a corporate setting, but I don't really have the training or a salable product right now. I could sublet my office space to help pay the rent, but then I won't have the space available if I do find more clients. I could try to sign on to some managed care lists, but I don't want to work within those rules." On and on he went, proposing ideas based on his fears of survival and then rejecting each one.

"What would you really love to do?" I asked.

He snorted. "I'd love to stay in my private practice, have a full caseload, and work with couples. What difference does it make? I can't make a living at that anymore. I figure I've got three months before I close my doors and collect unemployment."

I made a provocative request. "If you are going to close your doors, how about going out in style? Give yourself three months to build up your practice. Take actions based on what you'd love to do, instead of what you fear you must do. I'll show you how to design a love-based business strategy, one where you pursue actions to build the business you would love to own."

He was desperate enough to think this made sense. We inventoried his resources and assets. His assets included an ability to write, his outgoing personality, and some experience as a presenter. He also had a small amount of savings, about $2,000. I asked him to use his savings to seed the rebuilding his practice. He was appalled—this was all the money that stood between him and bankruptcy. I told him that if he was moving in the direction of love instead of fear, he would devote all his resources without hesitation. Having just spent a large amount of time, effort, and money on helping his wife recover from an illness, he agreed that this is was true; he did all this without a second thought for her, and would do the same for his business if he really loved it. His wife heartily agreed with this plan and urged him to "go for it" and give his practice a second chance.

Curt and I developed a long list of actions, many drawn from the list of strategies you already know, outlined in chapters 6 through 10. An early action Curt took was writing a heartfelt, short article containing a success story about counseling a couple going through a crisis. He contrasted their struggles and eventual decision to stay married to his experience of helping his wife through her illness. He went to a printer and spent part of his budget to print five hundred copies of the article in the format of a practice newsletter. He mailed this newsletter to everyone he knew, personally and professionally, not just to promote his business, but out of love for those friends, patients, and colleagues who had stood by him while his wife was ill, wanting them to know about his experience. He loved doing this, because it helped him to define the essence of his work and also reaffirm his commitment to his wife and family. He gave a copy to his minister and was invited to speak to the church, which he did. The county health center director saw the letter and asked him to speak to the staff. We were four weeks into his three-month time-table.

So far, no new referrals had come in, but Curt had a lot of energy and was doing tasks that were inspiring to him. Each time Curt became scared, I directed him back to a list of actions to take, so that he stayed busy building a business that he could love. I asked him to take some of his budget and go to a workshop, signing up for any training that would help fuel his creative juices. He felt this was a luxury he could ill afford, but after attending a weekend workshop about new techniques in couples therapy, he admitted he felt invigorated and energized.

One of the actions on his to-do list was to send a dozen colleagues his newsletter and then invite them to meet with him at his office to talk about their success stories (therapists rarely get to share the cases that go well). Another was to record his article on tape, which he did on his home stereo system, and then duplicate it. He made one hundred copies, each one twenty minutes long. First he introduced himself, explained his basic message, and then read his article. He closed by saying that he would welcome any comments or thoughts listeners might want to share with him about similar struggles in their own lives. I asked him to distribute all one hundred copies by the end of thirty days. Each time he gave a talk, he gave away tapes to the audience for free. Each tape had his office number printed on the outside. He began to get referrals and calls from the distribution of the tapes. Some people called just to thank him for his inspiring story. He loved this—and happily gave out more tapes. I also requested that he use a business affirmation daily: "I can prosper and build a strong practice by doing the work I love."

After eight weeks of nonstop, concentrated "loving action" his business began to turn around. New clients called—people who wanted to work with him regardless of insurance. His colleagues referred clients to him. The minister of the church referred clients. I asked him to see each and every success as a signal not to slow down, but to do more in the direction of love. He maintained a list of possible actions and took steps each day. I told him that no action step was beyond his reach if it would result in building a business he would love. After going through the hard work of nursing his wife back to health, he knew that to get certain results, he sometimes had to do more than he thought he could.

A year later he is in full-time private practice, primarily seeing couples. He still has open spaces in his calendar, but he has enough work and money to make it unnecessary to take a part-time job to supplement his income. "I have the energy to do a lot for my business, as long as it is love-based," he says. "I find I just don't mind the work, even though I am probably working harder at my business than I ever imagined I would or could. I can honestly say that I love what I am doing. I get great results and have really great clients to work with."

SEND LOVE TO YOUR PRACTICE

Years ago I developed a meditation to enhance therapists' feelings of goodwill and love toward their businesses. I teach this same meditation in almost every presentation or class I lead, because it does so much good, so quickly, providing therapists with a quick antidote to fear-based thinking. In the space of the five minutes it takes to complete the meditation, I see therapists make a shift. As they contemplate sending love to their businesses, their faces change. Furrowed brows become smooth, tense jaws lift up into soft smiles, hunched shoulders relax. Here's a written transcript of the meditation. Ask someone to read it to you or make your own tape. Then sit back, listen, and send love to your practice:

There are so many areas of our business we don't love. These are usually the ways we feel bound, pushed, or burdened by our practices. This is normal, because a business has many needs and demands, and we must respond to those needs to keep our business viable. But just like any other entity, it does better if we respond to it with love. This is one way to send love to your practice.

Close your eyes. Relax your body and your mind. Breathe easily and comfortably.

Think about your practice, exactly as it exists today. See it or sense it, in your mind's eye, as a separate entity from you. With your eyes closed, as you think about it, locate it in space. Maybe you see it off to the right of you, or above you. Notice exactly where you locate it, in your mind. Notice any emotions you experience as you think about it. Notice any critical thoughts or judgments you carry about it. Notice any body sensations you feel. Pay close attention to areas of tension in your body.

Now put your practice aside, momentarily, and think of a person, place, or thing that you love unconditionally, with your whole heart and mind. It might be a place in nature, or a pet, or a person or even some activity. Think about the person, place, or thing that you love with your whole heart and feel that pure, unconditional feeling of love in your body. Allow that feeling to expand, so that you have a strong sense of pure, easy, unconditional love in your body, emanating from the area of your heart.

Imagine that you are sending or directing that feeling of love to your practice. The love flows from your heart to wherever you have located your practice in space. Send love unconditionally to your practice, to every neglected, unappreciated, misunderstood, irritating aspect of your business. Imagine that your practice is capable of receiving the love, taking it in like a sponge absorbing water, or a plant absorbing sunlight, easily and naturally, so the more love you send, the more your practice absorbs. Now imagine you are standing inside your practice and feel the love yourself. Send love to yourself and your practice.

Think of an affirmation or an image that will help you to hold onto this experience, so you think of your practice with a loving heart, every day. What specific actions will you take to hold this love in place?

Now open your eyes.

Here's the shift one therapist expressed after this meditation:

"When you said to see my practice as it exists today, I realized that I am rarely completely honest about my practice. I tell little white lies to others who ask me how my business is going, such as that I have fifteen clients instead of the twelve I really have, because I am ashamed. It's fudging a little to make myself feel better, but it's still a level of nonacceptance that bothers me. I often hope someone won't ask about how my practice is going because I'm not going to want to tell the truth.

"Doing this exercise, I really got a new awareness. When I sent feelings of love to my practice, I saw how I need to be accepting of what currently exists. It's similar to those times I am able to look at my teenage daughter with love, instead of judgment. Sometimes I look at her and all I can see is where she doesn't measure up to my judgments. I wish she had a cleaner room or better grades in school. But those rare, wonderful times when I see her with unconditionally loving eyes, I see who she really is and how perfect she is, right in the present. This is the first time I ever did that with my business. I see that my practice is perfectly acceptable. It's a tremendous relief to just look at my practice with loving eyes and stop judging it. It's fine now, and it will be fine when I have more clients. I don't need to be ashamed."

STOP SUFFERING

For some reason, many therapists I meet seem to believe that a certain amount of suffering in a therapy business is normal. Thinking that you have to put up with aspects of the business that make you unhappy is based on your fear of survival, not on fact. When you are in the survival mode, you decide you must do things in your practice that you don't want to do, because everyone else you know does it that way. You are afraid to step outside the norm and run your business your way. Your fears of survival may influence:

- the hours you agree to work
- your arrangements regarding billing, payment, or insurance
- agreeing to see clients you shouldn't
- having a weak missed-session policy
- charging less than you deserve
- working in unhealthy, unattractive office space
- working without adequate training or supervision
- taking on too much stress
- spending unpaid time filling out excessive paperwork
- having an impossible caseload
- working without adequate staffing or administrative help
- being bored with clients and your practice

Because I have access to so many therapists and information about their therapy practices, every time I hear an example of fear-based policy in a private practice, I have several counterexamples of how other therapists set up things differently, with success. You can set up your practice to reflect your values and vision, make money, and attract clients. Your business becomes an *anxiety-free zone,* a place where your business challenges can be resolved without fear or anxiety. Every problem you have about your practice probably contains the seeds of a solution. You may not initially like the solution, but one exists.

As a business coach, I see a lot of resistance from my clients prior to taking action to make necessary changes in their practices. Your resistance to taking action to correct a business complaint is also fear-based. The problem you live with is more familiar and palatable than an unknown problem. Move beyond your resistance and take pro-active steps to correct anything and everything that creates suffering for you within your business. You will end up with a practice that looks and runs more like your business vision—the practice you aspire to build.

It's great to correct complaints during a group brainstorming session. At these sessions, each therapist presents a complaint, and then listens, without defensiveness, to the solutions offered by the group. The solutions from the group are rarely ideal. Mixed in with good solutions will be those that are too obvious, too drastic, or creative but impractical. Your tendency will be to push away all solutions, both good and bad, that will require a change in your mindset or behavior. Watch for your resistance: "I can't do that because" or "I thought of that and rejected it because" or "That won't work for me!" Instead, just listen. Reject nothing. A poorly thought-out solution may still contain the seeds of a great idea. Think: "80 percent of this solution won't work, but 20 percent is really helpful. How can I adapt this 20 percent and use it in my business?" Finally, select or synthesize a solution based on the ideas offered and correct the problems and complaints you have about your business. Listen in on a brainstorming session from one of the groups I lead.

Complaint: I hate to work evening hours, but most of my clients can't schedule appointments during the day. Working nights means I am away from my family four late evenings each week.

Brainstorming solutions from the group:
- Target your services to those who can see you during the day—retirees, self-employed people, college students, housewives, professionals with flexible lunch hours.
- Give your clients examples of how those who see you during the day set it up at work. My clients take lunch hours from as early as 11:00 A.M. to as late as 3:00 P.M., to come to daytime therapy appointments.
- Work Saturday mornings and Sunday afternoons to replace all weekday evenings.
- Run one or two groups on a weeknight evening and ask those who can only come in after work to join a group.
- Stop offering evening hours so you won't be tempted to work at night and see what happens.
- Set up an office downtown near large office buildings to minimize travel time for clients.
- Offer sessions by phone for those clients who can't get to your office.

- Offer half-hour sessions to see more clients in the morning before work or at lunch time, supplement with an additional longer session once a month.

Complaint: I don't like the office space I am subletting a few hours each week. It's ugly and impersonal, but the rent is affordable and the location is convenient.

Brainstorming solutions from the group:
- Bring in a few items that make it feel more like yours. Carry a few decorative pillows for the couch, or a small vase and cut flowers to put on a table.
- Bring a tape player to the office and put on soothing music for yourself to listen to between clients. Use incense or subtle scents to add more sensory appeal.
- Ask the other therapists that use the office to contribute to an annual decorating budget.
- If others won't contribute to the decorating, do it yourself. Consider it money well spent if it makes you eager to spend more time in the office.
- Lease or purchase an office yourself with multiple treatment rooms, decorate it the way you want, and sublet it to others.

Complaint: I'm a massage therapist and I find that my work is getting boring. It's the same thing each day, without much variety. My clients don't talk much, they just want their same, standard massage. My mind wanders a lot.

Brainstorming solutions from the group:
- Use a pre- and post-checklist to find out the effects of massage for your clients.
- Work more deeply as a therapist. Get more training to help you stay enthusiastic and then bring your enthusiasm into each session.
- Take more risks. Do something different each time. Talk. Sing. Use aromatherapy. Have more fun. Be bold.
- Diversify your services. Get trained in hypnosis and begin to offer a hypnotic meditation to begin and end each massage to help clients relax.

- Ask your clients to keep a journal of their week to notice how massage affects their lives.

Exercise
CORRECT YOUR COMPLAINTS

List ten complaints about your private practice, and list at least three good solutions for each complaint. Can't think of any solutions? Ask others for help until you get lots of ideas. Don't resist any advice. Write down all possibilities. Adapt freely until you find a solution that will work. Take a step to resolve one complaint each week. Build a business that runs according to your vision and values. Use this format:

Complaint:

My solutions:

Solutions from others:

Obstacles in my way:

Steps I will take to overcome the obstacles and correct the complaint:

Time line for completion:

OPTIMIZE YOUR TIME

As a therapy business owner, my time is my most precious asset. I want to have concentrated blocks of time so that I can work effectively at a given task, with the least effort possible. Jeff Raim, a business coach from Wyoming, taught me a great way to organize my time, dividing my week into "work," "buffer," and "spirit" days. By Jeff's definition, work means activity that brings you *both* joy and money. Spirit means time that replenishes your soul. Buffer is a catch-all phrase meaning everything else. When Jeff first coached me to think about rearranging my calendar into work, spirit, and buffer days, I told him that by his definition I had no work days, only work "moments." I worked five to six days a week in private practice and I made good money, but my work didn't always bring me joy. Parts of it were tedious and difficult. Jeff held to his definition and said in that case, I had to count my work as buffer time. I also had no spirit days. I didn't work Saturday afternoons or Sundays, but I used my down time to run errands, do a little paperwork, and then maybe see a movie or go out to dinner. According to Jeff, because this did not replenish my soul, this also counted as buffer time. (Jeff is tough!) I looked at my calendar and admitted to Jeff that I had weeks of buffer time. Jeff said he was not surprised that I complained about feeling overworked and tired. He coached me to reorganize my business and the rest of my life. First he helped me solve a number of complaints about my work, so that I had more joy in private practice. He then insisted that I take one full spirit day each week, free of errands and work-related tasks. Jeff suggested that I pencil the words work, spirit, and buffer into my calendar, so that my days were preplanned. Spirit time was to be penciled in first, taking priority. It was a new experience for me to make sure that I had quality time for myself, first. After doing this for a while, I realized how much a full spirit day each week improved the quality of my work days. Since that time, I have moved in the direction of having weeks filled primarily with work and spirit time, Jeff's goals for me, with a sharp reduction in buffer time. As a result, I am more productive and enjoying life much more.

Exercise
REORGANIZE YOUR TIME

Divide your calendar using the categories of spirit, work, and buffer time.

work = activity that brings you both joy and money
spirit = time that replenishes your soul and helps you recharge
buffer = everything else

Notice how your calendar looks now, and begin to look at what you can do to have primarily work and spirit days in your week, with a reduction of buffer time.

FOCUS ON THE "HOW" INSTEAD OF THE "WHAT"

One reason I enjoy business is that it gives me a place in my life to be a linear thinker. Business tends to be solution-focused. As a therapist, I often spend hours thinking in multiple dimensions and many shades of gray. In contrast, I find the direct, pragmatic thinking that's most useful for business a refreshing change. To enjoy business, focus on strategies—the combination of steps that help you reach a desired outcome. Given a business problem, design a strategy. Focusing on strategies means that you attach to your goal, but you stay unattached to the strategy. This way you can let go of one strategy that's not working and easily try another. As you try to reach your goal, you will run into obstacles. It's a given. The obstacles can consume your thinking, becoming the "what" in the equation. Your challenge is to stay focused on the "how"—the strategy.

Both simple and complex business problems can be resolved with carefully designed strategies. When you begin to feel that the problem is hopeless, you are focused on the what. Think about the *how*. Name the strategy, to help you stay focused. In chess, almost every series of moves has a name: the French Defense, the Four Knights Opening, Kings Gambit Declined. Naming your strategy makes the game easier to play—it leads you to understand that you can control the outcome of the game by preparation and skill, in this case your familiarity with remembering and using a series of proven moves. You can transfer this thinking to business. Similar to playing chess, some of the moves in business can be anticipated, others require creativity. Flexibility is key; if one path isn't working, shift and try another.

Let's pick a common problem in business, one that you face every day, and then name and design a strategy to make it easier to handle. In an early chapter we discussed that the nature of private practice is uneven— it goes up and down. This up and down nature is common to areas of any business that are market-driven. The stock market, for example, has a volatile nature. Experienced stockbrokers have strategies to deal with the volatile nature of a stock. One is called "averaging." It consists of buying a stock at regular intervals, whether it is high or low, which evens out or averages your buying pattern and minimizes volatility. You need a strategy to modify the uneven nature of private practice, too.

Ebb and Flow Strategy

The purpose of this strategy is to modify the uneven flow of business. Have a series of steps to even out times of either too little or too much business.

Too much "ebb"?

- *Diversify:* Have at least three different profit centers, so that the ups and down get spread out and you can move between one thing and another when business is slow. For example, you can see clients, teach, write articles for publication, sell products, or speak professionally.
- *Develop a referral engine:* Build a self-generating engine that keeps going easily and yields a steady, slow stream of referrals. Try to schedule networking lunches with a different referral source each month; give free monthly introductory lectures sponsored by outside organizations; send out a mailing every quarter to past clients and others; expand your mailing list by ten names each week.
- *Build a strong cash reserve:* Save money to build up a financial reserve to tide you over in lean times. Pay yourself first—before you pay bills, put 10 percent of your earnings each week into a savings vehicle. Budget carefully, cut costs, and don't pay for a business expense unless it will yield back double in profits.
- *Add value:* Keep doing more for existing clients to improve retention and referrals. Think about ways you can benefit your clients. Write a short article for clients each month and give it away for free. Take a new training each quarter and let clients know how it benefits them. Continually enrich your office space with expressions of the values most important to you and your work—reading material, quotes, music, artwork, etc.

Too much "flow"?

- *Resist the pressure to do more:* Maintain your boundaries and your spirit time in the face of too much business. Start by developing a waiting list and a good Rolodex of referrals you can make.

- *Hire staff:* This is the time to let others help you organize and manage the influx of new business. Have someone other than you book your appointments. Delegate all administrative activities. Get a reliable office manager.
- *Leverage your time:* See the maximum amount of people you can in the least amount of time. Some ideas include: running more groups, allocate hours to training or supervising other therapists, referring excess clients to those your supervise and train.

Exercise
DESIGN A CUSTOMIZED BUSINESS STRATEGY

What is a business problem that concerns you? Name the problem and then creatively name a strategy. Combine a series of action steps to create a strategy that will handle the problem. Clearly delineate each step with specific examples that you will follow.

State the business problem:

Name the strategy that will fix it:

Define its objective:

Articulate each step:

Give specific examples of how you will take action:

MODEL SUCCESS

Sometimes the easiest route to success in business is to observe what others have done and replicate it. Instead of envying another for his or her success, try to understand the strategy behind the success and then imitate the strategy. This is a great antidote for envy, which we all feel from time to time. When I started my practice, of course I was envious of others who had bigger practices or built-in referral sources. I was embarrassed about feeling envy—it wasn't a "nice" emotion. At the root of my envy was desire. I longed for something that felt way beyond my reach. As I got more interested in the business of therapy, I began to get very curious about the how—the strategies that led to others' results. Curiosity was a great cure for my envy. I began to interview other therapists to hear their strategies. I made notes of strategies and sometimes tried to reproduce them. But I found it tricky to understand all of the essential elements to include in a strategy—what was important to model and what was not?

Richard Bandler, one of the founders of neurolinguistic programming (NLP), relates the following story. Bandler was involved in a research study trying to replicate the results of several renowned therapists. He was closely observing Milton Erickson, considered to be the premier hynotherapist of his time. Bandler closely observed Erickson's methods and techniques as closely as he could, hoping to get similar results with clients. Even though he studied transcripts and repeated every word that Erickson used during hypnotic inductions, Bandler's clients failed to go into trance. Or if his clients did go into trance, they didn't get the same healing results that Erickson achieved. Bandler realized that he must be missing essential elements of the "Erickson model" that he had considered unimportant. He determined to include everything that Erickson did when hypnotizing a client. He learned to sit like Erickson sat, breathe at the same rate, blink his eyes in the same pattern, and mimicked Erickson's deep, gravely voice. As Bandler demonstrated this to the audience, assuming a twisted posture and talking in a low voice (Erickson was an old man, stricken by polio when Bandler studied him), many in the audience laughed. Bandler, a young healthy man, looked ludicrous pretending to be the older, wheelchair-bound icon of hypnosis. But Bandler was trying to make a point. At that time in his career, he didn't know which of many elements was essential to the Erickson model, so he adopted them all. By modeling everything, Bandler was able to achieve much more consistent results with his clients (although they, too, may have been bewildered by his posture and mimicry). After he got the results he wanted, he began to refine the model, eliminating one element at a time—first letting the voice go, then the bent posture, then the labored breathing, always checking for results until he could determine what was essential to keep and what was not.

This is a powerful modeling strategy. When trying to replicate what works for another person, don't discount any elements at first. Consider everything. Try to define a complete strategy. Once you begin to replicate results, then you can refine your strategy to ascertain the essential elements. At this point you will be able to adapt the strategy to fit your style. Here's an example of how to design a replication strategy, by stating a desire, defining the elements of the model, and then deciding on a strategy to follow:

Stated desire: My colleague has large therapy groups that fill up easily. My groups are smaller and hard to sustain. I want to have large groups that fill up easily.

Identifying the elements of his model: I talk with him and ask him how he manages to keep his groups full. He tells me he makes group a priority for clients and evaluates each new client as a possible candidate for group. He says he feels so strongly about the importance of group therapy as a method of treatment that he has refused to work with several clients unless they agree to attend a group. His fee for group is considerably lower than his fee for an individual session, so that his groups are attractive to those paying out-of-pocket. I observe that he continually attends training sessions and workshops that relate to group therapy, to stay inspired, even though he is a senior therapist. I have overheard him introduce himself as a therapist who specializes in running large groups. He has built a wonderful, big space for running his groups.

Designing my strategy: I adopt his model as best I can understand and follow all the steps, before I judge or eliminate any from the strategy.

Steps for me to take:
1. Change my basic message to say that I enjoy running large groups.
2. Find a bigger space in which to run groups.
3. Tell new clients that I consider group therapy a priority in their treatment plan, when appropriate.

4. Restructure my fees so that group pricing is considerably more attractive than individual sessions.

5. Schedule to take more training, to immerse myself in methods of group therapy.

6. Learn to value group therapy more.

7. Budget sufficient resources (time, energy, and money) to follow this entire strategy *until I see similar results.*

Exercise
REPLICATE SUCCESS

Think about something you desire for your business. Find someone who gets the results you desire, whom you can model. Observe or interview that therapist to try to understand all the elements of the model. Design a strategy that replicates his or her results.

1. Stated desire (what you want that you have seen modeled in someone else's practice).

2. Elements of his or her model (all of the elements you can define based on observation and/or interview with that therapist).

3. Your strategy (series of action steps that you will take to replicate this model; don't forget to include a timeline, specific budget, and all resources you will devote to fulfilling this strategy until you see similar results).

All these strategies will help you run a smoother operation, as you bring more of your loving attention and care to your business. In the next chapter I will show you another way to increase your pleasure in running your business by learning how to go beyond the traditional medical model and develop an innovative personal-growth business model, to help you stay on the cutting edge of your profession.

12

The Personal-Growth Model

Gerald Celente, author of *Trends 2000,* says that a major trend surfac-
ing in our aging, relatively affluent population is the desire for high-
quality longevity. We want to live well regardless of our age. We yearn for
long-term physical and mental health—to stay interested in life until the
day we die. This trend points the way for an expanded role for the therapy
profession, *if* therapy can move from a traditional medical model, which
emphasizes treatment of pathology, toward a personal-growth model,
which emphasizes personal development over one's life span.

There are at least three advantages to shifting your entire practice or a
part of your practice toward a personal-growth model:

1. *You lead the way in helping clients to have an optimum life.* Many therapists hold back from learning new methods that would help their
   clients because under the current medical model, little acknowledgment
   is given to the more innovative methods of therapy. As a personal-
   growth therapist you can consider a wide range of techniques and
   methods to help your clients, putting you at the forefront of therapy.
2. *You assume total financial control of your practice.* A personal-growth
   practice operates as a fee-for-service business. The responsibility for
   profitability rests entirely upon you, as the business owner. This is good
   for you and your practice, because it requires you run a sound fiscal
   business. You need to articulate your basic message, connect with the
   community, find out what the public wants, produce tangible results,
   and examine or create new ideas and methods that keep clients
   engaged.

3. *You won't get bored.* Experienced therapists complain of burnout as they do the same basic work, day in and day out. This model encourages you to keep learning and to stay on the cutting edge of healing technology. Similar to other businesses that rely on a market-driven process of innovation, in a personal-growth model of entrepreneurial business, you may see more new methods surface to meet the market demands. You can keep your interest in your work high as you learn or help design new methods and techniques to help your clients reach their goals.

Maybe you already have a practice that is geared in this direction, providing services outside the traditional therapy model. You may offer alternative methods of healing, including personal coaching, body psychotherapy, movement therapy, expressive therapy, spiritual or meditative practices, acupuncture, guided imagery, or energy healing. While one aspect of building a personal-growth business is having a wider range of services, you also need to consider adopting a slightly different business model—shifting to a more holistic, yet purely business focus.

In this chapter I will suggest ways for you to become even more entrepreneurial and more of an educator. We will examine how to link your work with others. I will also show you how to use a process of *circular positioning* for your practice. To help you understand how to create a personal-growth business model, let's first examine one therapist's practice. As you read this case example, you will see that the therapist is demonstrating many of the strategies I gave you earlier in the book, but she takes some of them further, adding new ways to connect her practice to others. The personal-growth business moves away from the medical model, allowing you to think "out of the box" and unleash your creativity in regards to building a practice that will embody your passion. Following this example, I will walk you through the model step by step, so that you understand:

- the five personal-growth stages of development
- a range of services you will want to offer for each stage
- the specific actions that will move your practice forward
- how to build circles of community around your practice

A PERSONAL-GROWTH PRACTICE

When I first met Betty Caldwell she was in the middle of a career transition. Betty, who has a masters in counseling, worked full-time as the vice-president for fundraising for a national nonprofit organization. But her real passion was in a less traditional area—that of energy healing. She had just completed a rigorous multiyear training in energy healing and was leaving her corporate job to start a private practice.

As Betty and I talked during our initial coaching session, I was impressed by her desire to create not only a private practice, but also a global network of healers. With her background in organizational development and fundraising, she was uniquely positioned to create a nonprofit network. (Today she is founder and president of the Healing Dimensions Foundation, located in Columbia, Maryland.) But on that day two years ago, it was clear to both of us that for Betty, developing her own private practice would be the greater challenge. She needed to build a practice quickly; it would be her sole source of financial support, and she told me, with concern, that only a small percentage of energy healers find ways to become completely self-supporting. We talked about a business plan based on a personal-growth model rather than a traditional medical model, so that the structure of her practice would make use of her previous business experience and complement the creative, untraditional nature of her work.

As I saw it, her task was threefold. We examined:

- who she needed to *be*,
- what she needed to *do*, and
- how to *position* her practice for success.

For example, we discussed that she would need to be pioneering, articulate, and entrepreneurial in order to build a nontraditional, self-sustaining business in an unproven market. She would also need to become an educator. We looked at how she could grow quickly and balance her time between building her foundation and building her practice. To position her practice to fit into her local community required that she use circular positioning, a process of linking her practice to others.

Above all, Betty needed to be articulate. Since she was passionate about energy healing, we looked at how she could transfer that passion to her brochure and a series of white papers. She worked hard to find the words to express the importance of energy healing as she wrote and rewrote her practice brochure and pages of text for a foundation website, trying to explain her work without using any jargon.

Here's a good example of her success in this area: A surgeon asked Betty to attend an operation and use her expertise as an energy healer to help soothe a nervous patient prior to undergoing arthroscopic surgery. As Betty sat talking to the patient, she sensed a great deal of tension within the patient and began to use her energetic techniques to "clear" the tension, which turned out to be related to a traumatic incident during an earlier surgery. The patient immediately felt much more relaxed and sailed through the operation. In the recovery room after surgery, Betty again used her energy healing to dramatically reduce the patient's postoperative pain. At the end of the day, Betty was in the staff locker room getting out of her hospital scrubs and putting on her street clothes. A nurse came in who had observed Betty working with the patient earlier. She asked what kind of work Betty was doing in the hospital. Betty was about to explain the concept of energy healing and the methods of clearing trauma, but realized that the nurse was not interested in the "features" of the work—the technical jargon; she was asking about the benefits.

"I am here because the surgeon asked me to attend the operation. I helped the patient release some feelings of fear based on an earlier surgical experience, which made her more comfortable during the operation. In the recovery room, I again used my energy techniques to help her feel relaxed and at ease so that she needed *no further medication* for the pain," Betty said. When the nurse heard *no further medication,* she stopped in her tracks to listen. Now she was eager to hear more about energy work. This is a great example of the skill Betty exhibits in articulating her work, making the esoteric aspects of energy healing easier to understand.

Four years before leaving the corporate setting, Betty had begun saving, to build a reserve to see her through the transition. She tracked and monitored her finances, lived more simply, and cut expenses. She realized that in order to leave her full-time employment as a fundraiser and run a personal-growth business, operating strictly on a fee-for-service basis, she would need to be alert and careful with money. She set a goal to build a self-sustaining practice within two years. Having reached that goal she now has further financial goals in place.

Betty also set out to link her practice with others. One of these links took her by surprise. During Betty's first year of private practice, a close personal friend called with an emergency situation. The friend's daughter was in the process of giving birth and the baby's heartbeat was erratic; it had actually stopped beating for moments during labor. Could Betty assist in any way? Betty rushed to the hospital and for the next six hours sat beside the mother transmitting energy to key tension spots so effectively that the mother was quickly able to fall into a relaxed state. Betty then began to concentrate sending energy to the baby, to stabilize his heart. As the parents, grandparents, doctor, and nurse watched the fetal heart monitor, Betty was able to help the infant's heartrate remain calm, even during the peak, difficult moments of the mother's contractions. Betty had never done this type of healing in a hospital setting before. The attending physician was impressed and asked her to consider getting credentials at the hospital—an unusual step for an alternative healer to take. Betty was surprised by this opportunity, and saw this as a rare chance to link her practice with the hospital. She devoted months of time, expense, and energy to get credentialed. She is now the first and only energy healer certified to practice at Howard County General Hospital in Columbia, Maryland.

Another linking took place this way: Betty initially knew of very few "practice angels," those people who can refer a steady stream of clients. She thought back to a strategy she had used in the corporate world and hired a public relations consultant to increase her visibility. The consultant, in turn, hired a freelance journalist to write a five-hundred-word article about Betty. The consultant pitched the finished article to several magazines and newspapers. *The Business Monthly,* a Columbia, Maryland, newspaper was interested. Betty sent reprints of the article with a cover letter to a direct-mail list of fifteen hundred physicians, physical therapists, and other complementary-care practitioners. This mailing generated an important result. One administrator who saw the article called Betty and asked her to be part of the complementary medicine services at a nearby rehabilitation center. (She was impressed by the fact that Betty was certified at the hospital!) At the center, Betty will not only have a large office designed just for her and be an independent contractor seeing private clients, but she will also be part of the center's staff of professionals. She has been asked to teach staff physicians about energy healing so that they can collaborate with her professionally. This will benefit them as it benefits her. Again, Betty is a trailblazer, the first and only energy healer at the rehabilitation center.

As I write this, Betty is practicing from three locations: a hospital, a rehabilitation center, and a group office in an alternative healing center near her house. In addition, she now teaches a course called "An Introduction to Energy Healing" at the local community college, which offers continuing education units for her course to interested health practitioners. Every time I call Betty she has added a new venue for her work. Betty laughingly says, "It seems that my real job is to be a door opener." She holds the door open for other healers to follow behind her, as she continues to function as practitioner, educator, and activist.

THE STAGES OF PERSONAL GROWTH

Betty's work involves an alternative method of therapy, so the personal-growth model of business makes sense. But what if you are a more traditional therapist and want to shift your focus to include the concept of personal growth instead of pathology? Let me define what I mean by personal growth to help you to look at the differences between personal growth and a traditional medical mindset.

If you are a therapist working in a traditional medical model, you are required to diagnose, treat, and hopefully cure a patient's illness. To comply with today's medical model, therapy tries to provide short-term, low-cost solutions. In a medical model, problems are often viewed as pathology. Your role as a health provider is to be the expert, know the answers, and fix people fast.

In a personal-growth model your role is less that of an expert and more a partner in holistic healing. While you may still diagnose and offer treatment, you see a client's problems in a larger context. You not only offer services designed to help people resolve immediate issues, but also to help them further a process of personal development. Treatment becomes part of a long-term strategy of wellness, not just a short-term Band-Aid. The goal in personal growth is to improve, transform, or enrich a person's quality of life. A personal-growth model may embrace a wide range of Eastern and Western methods designed to extend and enhance the way we grow, live, and eventually die.

I developed a personal-growth services model based, in part, on the theory of psychologist Abraham Maslow, the father of humanistic psychology. Maslow organized human development through his famous hierarchy of human needs:

1. *physiological*—the biological needs we humans require to exist
2. *safety and security*—the need for shelter, protection, and structure
3. *belonging*—the need to have relationships and be part of a society
4. *esteem*—the need for respect from self and others

Maslow reasoned that needs take a stair-step approach: Until the lower needs get met, we humans can't address the higher ones. According to Maslow, meeting these four levels of needs leads to the potential for:

5. *self-actualization*—a state of fulfillment and high personal achievement*

In creating a personal-growth services model, I, too, have looked at a stair-step model of development, although my stages differ from Maslow's. Rather than focus on needs, as Maslow has done, I am more interested in looking at growth and movement—specifically a range of services you can offer to help a client move from one stage to the next. Although I organized the model to reflect five distinct stages, our actual personal development is rarely linear. In times of stress or loss, we all regress to "lower" stages of

---

*A. Maslow, 1954. *Motivation and Personality*. NY: Harper & Row.

survival and in times of calm, approach the "higher" stages of awareness. There is a normal back-and-forth movement to each person's development. You may find that your clients move between stages, at times needing services from one, at other times from another. It's not unusual to work with a client who needs services from two extremes of the model at the same time. For example, you may have a client who is at a survival level in terms of relationships, but at a pleasure level in terms of his or her career. If the services you offer are different from mental health services (for example, if you offer primarily physical services such as chiropractic, acupuncture, or massage that use little talk during sessions), you can still adapt this model for your type of work and allow the broad concepts to guide you.

Using the model, you have a definition of each of five stages of personal growth. Following their description, I have outlined an explanation of the presenting nature of the client and the services you can offer.

THE FIVE STAGES OF PERSONAL GROWTH

1. *Survival:* This is the stage when a client commonly decides to seek therapy. The client is in crisis, at a low point of existence. He or she is often in extreme emotional, psychological, or physical pain, with concerns about stability, self-protection, or personal preservation. The focus of therapy is helping the client to handle the crisis and survive internal or external conflict.

2. *Recovery:* At this point, the client is out of crisis and can look beyond intense self-absorption to relational issues. He or she is ready to explore a deeper connection to self and others. The client focuses on strengthening boundaries and getting relational needs identified and met. At this stage a client can "go deeper," using insight to create a stronger sense of self. The client can explore the underlying causal issues that contribute to current problems.

3. *Progress:* In the medical model, this stage signals the time when patients exit therapy—the crisis is past, the person is functioning, so therapy is over. In the personal-growth model, this is the stage when the interesting work begins. Clients can make tremendous strides in personal development now that the immediate crisis is resolved. This stage

involves services that help a client shift from functioning to satisfaction and that promote his or her feelings of confidence, competence, achievement, mastery, independence, and freedom.

4. *Pleasure:* At this stage, a client functions well independently and finds that much of life provides satisfaction and pleasure, instead of struggle and pain. A client in a personal-growth mode now wants to explore the subtler aspects of life, learning how to sustain feelings of pleasure, find meaning in everyday life, and enhance feelings of appreciation and love with significant others.

5. *Awareness:* This stage represents a "consciousness wake-up call" and often comes during a peak time of life, once personal and professional goals have been accomplished. The client becomes acutely aware of how precious life has become and wants to explore his or her legacy, reflect on life experiences, pursue spirituality, or create a wonderful last chapter of life. Even when a client reaches this stage, he or she is still growing and learning and wants to continue to find challenges and purpose in life.

Now let's look at the services you can offer for clients at each stage of growth:

Survival

Presenting nature of the client:

- facing personal, physical, or psychological trauma
- poor self-concept, poor self-care
- low point in life

At this stage, your services will include standard therapy services. The focus is on helping the client to:

- get out of crisis
- change self-destructive behaviors
- calm or shift affect (emotion)
- find solutions
- reduce the trauma and crisis

- keep safe
- establish or protect a fragile sense of self

Recovery

Presenting nature of the client:

- crisis stabilized
- occasional continuing upsets at work and/or home
- feels less desperate, still in pain

At this stage, your services will again include your standard therapy services. The focus is on helping the client to:

- stay out of crisis
- change self-destructive behaviors
- learn to appropriately express and feel emotions
- generate own solutions to problems
- set and maintain boundaries
- improve relational skills and connections
- consolidate gains
- explore and examine deeper causal issues below the surface
- connect more solidly with self and others

Progress

Presenting nature of the client:

- able to set and achieve goals, self-motivated, insightful
- has relationships that provide more pleasure than pain
- can cope with life problems

At this stage, you want to offer services that promote higher levels of self-value and a deeper connection with others. The client can begin to feel the reciprocal nature of relationships, taking in energy and love from others, digesting it completely to feed the self and then giving back without feeling drained or burdened. This is the stage when a client can learn to create a reserve of time, energy, love, money, peace, community, and good relationships to shore up any missing areas and prevent future crisis. The services can be delivered during individual or group sessions or you may offer workshops, classes, or other methods that help the client to:

- develop a life vision
- define large goals
- build stronger ties to family, friendships, and community
- find spiritual direction or a calming, meditative practice
- enhance self-care and show better care to others
- develop creativity and artistic expression
- sustain previous gains, enhance the quality of life

Pleasure

Presenting nature of the client:

- has a peaceful and enthusiastic outlook
- relationships include an extended, loving community
- life offers opportunities for pleasure and profit

At this stage, you want to have services that appeal to a person whose life is in order, but who still wants to grow and deepen awareness. Research shows us that the best way to stay strong and vibrant into old age is to continue to learn and grow. The task at this stage is to go deeper into areas of personal satisfaction and community building. The focus is on offering therapy sessions, classes, or workshops that help the client to:

- deepen practices of spirituality, meditation, or contemplation
- sustain pleasure and a playful outlook
- appreciate nature, heighten relaxation, recharge energy, and get nurtured
- open his or her heart to significant others with love and passion
- enhance social interest, compassion, ties to humanity
- maintain good physical health and well-being

Awareness

Presenting nature of the client:

- desire to create and be of service are primary motivators
- has clear vision, purpose, and mission
- all relationships support sense of happiness

At this stage you can help a client begin to create a legacy, deepen his or her awareness of how precious life is, and stay engaged in the process. Help a client identify and explore new areas of attraction, support him or her in giving back to the community or finding new passions to keep life meaningful. Have services that help a client to:

- feel supported, inspired, and reinforced
- live a life based on integrity
- resolve issues of "old business" and practice forgiveness, to have peace of mind
- open doors on life's further possibilities
- give back to others

In addition, embody these concepts within your services to help clients at the awareness level continue to grow and change:

- truth, rather than pretense
- integrity, rather than incompleteness
- aliveness, rather than retirement
- fulfillment, rather than disappointment
- simplicity, rather than entanglement
- effortlessness, rather than difficulty
- meaningfulness, rather than futility

WHO YOU NEED TO BE

As you can see, the personal-growth business model requires that you think about yourself and your business in a new way. You are helping people get to a more advanced level of behavior, thinking and feeling, but it's hard to help someone walk a path you haven't traveled first. For example, you will find it difficult to help a client learn to live a life of integrity if you are not actively working on this goal yourself. What I love about this model is that it pushes me to constantly grow and take on new personal and professional challenges, just to stay current with clients. To have a successful personal-growth business, you *ideally* need to be:

- continually passionate about your work
- an articulate educator
- at the top of your profession
- a skillful master of your methods
- highly collaborative
- interested in building a larger vision
- grounded in your desire to serve others
- an entrepreneur who loves the business
- confident about what you have to offer to the world
- self-aware, continuing to grow personally
- a model of the services you offer to others

Let's explore this last attribute further. A personal-growth business operates by attracting ideal clients. You are no longer in the medical role of an expert who can tell others what to do without following his own advice. To be a model of your services means that you embody what you sell; you set an example in these ways:

- *Be on a strong financial track.* It's hard to be an effective therapist when you are overly concerned about money. Get business coaching and financial advice so that your business prospers. Have a plan to help you achieve financial independence.
- *Decorate your office so that you love spending time there.* If you love to spend time in your office, you will be happier when you are at work. Bring in fresh flowers, a favorite painting, comfortable furniture, and surround yourself with colors that make you feel good.
- *Get all your personal needs met outside of your practice.* Too often overworked therapists have a practice but no life. I want you to have both. Devote time to hobbies and satisfying relationships outside of your work.
- *Get your own therapy, ongoing clinical supervision, and business coaching.* Remember to set aside resources for therapist self-care. Get the support you need first, so that you can give to others a full well, not

an empty tank. Have a strong professional network that encourages your success.

WHAT YOU NEED TO DO

Beyond who you need to be, you also need to take certain actions within your business. These actions are similar to others we have discussed, but in this model I want you to focus on your creativity, your ability to project optimism, and a strong sense of vision. Here's a checklist of what you can do to build a personal-growth business:

- *Focus attention on the depth of services.* You have looked at a long list of possible services to offer using the personal-growth model. Pick no more than one or two per stage. More important than breadth of services is how deeply you are able to work with others. This model pushes you to become expert in a few services and then orient your practice around your strengths.
- *Think outside the box.* This is a practice where your creativity and your ability to be different and spot trends will be a major asset. Instead of having to do things the traditional way, you can be inventive. Your practice may not look the same as anyone else's; this can be a strength. To be distinctive, play to your strengths and your passions.
- *Work from a model of abundance.* Shift from a mode of competition to one of collaboration in order to stay focused on thoughts of abundance. Give a lot to others, keep connecting to larger and larger networks and bigger circles of influence, and you will see that there is plenty to go around. In a personal-growth business, your best referrals will come from the relationships you have built with others. Your network, along with your creativity, are your major assets. Do as much as you can in collaboration with others.
- *Have an overarching vision.* Get ready to work with clients over the long term. In a personal-growth practice you may see clients for many years, perhaps in a revolving-door method where they come in and out of your office at different stages of their personal development. See the

big picture of health and wellness, so that your practice is part of a large vision. Make sure you follow the guidelines in chapter 9 for adding value, so that your practice has a lot to offer. Keep your emphasis on excellent services of a high nature.

POSITIONING YOUR PRACTICE

Ideally, a personal-growth business model relies on a holistic world view— you see how your practice is part of a larger whole. In a personal-growth business, your strength comes from connection as you link yourself and your business with others. More than networking, this linkage is about building community. The easiest way to build community is to recognize the connections with community that already exist for you and strengthen them. Your practice is already positioned within several communities. For starters, you have a position within your neighborhood (your local community), within your professional community, and within the society at large. The links may be dormant, because you do little to activate them. Isolation is the biggest obstacle to the success of a personal-growth practice; your task is to become more aware of the existing connections and activate or nurture them.

Here's how to begin the process of *circular positioning* and enhance the circles of community that exist around your practice. Think about a series of concentric circles, with your practice in the middle. Each circle represents a community that surrounds your practice. Make a diagram and name the circles of community that link to your practice. Don't be concerned as to whether the connections are active or dormant at this point.

Pick one circle. Think how to add value to that circle. Don't contribute money—get personally involved and give something of yourself to this community for the purpose of improving your world. Feeding the circle will enrich your immediate environment, one form of reciprocation. Circular positioning is different from networking, which is promotional in its nature and yields a quantity of superficial relationships. With circular positioning you build deeper relationships, because you have directly contributed to bettering people's lives. It's these relationships that are the basis for reciprocation—which may take many forms, including forms that benefit your practice. What comes back is often in the form of deeper relationships with the people in the community you have chosen to add value to. As you connect to people and let them know about your passion for your work (by articulating your basic message), referrals and opportunities circulate back to you.

Here's the catch: The reciprocal nature of circular positioning only works if you contribute from a desire to really enrich a particular community. It's a natural phenomena; as you build a base of stronger relationships based on adding value to a community, the community naturally reciprocates to add value back to your life (and often to your business). I call this "karmic marketing," because with this strategy, what goes around, comes around. Here are three case examples of circular positioning that I observe within my local community.

Lucy Banks is a psychotherapist in Virginia who codirects a therapy practice of thirteen therapists, most of whom specialize in marriage and family counseling. A veteran social worker for twenty years, she has directed this practice for eight. Since she is well established, referrals come in regularly. Her main challenge is how to feel continually invested in her work and stay fresh after so many years. She also wants to control her therapy hours so that she has sufficient time to devote to her own family. When she and I talked about the concept of circular positioning, she felt confused about how it worked for her. "I have a strong connection to my local community, since I have children at home. For example, I volunteer time at their schools and the neighborhood swimming pool. I get known through these channels, and I develop relationships with other parents and teachers, but these are not relationships that feed my busi ness. Often when people within these communities want a therapist they will ask me for a referral, but because I want to maintain strong boundaries between my social and professional relationships, I don't offer my own services. I refer out to other therapists."

"And do those therapists you refer to reciprocate in kind?" I asked.

Lucy smiled. "Of course they do. I see how this works. It's reciprocal, one step removed."

This is a good example of circular positioning at the local level. Lucy gives time and energy to neighborhood projects, to have a better place to live and raise her family. In the process, she builds quality relationships.

Even though she doesn't exploit these relationships for herself, she makes referrals to others in her professional community and that generosity gets reciprocated.

When Deany Laliotis, a therapist in Maryland first got training in EMDR (eye movement desensitization and reprocessing), few people knew about this therapeutic method. Deany was fascinated by the results she obtained with clients using EMDR and continued her training to become one of the first EMDR facilitators (the senior level of training) in the Washington, D.C., metropolitan area. She desired to build a stronger professional EMDR community. Deany assisted at weekend certification programs, started several small supervision groups for those who had just learned the process, and made herself available for consultation and support to the growing community of therapists interested in EMDR. Much of this was done with no thought of financial gain; she was passionate about the methodology and wanted to build a stronger community around herself. She began to gain a reputation based in part on her generosity to the professional development of others, as well as her expertise in this area. Deany, who has a waiting list for her private practice, acknowledges that her efforts over the years to give back to the professional community have generated substantial business for her practice, but that was not her motivator. She contributed primarily based on her belief in the method and a desire to help colleagues reach a level of expertise.

This is a good example of circular positioning at the professional level. Deany gives time and energy to the growing community of therapists trained to use EMDR. In the process, she builds her reputation and relationships with the therapists she assists. Even though she never exploits these relationships or markets directly to therapists for her own practice, when a local therapist wants to make a referral for a client to see a "master" of EMDR, Deany is often the first person who comes to mind.

Rudolph Bauer, Ph.D., is considered a "therapist's therapist." He and his wife, Sharon, also a psychotherapist, take time away from their busy practices to lead a two-year Gestalt therapy training that combines psychology and eastern methods of awareness, considered a "must" for many therapists in the Washington, D.C., area. They also formed a meditation center to respond to the desire of therapists and others to learn more about methods of meditation. Rudy and Sharon sponsor regular weekly meditation sessions as well as large weekend workshops and lectures, where they host a variety of international meditation experts from various cultures. For example, a recent lecture his center cosponsored to introduce a revered teacher from China attracted two thousand people.

This is a good example of circular positioning at the societal level. The Bauers give considerable time and energy to further a broad community of people who want to integrate methods of Eastern meditation and into their Western lives. This is no small task and requires a willingness to deal with sometimes wonderful and sometimes unpredictable results. The Bauers do this without any thought of building their own practice or receiving monetary gain; instead, they are passionate about a larger vision, the "integration of the field of energy and psychology." But over the years as they work to build community, I observe that their professional stature grows as those within the community recognize and appreciate their efforts. For Rudy and Sharon, the reciprocity comes in terms of "energy, mutual interest, and ever-deepening relationships."

Exercise

POSITION YOUR PRACTICE WITHIN
CIRCLES OF COMMUNITY

Create a diagram of concentric circles, and place your practice at the center. Name each circle to reflect the links to existing communities that surround your practice now. Add as many circles as you need to represent the position of your practice. Pick one circle (one existing community) to start with.

1. List all the ways you could help to build this community and add value to it in a form other than donating money.
2. Create a plan of action to begin the process of adding value to this community.
3. Focus on the pleasure of making connections with others.
4. Try to improve your environment and your world.
5. Follow your passion.
6. Notice what comes back over time.

Using this model will help you stay connected to others as you move forward and create a larger vision. Learning to love your business and creating a personal-growth business model will make your practice shine. Now let's look at what you need to do to hold onto your success so that you maintain your practice in good shape over the long term.

13

Holding Onto Success

When I was fifteen, my parents bought a house that was built in 1900, which they still own and live in. The first impression I had when my parents took me and my sisters to see it was how solid the house looked compared to the small tract house we were moving from. This house was built to last—and it does, as long as it gets the necessary help from its owners. I have witnessed first-hand the amount of maintenance and attention an old house requires. "Once in a while the house actually doesn't need much," my mother says, but the rest of the time the paint by the window is peeling, carpeting needs to be replaced, the roof leaks into the garage, or the foundation wall displays a small crack. Even in a very well-built house, overlooked minor problems can turn into major difficulties given enough time.

As your well-built, ideal practice ages, it will need your loving attention and care to stay viable. The complaint I hear most often from therapists with established practices of fifteen years or more is, "I was doing so well for years that I guess I got complacent. Now my business has slid into trouble." After reaching your goals of building a great practice, I want to make sure you hold onto your success for a long time in the easiest, most effective manner possible.

Keeping your practice strong over the long-term means attending to three areas: who you need to be, what you need to do, and how to position your practice. To hold onto success:

- *be* motivated,
- *do* maintenance, and
- *position* your practice to take advantage of three levels of collaboration.

MOTIVATION

Over the past four years that I have been a business coach for therapists, I notice that those I coach tend to make real progress toward achieving their goals during the time we work together. The problem comes when the support and structure of the coaching sessions end. Then my clients begin to procrastinate and miss deadlines. Action slows down. Phone calls don't get made. Plans for expansion take a back seat. Within six months, clients find themselves back in their familiar patterns, feeling stuck. They email me or leave phone messages, sounding perplexed and frustrated. "I'm not getting as much done as I did when we worked together," they say.

I understand how difficult it is to hold onto gains and keep moving forward. In a sole proprietorship you wear a lot of hats. You are owner, office manager, and, of course, the one who delivers service. You will gravitate to those roles you most like to do. If you like to deliver service the most, that's what you will tend to do, overlooking the other roles you need to attend to in order to keep your business going well. The key ingredient to performing well in *all* your roles will be your degree of motivation.

Motivation is the fuel that inspires us to action and, for that reason, it is an important business quality to cultivate. Motivational researcher John Keller created a model of motivation to use for learning that highlights four components, which I have adapted for business. According to Keller, to stay motivated one needs to:

1. Arouse interest.
2. Create relevance.
3. Develop an expectancy of success.
4. Produce satisfaction through intrinsic and extrinsic rewards.

Let me show you how to be a motivated business owner using these four components.

AROUSE INTEREST

Margaret has been in practice for fifteen years and tells me right away that she is bored. Her goal in hiring me as a business coach is to get out of her rut and feel more upbeat. Session by session she increases her zeal. I am enthusiastic about her, as a person, and about her desire to accomplish her goals, and my feelings are contagious, she says. I keep her focused on taking action and the more she does, the more enthusiastic she gets. But how will she sustain her intensity once the coaching sessions come to a close? She needs to learn to arouse her own interest.

Keeping your interest at a high level is an important element to staying invested in any career over time. One way to arouse your interest in your work is by continually learning. Expose yourself to new ideas and experiences, for the purpose of staying fresh. Sustaining interest doesn't just happen; you must plan for it and dedicate a percentage of your budget to it. I think you'll want to go beyond courses in continuing education training, and pursue more far-flung experiences. The longer you stay in practice, the more you must challenge yourself in this area. One colleague does this with style. Each year he picks an area of the country he has never visited and looks for a weeklong course he can take in that location. Some of these courses have only a thread of relevance to his work. Part of the fun for him is in synthesizing new learning into his practice. For example, he signed up for a week of nature photography in New Mexico and spent the next year "seeing" new things about old clients.

Action Plan: Dedicate 5 percent of your budget each year to new experiences and/or training that will keep your interest aroused.

CREATE RELEVANCE

As we ascend on the stages of personal development, we are drawn to finding meaning and purpose in our lives. Finding meaning in your work is another key to staying motivated over time. You can create relevance by continually integrating your practice into a larger world view. You will find that your motivation to take on new tasks grows as the meaning of your work evolves. When the purpose of your practice means more to you than just providing a source of personal income or a service for a small pool of clients, you will be inspired to take larger steps.

Create relevance by identifying a theme for your practice that expresses your overarching purpose as a therapist. Recognize that your business goals and tasks are the way you manifest this larger vision and how you connect your small practice to a larger world view. Remembering your purpose can make difficult tasks more doable.

Relevance was a key motivator for me in my efforts to write this book. Soon after I started my initial outline, I got a bad case of writer's block. I had already done significant preparation—I had several years of notes from teaching the material and transcriptions of class audiotapes. I even had encouragement from an editor at a major publishing house. It didn't matter—I was blocked. What helped was asking myself a number of questions that I couldn't answer at first. I quietly contemplated the questions for several months: Why should I write this book at this time? What did I really have to say that was important to others? What was the bigger purpose? When I could finally answer these questions to my personal satisfaction, the motivation to proceed naturally emerged and the book began to write itself.

Action Plan: Define the larger purpose of your work. Articulate a theme that helps you feel that your work fits into a bigger picture of life. Write the theme on a card and post it in places where you will see it often.

DEVELOP AN EXPECTANCY OF SUCCESS

It's hard to feel motivated when you expect to fail. One therapist told me that he can come up with a great idea for his practice on a Monday morning, but by noon he will have talked himself out of it. His negative thinking is self-protective; he doesn't want to look stupid, make a mistake, or fail in front of his peers. Another therapist recently reminded me that she has to do battle on two fronts—she must contend with her own negative thinking as well as the fear she hears voiced by colleagues. She says that even when she feels ready to take a risk and try something new, if she mentions it to her peers they actively discourage her because "no one can make it in private practice these days."

In cases like these I am convinced that my biggest value as a business coach is not in the information I impart, but the fact that I remain so optimistic about what is possible for my clients to achieve. Some of the optimism comes from experience; I have seen hundreds of therapists take large and small steps to become successful despite their initial reservations about their business abilities. I have seen that therapists can do very well in private practice regardless of any number of factors, including location, type of profession, or years of experience. For me, the concept of having an ideal practice is not extraordinary; it's a normal, expected outcome of business coaching.

As a coach, I don't always know how a particular therapist will proceed to accomplish his or her desired goal; I just know that it's possible. As a result, I don't get overly concerned with small setbacks in the pursuit of that goal. I stay focused on an expectation of success. If I hold onto this expectation firmly enough, I can usually impart some of my mindset to my client. The next thing I know, he or she has taken action and great things begin to happen. Based on this, I have learned not to underestimate the power of simply staying open to the idea of success.

If you can do this for yourself, it will help you in many ways in your own business. It will also give you a powerful therapeutic tool to use with others. I saw a thirty-year-old psychotherapy client who was in a dead-end job. She had a very sad history of contending with serious problems throughout her childhood into young adulthood that left her feeling depressed and hopeless, especially about her ability to support herself financially. One day, after hearing her anxieties regarding money, I simply said, "You know, you have an unlimited earning potential." She looked at me like I was crazy, but I held firmly to this stance. (I actually believe it is true, not just for her, but for many people.) I began to repeat this to her often. Within two years she tripled her salary. She continually surprised me with the resourceful ways she found to get additional training, find better positions, and meet her employment goals. She did the work; I just "held the hope." When she was ending her therapy, she told me, "You had a belief about my ability to support myself that was crucial to me taking any actions. Now I can take it back from you and hold onto it myself. I know it's true."

How can you hold onto an expectancy of success for your business? One way is to inspire yourself by reading biographies of others who have succeeded despite difficult odds. You can always find accounts of people who faced more problems than you do, yet accomplished awe-inspiring goals. Read business magazines, like *Fast Company,* that offer first-person accounts of the successes of contemporary entrepreneurs. If you give yourself enough case examples, you will see that succeeding in business is not unusual. It happens every day.

Action Plan: Surround yourself with inspiring stories and examples of others who express optimism and a belief in possibility. Join a group of active businesspeople (such as the chamber of commerce) who can help normalize your desire for business success.

PRODUCE SATISFACTION THROUGH REWARDS

The easiest way to motivate yourself to complete difficult tasks is to utilize a reward system. While in college, my son once worked for a tele-marketing company selling subscriptions to magazines. As he described it, the work was unusually tedious. He sat at a small desk, elbow to elbow with fifty other telemarketers in a large room. Each telemarketer had a long list of phone numbers to call. My son called number after number, and as soon as he got a few words into his prepared pitch, the person on the other end of the line would hang up. Once in a great while he would get to talk longer, and once in a really great while, this would result in making a sale. When he made a sale, he would ring a big metal bell attached to a wall in the office. His manager would run over, applauding, and pat him on the back. Everyone else would look up from their phones and give him the thumbs-up sign. This reward system was extremely effective and helped to keep him and others motivated to sit hour after hour, facing hundreds of rejections.

There are two types of rewards that increase motivation: intrinsic (self-focused rewards) and extrinsic (externally focused rewards). To stay motivated, you need a combination of both. Intrinsic rewards include feelings of satisfaction, joy, and pride. Extrinsic rewards may come in the form of money or other tangible markers of success.

In motivating myself, I find that it is helpful to structure my own rewards at set intervals. For example, I usually schedule difficult tasks early in the day. I will spend a morning completing administrative tasks, so that by noon I can "reward myself" by spending time in my garden or going for a walk. I also have a circle of friends and peers who I can call for a quick verbal pat on the back when needed—another reward. I ask this circle to hold me accountable for certain goals and report my progress to them regularly.

One easy way to reward yourself is to keep a list of your "wins" for each week. When I coach a therapist by phone from across the country, he or she will send me a coaching "prep form" by email just prior to the call. The prep form asks for an accounting of the therapist's wins, current challenges, and specific goals for the phone consultation, which keeps our coaching call highly focused. My clients tell me that the act of writing out their weekly wins acts as an intrinsic reward, giving them feelings of satisfaction, and they are reminded about the tangible results they achieve over time.

Action plan: Keep two lists each week—one for wins and one for current goals. Break down the goals into small action steps. The smaller the steps, the more chance for frequent rewards—you will accomplish many small steps versus one large step. Have someone you account to each week who can hold you to your tasks and celebrate your progress.

ACTIVE MAINTENANCE

Active maintenance is a form of patrolling your practice, looking for areas to repair, all the while using a system of upkeep. You maintain your practice in good shape by having a plan. You have a plan that allows you to detect any small warning signals that alert you that you need to take action. Similar to a house, where signs of wear and tear can signal you to step up your maintenance, your practice will show signs of wear and tear, too, if you look. These are your signal to make some corrections. Signals include small worries, anxieties, or doubts that begin to show up repeatedly in your mind about your practice—these are often similar to the small cracks in the foundation of a house and need to be evaluated for seriousness. Even when your practice is doing very well, you can be alert to the following warning signals that indicate that you need to do active maintenance:

- You lose track of your cash flow and don't know what you have earned or what you have spent during the last three months.

- You are currently busy but have no new referrals coming in during a ninety-day time period.
- You feel bored or tired and the feeling lasts for more than sixty days.
- You are feeling jealous of other colleagues who are doing better than you.
- You have a small, steady exodus of clients, without replacements.
- You become a victim of slippage—you are juggling so many tasks that things inevitably slip through (you double-book appointments, neglect to send out bills, fail to return phone calls).
- You feel resentful of some aspect of your practice—clients, workload, or hours.
- You lose sight of your vision and have trouble finding relevance for your work.
- You procrastinate on following through on good ideas that would benefit you.
- You haven't taken one full spirit day for yourself in a three-week period.

If you recognize yourself in this list, it's time for active maintenance. In the first chapter, we organized the elements of practice-building into three categories, based on building a house—preparation, building blocks, and finishing touches. The easiest way to maintain your ideal practice after you recognize a warning signal is to decide which category it falls into.

Is the problem indicative of worries and anxieties? Are you feeling a lack of confidence or increased confusion? Can't see the bigger picture? That's a preparation issue. You will want to review the chapters on vision, support, and mindset, and allow yourself to go back through the exercises to rebuild your conceptual, psychological, and emotional foundation.

Is your problem indicative of inaction? Need more money or referrals? Are you feeling like you are isolated, too small to compete, or desperate for some new ideas? Go to the building block section and refresh your framework of strategies regarding profitability, generating referrals, expansion, diversification, or adding value.

Is your problem that you are losing interest in your practice over time? Feeling burnt-out or tired by the hard work of a therapy business? You need to reinspire yourself by reviewing the finishing touches section. Look at all the ways to love the business more. Find easier, more effective methods. Send love to your practice. Increase your creativity and outlook by using the personal-growth model.

CREATE A MAINTENANCE METAPHOR

Unless you understand and accept the needs of your business, you will not be able to happily give it what it needs to grow and flourish. It helps to find a metaphor that explains the needs of your business to encourage your acceptance. The metaphor must be broad enough to help you organize the daily work of maintaining your business and to have pleasurable associations for you. Earlier in this book, I used the metaphor of building a house as a way to understand how to build your practice. I picked this metaphor because it clearly describes the steps needed to build a strong business, and it had good associations for me, since my husband is an architect and I am fascinated by the home construction process.

I am going to offer you a different metaphor for maintaining your practice—that of gardening. I learned to garden ten years ago, when I moved to a house with a sunny side yard. I created a small kitchen garden planted with herbs, perennial flowers, and seasonal vegetables. Even though it is limited in size, it yields a surprising amount of flowers and produce.

The needs of the garden are predictable and unrelenting. In the early spring I clean up the planting beds that are filled with debris, leaves, sticks, and old plants. I prune the roses and replace plants that did not survive the winter. I fertilize beds. I spend hours planting, weeding, and irrigating. Eventually I'll get to pick spring flowers and make bouquets. As summer approaches I harvest my vegetables and weed or water daily. By late summer, my interest in the garden always begins to wane. I do very little and usually just visit the garden to pull out some late summer vegetables, avoiding the weeding that should get done. I know I am only postponing the cleanup for the fall, but I have no desire to do any more. By late fall I hurriedly clean and prune, fertilize beds, and prepare for a dormant season. Then I rest during the winter and read gardening books, dreaming of new perennials to plant or finding a space for one more climbing rose bush.

My practice has similar maintenance needs. At times I am seeding the practice by thinking of new groups to run, making notes for the next book I want to write, or taking steps to establish new referral sources. I spend time eliminating or pruning the practice by cutting expenses that no longer serve me well. For example, after three years of paying for advertising in a directory of mental health therapists with no results, I ended my contract and "transplanted" those funds to other sources of advertising. With a business, as with a garden, something is always needed. Using this metaphor I can appreciate the cycles or even the seasons of my practice. For example, as my practice matures, I notice it takes less work. Just as a mature garden with established plants needs less attention than a new garden, an established private practice requires less than a start-up practice will demand.

Find a personal metaphor for your practice that has meaning for you, one that gives you a framework for spending the time and attention on your practice that it needs. Use your metaphor to make maintaining your business feel easier and more pleasurable.

Exercise
THINK ABOUT YOUR PRACTICE AS A GARDEN

If you think about your practice as a garden, what do you need to do this week, month, or season? Think about each category listed and translate it into actions you will take to maintain your practice:

fertilize	seed	irrigate
weed	plant	prepare
organize	transplant	rest
prune	harvest	dream

ENGAGE IN PROACTIVE MAINTENANCE

Proactive maintenance is a preventative maintenance system for keeping your ideal practice in good shape when nothing is wrong—when there are no warning signals. It's like changing the oil in your car every three thousand miles—you just want to keep your well-running business in top condition. To do preventative maintenance, keep the three categories of practice-building in mind—preparation, building blocks, and finishing touches—and focus on one category each month, formulating a goal for each. For example, one month spend time improving your mindset by further developing an entrepreneurial quality from chapter 5. As you review the list of qualities, perhaps you don't yet embody "persistence." Create a goal that helps you to become more persistent, such as "This month I will focus on the items I never get around to on my to-do list and follow through on each one to completion."

The next month, pick a different category and a different goal. There is enough material in the book to keep you busy for many years. As you move back and forth between the different chapters, you will become a stronger businessperson. In the process you will sharpen your business capabilities and your practice will thank you.

You can also use the pre- and post-test in the Appendix for this purpose. The test gives you sixty items to check, under six categories of practice-building. Increase your score until you can check each one. Then add your own items to the list and work to check them as well. The Generating Referrals checklist is another tool in the Appendix that can help you stay proactive. Each month consult the checklist, picking one item to complete and check off.

COLLABORATE WITH OTHERS

The easiest way to hold onto success is by letting other people help you. Small business collaboration falls into three areas:

1. *People you hire*—staff, consultants, supervisors, or coaches who help you to reach outcomes or accomplish specific tasks
2. *People you attract*—peers and colleagues with whom you may or may not actually do business, but who offer support, advice, and brainstorming

3. *People you are attracted to*—those mentors and models of excellence who you seek out so you can shift to a higher level of accomplishment or awareness

Hiring others is essential when you feel overwhelmed, overworked, or under pressure. Sometimes you need a staff—a full- or part-time book-keeper, secretary, receptionist, or others to delegate work to and ease the pressure. Most therapists in practice delegate some aspects of billing, administration, public relations, promotion, or accounting. Feeling over-whelmed may also signal the need to hire a coach. When I first began to write this book, I knew little about publishing, other than watching two col-leagues in two years become frustrated in their failure to find an agent or a publisher for their manuscripts. I knew that I needed help to get a different outcome, but didn't know how to proceed. Hiring Maggie Klee Lichtenberg, a book marketing coach who specializes in helping new authors, was the perfect solution. Maggie greatly reduced my feelings of confusion, acted as a knowledgeable consultant and guide during the process of writing a book proposal and, later, helped me to evaluate offers. With the wide variety of business coaches/consultants who work by phone, you can probably find expert help on any area of your practice, within reach. See the Resources in the Appendix for some coach referral networks.

Attracting peers is a way to ease feelings of isolation. Collaborating with peers is often the fastest route to take to shift business from work to fun. As you attract others based on a similarity of goals or shared enthusiasm, you build a circle of encouragement for yourself. You may decide to pursue business endeavors with this circle of peers, or mutually share support, ideas, and encouragement.

Sometimes the answer to a problem is to collaborate with a colleague. For example, maybe you refrain from giving presentations because of the stress involved in public speaking (the number one fear in adults). It might feel easier to share the platform with an associate, for moral support and to lessen the workload. A massage therapist scheduled a series of monthly introductory workshops. At these classes she offered a lecture and then an hour of teaching simple massage exercises, which people did with partners. Sometimes she had difficulty monitoring the exercises and attending to the entire class as well. Her solution was to ask a colleague, a yoga teacher, to assist her. The yoga teacher was happy to comply. She recognized this as an opportunity to learn something about massage and help out a colleague. Her assistance allowed the massage therapist to relax. The yoga teacher monitored those participants who had difficulty following the instructions. Both shared the work of setting up the room and debriefed together, sharing impressions to make the next class even better. When the yoga teacher needed help with her workshops, the massage teacher reciprocated in kind.

You can combine the first two collaboration levels—hiring others and attracting others—to help you overcome many business challenges. Brenda, a physical therapist, had a therapy practice with three other therapists, all independent contractors. Brenda paid the therapists a flat fee for each client they saw, keeping a percentage of the full fee to cover the administration, billing, advertising, and space rental. This arrangement, not unusual in a small practice, allowed her to cover her business expenses, with little profit left over. She was dissatisfied about the amount of managing and administrative work required to yield such a small amount of profit, and wondered if she should close down. After a careful evaluation, she saw that she could increase her profit picture with more volume. If she hired three more therapists to work evenings and weekends, the times when the office normally sat empty, her expenses would stay roughly the same and her profits would increase.

The solution to expand seemed obvious, but Brenda felt frightened at the thought of doubling in size, a common emotion to feel prior to making a change. She needed more collegial support. I asked her to find and interview three other therapy business owners who had a successful, six-person business of any kind. She found an occupational therapist, a physical therapist, and a psychotherapist and was surprised that the owners were happy to talk to her about the pros and cons of operating a larger practice.

Together, Brenda and I developed a business plan modeled on the information she had gathered from interviewing the other therapists. We paid close attention to issues these therapists highlighted during her interviews with them, including difficulties with scheduling six therapists, communication problems with therapists who worked during off-hours, and how to make sure that the flow of referrals stayed steady. Within six months Brenda doubled in size; with the increase in patient volume, she made a respectable profit for the first time. She was ecstatic with her results. "I finally get what it takes to make my business dreams a reality. I don't have to do it alone. I can get help—hire a coach, talk to peers, and do it the easy way," she said.

The third level of collaboration, your attraction to mentors and models of excellence, helps you jump to the next level of professional or personal expertise. This collaboration may take the form of you finding ways to "hang out" with leaders of your profession, those key people who inspire you and move you forward. We therapists usually consider other therapists our mentors, and attend training sessions or conferences to gain exposure to them. You can also begin to identify business visionaries who inspire you as well. One magazine I like to read is *Fast Company,* which includes first-person narratives by young, articulate CEOs who discuss trends and new directions.

CREATE FULL COLLABORATION

Pat Williams is a good example of a therapist who used all three areas of collaboration to successfully launch a new business in a remarkably short period of time. Pat was a psychologist in private practice for fifteen years, who also worked as a corporate trainer and as a personal/business coach. In 1998, he developed a virtual training forum for therapists called TherapistU, which offers classes by phone for therapists who want to develop skills in coaching. Pat, who describes himself as a "non–business person" who has drive, energy, but not a lot of business knowledge, fills in his gaps in business by using the first level of collaboration—hiring others.

When we met in 1997, I was one of five business coaches he had hired serially over a two-year period to assist him in defining his business plan. He hired coaches who could advise him in everything from business planning to public relations to advertising. Pat calls this group of business coaches his "outer circle."

Collaboration tip from Pat: "I wanted to learn from the best, so I hired a number of good coaches with a variety of strengths and different specialties and ran my business vision by all of them. Each was able to contribute a different perspective to my overall ideas and plans. The coach I work with now is a specialist in strategic planning. My next coach will specialize in building national organizations. Each one takes me a step further."

At the same time that he was hiring business coaches, Pat began to reach out to other therapists within the international coaching community for brainstorming and support, with the idea of a possible business connection in the future—the second level of collaboration. Pat, a gregarious and enthusiastic man, routinely attracts a wide circle of friends and colleagues. He makes it look easy, but as I talk to Pat it is clear that he does a lot to build what he calls his "inner circle." He is not shy about asking for advice and assistance from those colleagues he barely knows. For example, to begin to generate interest in his new venture, Pat asked to interview fourteen therapists who also worked as coaches, some of whom he had met and others he had only talked with by phone. He taped the interviews, with the permission of each therapist, and compiled them into a taped set called "New Directions for Therapists: Building a Successful Coaching Business." This tape set became the primary marketing and educational tool for TherapistU. Pat then asked these same therapists to be part of his informal advisory board, and to join him on a conference call each month to talk about the progress of his company. Two members of the advisory board wrote curriculum for TherapistU, which Pat licensed, and became part of his faculty. The other members of the advisory board genuinely like Pat, support his work, and are available to give him advice and ideas to help him succeed.

Collaboration tip from Pat: "I always ask people to be part of my inner circle hoping for mutual business, to create a win/win situation. I hope they will benefit in some way from the organization they are helping me to build—some by becoming teachers, others by having products we can sell on the web page, others by knowing I am referring clients to them."

Pat also devotes time and resources to spending time with mentors he is attracted to—collaborating at the third level. One of these mentors is Dave Ellis, author of two of the texts that Pat uses in the TherapistU curriculum. Pat recently attended one of Ellis's workshops and met with him and his staff. Ellis was happy to hear how Pat uses his books, and a new level of collaboration has opened up for Pat with Ellis's organization.

Collaboration tip from Pat: "I look for a high level of integrity and generosity in a mentor—I believe passionately in what I am doing and want to work with others who demonstrate the same spirit."

STAYING FULFILLED

Several years ago I sat in on a meeting of business coaches who were debating the distinction between a full practice and a fulfilling practice. Some coaches believed that the best outcome of coaching was to help business owners develop a waiting list of customers and clients; others argued against using the degree of growth as an indicator of a business owner's satisfaction. At the end of the meeting, we agreed that full and fulfilling were not the same thing. You can build a practice with a waiting list, but feel unfulfilled if it does not offer you the opportunity to do work that brings you sufficient joy. You can have a practice that allows you to do the work that you love, but if you are not making money or attracting clients, you may feel unhappy.

This book is set up to help you custom-design a fulfilling practice—one where you work the hours you choose, make the amount of income you want, do the type of therapy you love, and see only those clients that appreciate and benefit from your services. Custom-designing means that as you go through each chapter, you select those ideas and strategies that match your integrity, your professional code of ethics, and your aligned vision. You refer to your business plan, but you don't ignore your gut feelings. The goal is to make sure you are building your business not just the *right* way, but *your* way. I encourage you to individualize not only the business you build, but the way you build it by choosing your own timeline for your goals, so that you develop your business at your own pace, with a sense of comfort and control.

A custom-designed practice has special meaning, because it reflects who you are today and who you aspire to become tomorrow. The better you fit your practice to meet your business and life priorities, the longer you will wish to stay in practice. And I want you to work profitably and joyfully in practice for a long time, because the existence of your successful practice directly affects the existence of the future of the therapy profession.

I am very concerned when I hear about the numbers of therapists leaving the field. My larger purpose as a business coach is to see all therapists—physicians, psychologists, social workers, counselors, personal coaches, life coaches, nurses, energy healers, chiropractors, massage therapists, physical therapists, acupuncturists, and body workers—not just survive, but thrive for a long time. According to a recent survey in a national newsletter, 20 percent of all mental health therapists in private practice are leaving the profession each year, due in part to their inability to operate a practice profitably. Another study published in a professional journal finds half of all licensed counselors in the state of California may terminate their private practices in the next ten years based on a lack of being able to make it in business. I am saddened by this waste of much needed talent. I believe that we therapists offer valuable and important services for the public, services that are greatly needed but often underappreciated.

Earlier in this chapter we explored the idea of creating relevance as a key to staying motivated, and I suggested that you do that by defining a larger purpose for your work. One larger purpose for all of us to consider is the life-giving, nutritive culture that we, as therapists and healing professionals, promote by our existence in private practice. In this larger world view, we represent an industry composed of therapists of all kinds who work in private practice, rather than within large corporate organizations. By opting to work in private practice, we ensure that our various professions remain client-focused and responsive to the needs of the end-users, rather than to investors or stockholders. To keep our industry strong, your role is to keep your individual practice profitable and strong. As you continue to build your fulfilling private practice, you contribute to the stability of a noncorporate, privately-owned, therapy industry that offers the public necessary additional choices and options that can improve the quality of life.

Earlier in the book we talked about the need of the therapy business owner to reconcile the concepts of service and profit. In this more global view of a client-focused therapy industry, profit and service are intertwined; those of us in profitable practice make it possible for the public to be well-served and in doing so, further the goal of a healthier, higher-functioning society. As you build and maintain your practice, you do your part to add to the health and well-being of others in your community and your society. And if you have built an *ideal* private practice, your efforts will be reciprocated as you reap many rewards.

Appendix

> ## THE PRIVATE PRACTICE SUCCESS PROGRAM™
> ## PRE- AND POST-TEST
> A personal checklist for building an ideal private practice.
> *Give yourself 1 point for each checked item. Each section
> has ten items.*

VISION

*Your business vision is the life energy that brings meaning and focus
to your private practice.*

☐ I understand the concept of a business by design—that if I don't make
choices for my business, circumstances will.

☐ I am aware of five future trends that will effect my business in the next
two years.

☐ I know my unique strengths and talents as a therapist.

☐ I've identified my top three points of integrity.

☐ I have a vision for my practice that is oriented around my integrity and
my unique talents, and that is set into a predictable future context.

☐ I have a written vision statement.

☐ I have a written purpose statement.

☐ I have a written mission statement.

☐ I am moving forward on the first five action steps of my mission statement that will help me fulfill my business vision.

☐ I have articulated my vision to other trusted associates in my "circle of
encouragement."

_____ total score

MINDSET

*To be successful in private practice, you need to think like a success-
ful entrepreneur.*

☐ I know how to identify and overcome the barriers the public faces in
regards to therapy.

☐ I can tap into my "inner entrepreneur" to give me motivation to move
forward on my business goals.

☐ I recognize the thinking traits of successful entrepreneurs and know which ones I need to adopt.

☐ I know how to construct a powerful business affirmation.

☐ I am working with a personalized affirmation that supports my specific business goal.

☐ I use one of three methods to clear away my negative beliefs about business.

☐ I am clear about the direction I need to take to build the practice I desire.

☐ I surround myself with positive people who want me to succeed.

☐ I am becoming more businesslike in my thinking.

☐ I have created an advisory circle to support my efforts.

_____total score

REFERRALS

A healthy private practice can be identified by a steady flow of referrals.

☐ I have a well-crafted basic message that I use as an introduction.

☐ I know three ways to overcome the initial price barrier.

☐ I can list five benefits of my services, with specific success stories.

☐ I know how to ask for referrals in a manner that reflects the integrity of my practice.

☐ I have cultivated four " practice angels" who refer clients to me.

☐ I have a menu of options for new clients and have packaged my services in five different ways.

☐ My promotional materials focus on the solutions I offer to others.

☐ I educate existing clients about the value-added aspects of my practice.

☐ I support all termination and treat each client respectfully as a lifetime relationship.

☐ I have more than one profit center and revenue stream.

_____total score

MONEY

Treating your practice like a business means understanding how to become highly profitable while doing the work you love.

☐ I have reconciled the difference between profit and service.

☐ I am well within the profit formula guideline for a therapy business.

☐ I know how many billable hours I will work this year and what my fee needs to be.

☐ I understand the hidden costs in my practice.

☐ I have a written business plan.

☐ My current fees are based on the "right" criteria.

☐ I am very comfortable discussing my fee structure, my missed-session policy, my payment policy, and other issues regarding money with clients.

☐ I know the steps to take to increase my profits immediately.

☐ I know how to raise my fees without alienating existing clients.

☐ I am building a practice to sell, not just to own.

_____total score

LOVING THE BUSINESS

The hallmark of a successful entrepreneur is that running the business contains many elements of pleasure.

☐ I understand the difference between a fear-based and love-based practice.

☐ I am eliminating all "push" marketing in my practice.

☐ I have created a maintenance metaphor to help me give my business continual attention.

☐ I have reorganized my calendar to reflect a balance of work, spirit, and buffer time.

☐ I use an "ebb and flow" strategy to minimize the normal ups and downs of private practice.

☐ I have listed ten complaints about my current practice and have ten good solutions to correct them.

☐ I know how to model the strategies of other successful businesspeople.

☐ I use the three strategies of collaboration to make operating my business more fun.

☐ I know how to focus my energy on the "how" instead of the "what."

☐ My practice operates from a model of abundance, not deprivation.

_____total score

BEYOND A MEDICAL MODEL

Go beyond a medical model to create a full-service, personal-growth business.

☐ I know the five stages of personal growth.

☐ I have a list of services I can offer clients at any one of those stages.

☐ I am following all the items on the practice management checklist to make my practice a business, not a hobby.

☐ I know the distinction between what my clients want and will pay for out of pocket versus what I think they need.

☐ I have expanded my initial vision of my practice to include aspects of the personal-growth business model.

☐ I stay motivated using the four-step model, to keep my practice successful.

☐ I know exactly who I need to be in order to run a successful personal-growth business.

☐ I know specifically what I need to do in order to run a successful personal-growth business.

☐ I know how to establish my personal-growth practice using circular positioning.

☐ I am a model of the services that I offer to others.

_____ total score

Scoring

50–60 points: You are really working on the business and have a strong sense of how to set up and maintain your ideal private practice. Congratulations!

40–49 points: You're definitely on your way to having a successful practice. Keep going in the same direction. Motivate yourself to take the important next steps. Go for it!

20–39 points: Time to do some additional work on your practice and on yourself, so that you can meet your goals and learn to enjoy the business of therapy. Commit to spending the time you need to see results.

0–19 points: To get a strong start in practice-building, use this book as a handbook. Strengthen your business abilities by going through each chapter and completing each exercise.

THE TOP TEN BUSINESS STRATEGIES THAT GENERATE REFERRALS
A checklist of forty action steps that increase referrals.

---

1. ARTICULATE YOUR BASIC MESSAGE

Know how to speak about the essence of who you are and what you do—an essential step that creates a lasting result.

☐ Have a fifteen-second self-introduction that attracts referrals—your basic message.

☐ Get sponsored by organizations and speak to their members—on message.

☐ Write a valuable, monthly practice letter for existing clients—on message.

☐ Write a manual or booklet that expands your message; self publish; use it as the text for your workshops.

2. FOCUS ON THE BENEFITS

Too many therapists focus on promoting the features of their practice—their degrees and training. Potential clients want to know about benefits—the results they can expect.

☐ Think about the ways you have specifically helped clients "as evidenced by."

☐ Have several success stories you can talk about.

☐ Design your promotional materials to identify the solutions you offer.

☐ Use language that reflects what your clients want versus what you think they need.

3. OVERCOME THE INITIAL BARRIERS TO THERAPY

Make it easier for clients to first connect with you.

☐ Give a free, "high touch" introduction or preview of your work.

☐ Host gatherings of your colleagues and teach them what you know.

☐ Instead of a printed brochure, offer a twenty-minute "living brochure."

☐ Develop a mailing list of potential clients and send them your free practice newsletter every six months.

4. ASK FOR THE REFERRAL

You need to let others know that you welcome referrals. Asking for referrals is a legitimate way to communicate your business needs.

☐ Identify your ideal client profile, so that you know the type of clients you want to attract. Practice saying, "I have some openings in my practice I am looking to fill."

☐ Include the following on your policy sheet: "I welcome referrals, which signify your satisfaction and trust in my services."

☐ Ask the universe for referrals.

5. LEVERAGE YOUR MARKETING TIME

Marketing means educating others about your services. Use your time efficiently by educating more people using less effort.

☐ Meet and cultivate four "practice angels"—those influential people who are well connected in your community and can make multiple referrals.

☐ Identify your current referral network—list your existing and past clients and who originally sent them to you.

☐ Become a referral source—expand your Rolodex by getting to know fifty professionals who provide services your clients might need (in the process you expand the network of people who know about your services, too).

☐ Create your own advisory board; surround yourself with those who encourage your success.

6. DIVERSIFY

When generating referrals, it's not always who you know; it's also how many you know. Enlarge your network and expand your menu of services.

☐ Develop multiple profit centers and revenue streams—become a "cross trainer."

☐ Cultivate flexibility and diversity in your professional network.

☐ Read outside your field; join groups outside your profession; develop more hobbies.

☐ Package your services in at least five different ways; create a menu of options for new clients.

7. GO BEYOND COMPETENCY

To generate referrals in a highly competitive marketplace, you must be highly skilled.

☐ Become truly excellent in one aspect of your practice.

☐ Invest at least 5 percent of your annual revenue in training and development to maintain excellence.

☐ Lead with your strengths—orient your practice around your area of greatest expertise.

☐ Niche your services by the outcomes you deliver, instead of by the issues you address.

8. CONTINUALLY ADD VALUE

Existing and former clients will be a source of referrals if they perceive a high value of service in your practice.

☐ Enrich your menu of services each year.

☐ Articulate the added value to others—don't keep it a secret.

☐ Develop a full-service personal-growth practice.

☐ Anticipate your clients' future needs and be one step ahead of them.

9. HELP CLIENTS TO END THERAPY SUCCESSFULLY

Treat each client as a long-term relationship, not a short-term cash flow. Good endings generate future referrals.

☐ Educate your clients about how they can get the most out of their time in therapy with you.

☐ Help clients leave without shame or guilt—support all termination.

☐ Let clients know your policy about supporting termination during their first session.

☐ Act as if you have a waiting list, even when you don't.

10. BECOME A MODEL OF THE SERVICES YOU OFFER

The more attractive you are as a professional, the more you will attract your ideal clients.

☐ Get all your personal needs met outside of your practice.

☐ Be on a strong financial track.

☐ Get excellent clinical supervision and business coaching.

☐ Find solutions for all the complaints you have regarding your work.

THREE-YEAR BUSINESS BUDGET
Use this format for recording income and expenses
of a sole proprietorship.

Income	Year 1	Year 2	Year 3
Clients	_____	_____	_____
Consulting	_____	_____	_____
Speaking	_____	_____	_____
Reports	_____	_____	_____
Phone sessions	_____	_____	_____
Classes	_____	_____	_____
Workshops	_____	_____	_____
Products	_____	_____	_____
Other	_____	_____	_____
Total	_____	_____	_____

Expenses

Accounting	_____	_____	_____
Advertising	_____	_____	_____
Automobile	_____	_____	_____
Books	_____	_____	_____
Cleaning	_____	_____	_____
Consultants	_____	_____	_____
Dues	_____	_____	_____
Education	_____	_____	_____
Equipment	_____	_____	_____
Furnishings	_____	_____	_____
Insurance:	_____	_____	_____
Malpractice	_____	_____	_____
Disability	_____	_____	_____
Medical	_____	_____	_____

(Expenses cont.)	Year 1	Year 2	Year 3
Landscaping			
Meals/Entertain			
Parking			
Phone			
Postage			
Printing			
Repairs			
Rent			
Supplies			
Taxes			
Travel			
Utilities			
Other			
Total			
Income			
Expenses			
Net Profit			
(or Loss)			

RESOURCES

BUSINESS VISION

Abrahams, Jeffrey. (1995). *The Mission Statement Book—301 Corporate Mission Statements from America's Top Companies.* Berkeley, CA: Ten-Speed.

A useful guide to developing your vision, purpose, and mission statements. The book gives hundreds of examples of corporate mission statements from famous companies.

Bolles, Richard N. (1992). *How to Find Your Mission in Life.* Berkeley, CA: Ten-Speed.

This book is a companion guide to Bolles's What Color Is Your Parachute? *It's written to get at the deeper purpose in work and life, and takes you through several exercises to try to help the reader articulate mission and purpose.*

Celente, Gerald. (1998). *Trends 2000: How to Prepare for and Profit from the Changes of the 21st Century.* New York: Warner.

Details major trends in important areas to help readers make sound, profitable business, career, and personal decisions. Celente looks at the field of health care and personal-growth from an unorthodox viewpoint.

Ellis, Dave. (1998). *Creating Your Future: Five Steps to the Life of Your Dreams.* Boston: Houghton Mifflin.

A motivational roadmap for getting the most out of life. Invites readers to visualize and live a more meaningful and deeply fulfilling life.

Falkenstein, Lynda. (1996). *Nichecraft: Using Your Specialness to Focus Your Business, Corner Your Market and Make Customers Seek You Out.* New York: HarperBusiness.

Provides a simple-to-follow, nine-step blueprint for identifying and developing a niche and using it to sell your product or service.

Gawain, Shakti. (1983). *Creative Visualization.* New York: Bantam.

A beginning guide to using affirmations and visualizations.

Gerber, Michael. (1995). *The E-Myth Revisited: Why Most Small Businesses Don't Work and What to Do About It.* New York: HarperBusiness.

Required reading for anyone thinking about starting a business or for those who have already taken that fateful step. Outlines an accessible and organized plan, so that daily details are scripted, freeing the entrepreneur's mind to build the long-term success of the business.

Jones, Laurie Beth. (1998). *The Path to Creating Your Mission Statement for Work and for Life.* New York: Hyperion.

Inspiring and practical advice that leads listeners through every step of both defining and fulfilling a mission.

Morrissey, Mary. (1997). *Building Your Field of Dreams.* New York: Bantam.

Demonstrates how readers can tap into their "divine discontent" to identify their deepest desires.

Popcorn, Faith, and Lys Marigold. (1998). *Clicking: 17 Trends That Drive Your Business—and Your Life.* New York: Harper Collins.

Popcorn writes a fast-paced, fun book full of her thoughts and opinions about the coming trends. She explores many areas of the future concerning both lifestyle and work.

Seiffer, John. *The Seiffer Report.* (newsletter)
Available from: John Seiffer, web address: www.coachingworks.com

Seiffer is a business coach who publishes this free e-mail newsletter sporadically. He is an original thinker and has some very perceptive ideas about the future, as well as help for small business owners who want to achieve success.

Seligman, Martin. (1998). *Learned Optimism: How to Change Your Mind and Your Life.* New York: Pocket.

This is a good resource to use for working with a business affirmation; Seligman teaches readers how to refute negative thoughts using cognitive, rational self-talk.

Wheatley, Margaret and Myron Kellner-Rogers. (1996). *A Simpler Way.* San Francisco: Berrett-Koehler.

Wheatley is a visionary and management consultant who thinks out of the box and explores the underlying structure of business. She looks at the deeper elemental forms that make up business organizations and human life itself.

ENTREPRENUERIAL MINDSET

Bangs, David H., Jr. (1998). *The Business Planning Guide: Creating a Plan for Success in Your Own Business* (8th ed.). Dover, NH: Upstart.

Named as one of the most useful small business book by Forbes. Teaches small business owners how to ramp up their technical savvy on the business planning front, complete with information on using the Internet as a business planning tool.

Bangs, David H., Jr. (1998). *The Start-Up Guide: A One-Year Plan for Entrepreneurs* (3rd ed.). Dover, NH: Upstart.

Outlines a complete twelve-month action plan for creating a new business. It provides a practical framework to research and test ideas inexpensively, define and identify ways to reach the best markets, forecast sales and expenses, and use the Internet as a source for low-cost resources.

Brandt, Steven. (1997). *Entrepreneuring: The 10 Commandments for Building a Growth Company* (3rd ed.). Friday Harbor, WA: Archipelago.

Presents ten proven operating principles for building a successful company and covers key startup issues to help develop a solid foundation.

Edwards, Sarah and Paul. (1996). *Secrets of Self-Employment: Surviving and Thriving on the Ups and Downs of Being Your Own Boss.* New York: Jeremy P. Tarcher/Putnam.

Solid tips for small business success.

Gershon, David & Gail Straub. (1989). *Empowerment: The Art of Creating Your Life as You Want It.* New York: Delta.

An easy-to-use guide with methods for using affirmations, visualizations, and other metaphysical tools to achieve exactly what you desire out of life. The Straubs offer dozens of sample affirmations for all areas of life.

Jeffers, Susan. (1992). *Feel the Fear and Do It Anyway.* New York: Fawcett Columbine.

This is a classic text, filled with concrete techniques to turn passivity into assertiveness.

Lawless, Linda L. (1997). *Therapy, Inc.: A Hands-On Guide to Developing, Positioning, and Marketing Your Mental Health Practice in the 1990s.* New York: John Wiley & Sons.

A pragmatic guidebook that offers a developmental model of practice-building, outlining career development, business management, and marketing strategies.

Lonier, Terri. (1998). *Working Solo: The Real Guide to Freedom and Financial Success With Your Own Business* (2nd ed.). New York: John Wiley & Sons.

Dispels myths about self-employment. A good reality check for those dazzled by the glamour of "doing their own thing" and a terrific psychological spur to practicing soloists.

Lonier, Terri. (1998). *Working Solo Sourcebook: Essential Resources for Independent Entrepreneurs* (2nd ed.). New York: John Wiley & Sons.

An annotated listing of 1,200 resources on running one's own business, alphabetized from advertising to women-owned businesses. Brief, to-the-point notes and advice about techniques and new avenues to try.

Mindell, Arnold. (1993). *The Leader as Martial Artist: An Introduction to Deep Democracy.* San Francisco: HarperCollins.

Shows how confronting the challenges of today's business world requires the skill of a martial artist, and how to exhibit flexibility, balance, and keen awareness in the midst of group chaos and confusion.

Salmansohn, Karen. (1997). *How to Succeed in Business Without a Penis: Secrets and Strategies for the Working Woman.* New York: Random House.

Offers advice from real, successful women, a "chick list" of clever and aggressive career suggestions, and pithy affirmations from a woman who likes it on top.

Sinetar, Marsha. (1996). *To Build the Life You Want, Create the Work You Love: The Spiritual Dimension of Entrepreneuring.* New York: St. Martins.

Shows readers how to embrace the inner qualities of effective, fulfilled entrepreneurs—a practical handbook for anyone who wants to do what they love for a living.

Wheatley, Margaret. (1994). *Leadership and the New Science: Learning About Organization from an Orderly Universe.* San Francisco: Berrett-Koehler.

Using exciting breakthroughs in biology, chemistry, and especially quantum physics, Wheatley paints a brand-new picture of business management. This book explains the concept of vision and field theory.

GENERATING REFERRALS

Ackley, Dana. (1997) *Breaking Free of Managed Care : A Step-By-Step Guide to Regaining Control of Your Practice (Clinician's Toolbox).* New York: Guilford.

A solid approach to finding finding private pay clients, including a detailed plan for developing organizational consulting contracts.

Beckwith, Harry. (1997). *Selling the Invisible: A Field Guide to Modern Marketing.* New York: Warner.

Beckwith explains that what moves consumers today are not product features, but relationships. This short book shows how to market your service business by focusing on building business relationships as well as using sales techniques.

Cameron-Bandler, Leslie, David Gordon and Michael Lebeau. (1985). *The Emprint Method: A Guide to Reproducing Competence.* San Rafael: FuturePace.

A guide for understanding and modeling the successful strategies of others.

Davis, Jeri and Michael Freeman (Eds.). (1996). *Marketing for Therapists: A Handbook for Success in Managed Care.* San Francisco: Jossey-Bass.

For those who still operate within managed care, this book offers a step-by-step plan for marketing a therapy practice within that system.

Lambert, Clark. (1986). *Secrets of a Successful Trainer: A Simplified Guide for Survival.* New York: John Wiley & Sons.

Insider's guide to effective presentation of training material for both novices and experienced professionals. Good for beginners.

MacKay, Harvey. (1999). *Dig Your Well Before You're Thirsty: The Only Networking Book You'll Ever Need.* New York: Doubleday.

This is a surprisingly entertaining book about networking. Many of the ideas can be adapted and then applied to a therapy business. MacKay outlines a host of techniques he used to build an impressive network that feeds his successful career in business and writing.

Walters, Lilly. *Secrets of Successful Speakers.* (1993). New York: McGraw Hill.

Spells out presentation tips and ideas in easy-to-follow steps, each accompanied by interactive exercises. Useful for anyone who makes presentations or gives talks.

PROFITABILITY

Barnhart, Tod. (1995). *Five Rituals of Wealth: Proven Strategies for Turning the Little You Have into More Than Enough.* New York: HarperBusiness.

How people of all incomes can increase their financial status.

Bernstein, Barton & Thomas Hartsell. (1998). *The Portable Lawyer for Mental Health Professionals: An A-Z Guide to Protecting Your Clients, Your Practice, and Yourself.* New York: John Wiley & Sons.

Organized alphabetically, an A-to-Z guide that provides clear and concise answers to legal questions, including recordkeeping, confidentiality, malpractice, and client/therapist relationships.

Carlson, Richard. (1997). *Don't Worry, Make Money: Spiritual and Practical Ways to Create Abundance and More Fun in Your Life.* New York: Little, Brown.

Filled with ideas to help calm one's anxiety regarding money. Ideas to spark the interest of even the most overworked businessperson.

Chilton, David. (1998). *The Wealthy Barber: Everyone's Commonsense Guide to Becoming Financially Independent.* Rocklin, CA: Prima.

Shows readers how to achieve the financial independence they've always dreamed of. Chilton encourages readers to take control of their financial future and build wealth slowly and steadily.

Dominguez, Joe and Vicki Robin. (1993). *Your Money or Your Life: Transforming Your Relationship With Money and Achieving Financial Independence.* New York: Penguin.

Discover the difference between "making a living" and making a life. How to get out of debt and develop savings, reorder material priorities, and resolve inner conflicts between values and lifestyles.

Herron, William and Sheila Rouslin Welt. (1994). *Money Matters: The Fee in Psychotherapy and Psychoanalysis.* New York: Guilford.

Illuminates the problems of fee-guilt felt by therapists, and fee-avoidance by patients. Considers the meaning of money and the philosophy of a service that involves money, the patient's financial situation, and other questions that discomfort therapists.

Hill, Napoleon. (1990). *Think and Grow Rich.* New York: Fawcett.

Simple, basic financial techniques that can create lasting financial success.

Krueger, David. (1986). *The Last Taboo: Money as a Symbol and Reality in Psychotherapy and Psychoanalysis.* New York: Brunner/Mazel.

Discussion of a wide variety of approaches to setting fees and handling the financial aspects of private practice, using case examples.

Mundis, Jerold. (1996). *Earn What You Deserve: How to Stop Underearning and Start Thriving.* New York: Bantam.

Helps readers streamline their finances and change their views about money forever.

Phillips, Michael. (1997). *The Seven Laws of Money.* Boston: Shambhala.

Outlines seven, simple concepts that result in a healthy attitude toward money.

Stern, Linda. (1997). *Money-Smart Secrets for the Self-Employed.* New York: Random House.

Helpful resource that outlines a series of logical, easy-to-apply techniques addressing all of the major economic issues faced by a solo enterprise today—including taxes, expenses, and recordkeeping.

Whitmyer, Claude and Sali Rasberry. (1994). *Running a One-Person Business.* (revised edition) Berkeley: Ten-Speed.

Addresses the concerns of the very small organization. Standard business topics such as bookkeeping, marketing, and finance are discussed with the needs of the sole proprietor in mind.

LOVING THE BUSINESS

Cameron, Julia. (1996). *The Artist's Way: A Spiritual Path to Higher Creativity.* New York: J. P. Tarcher.

This book can free up your creativity, which you can then apply to your practice. Outlines a comprehensive twelve-week program to recover your creativity from a variety of blocks, including limiting beliefs, fear, self-sabotage, and other inhibiting forces.

Chopra, Deepak. (1995). *The Seven Spiritual Laws of Success: A Practical Guide to the Fulfillment of Your Dreams.* San Rafael, CA: Amber-Allen.

How to use personal understanding and harmony to promote material abundance. Each concept is explained and then the reader is offered a meditation and exercises to use. All of the concepts combine to give an elegant definition of abundance in daily life.

Covey, Stephen R., A. Roger Merrill, and Rebecca Merrill. (1994). *First Things First: To Live, to Love, to Learn, to Leave a Legacy.* New York: Simon & Schuster.

Covey teaches an organizing process that helps you categorize tasks so you focus on what is important, not merely what is urgent.

Fortgang, Laura Berman. (1998). *Take Yourself to the Top.* New York: Time Warner.

This career coach offers action-oriented plans to help readers take big steps, make changes, and become responsible for the choices they make.

Leonard, Thomas J. and Byron Laursen. (1998). *The Portable Coach: 28 Sure-Fire Strategies for Business and Personal Success.* New York, NY: Scribner.

Leonard's explanation of coaching includes principles to help you shape your life, career, and relationships so that they are satisfying and profitable.

Maslow, Abraham H., and Richard Lowry, (Ed.). (1998). *Toward a Psychology of Being.* (3rd ed.). New York: John Wiley & Sons.

Maslow's theory of self-actualization, hierarchy of human needs, and mental/emotional well-being help explain his ideas of motivation.

Richardson, Cheryl. (1998). *Take Time for Your Life: A Personal Coach's Seven-Step Program for Creating the Life You Want.* New York: Broadway.

Shows you how to switch from being stressed, unfulfilled, and overworked, to living a life you love and becoming a model of the services you offer.

Walsch, Neale Donald. (1996). *Conversations with God: An Uncommon Dialogue (Book 1).* New York: Putnam.

Walsch's account of his spiritual journey clearly explains the difference between fear-based and love-based thinking and how to shift your focus to the latter.

USEFUL WEBSITES

Private Practice Success
www.privatepracticesuccess.com

Lynn Grodzki's website offers articles, ideas, and tips for building an ideal private practice. Use the website to subscribe to the "Private Practice Success" free e-mail newsletter, and access information regarding classes, workshops, and coaching consultations.

Healing Dimensions Foundation
www.healingdimensionsfound.org

A nonprofit membership organization providing resources for those exploring the holistic healing arts. Has a referral list for healers and information about classes.

CoachU
www.coachu.com

The premier virtual university training and referring personal and professional coaches.The website has descriptions of coaching, a list of all the coaches trained by CoachU, and a bookstore.

TherapistU
www.therapistu.com

A virtual learning forum specializing in training therapists to become personal coaches, which can enhance their therapy practices and advance their personal development.

International Coach Federation

www.coachfederation.com

Professional organization of personal and business coaches that exists to build, support, and preserve the integrity of the coaching profession.

AssistU

web address: www.assistu.com

Provides referrals for virtual assistants, those well-trained administrative assistants who can assist you in your business tasks by working virtually, using e-mail, phone, and direct mail.

National Speakers Association

www.nsaspeaker.org

NSA is an international, professional organization for experts who speak for a living. They have state and regional chapters nationwide. They can be a great resource for therapists who want to develop more expertise and savvy as public speakers.

Practice Strategies

www.aamft.org/resources/practice.htm

Sponsored by the American Association of Marriage and Family Therapy (AAMFT), Practice Strategies *is written from the practitioner's perspective, with the awareness that clinicians cannot thrive in isolation. Each month the publication informs and educates mental health practitioners, regardless of discipline, about trends and information that will affect their practices.*

Psychotherapy Finances

www.psyfin.com

Subscribe to a national newsletter of resources for behavioral health providers, helping therapists work with managed-care providers as well as build a practice outside the constraints of managed care. Each newsletter offers real-life examples of therapists who have successfully niched their practices and gives specific tips and ideas for practice success.

Mental Health Net
www:mentalhelp.net

   Mental health directory guide and community. Hosts a multidiscipli-nary, peer-reviewed, internet journal that publishes articles on topics relating to mental health issues and advocacy.

Clinical Social Work Federation Web Sites of Interest
www.webcom.com/nfscsw/hotsites.html

   Complete listing of major websites for psychotherapists.

CONTACTS

How to reach therapists and/or business coaches referenced in the book

Wendy Allen, Ph.D., 27 East Victoria St., Santa Barbara, CA 93101, 805-962-2212 (voice)

Lucy Banks, LCSW-C, The Arbor Center, 10560 Main St., Suite 410, Fairfax, VA 22030, 703-352-9009 (voice), e-mail:lucybanks@aol.com

Rudolph Bauer, Ph.D. and Sharon Bauer, MSW, Gestalt Therapy Training Center of Washington, D.C., and Washington Center for Meditation Studies, 1834 Swann St., N.W., Washington, D.C., 20009, 202-667-6425 (voice)

Betty Caldwell, Healing Dimensions Foundation, 9462 Greco Garth, Columbia, MD 21045, 410-740-4659 (voice), e-mail: bcaldwell@healingdimensionsfound.org

Marilyn Ellis, LCSW-C, 1116 Clinch Road, Herndon, VA 22070, 703-450-2752 (voice), e-mail: ellism@erols.com

Lynn Grodzki, LCSW-C, 910 La Grande Rd., Silver Spring, MD 20903, 301-434-0766 (voice), e-mail: lynn@privatepracticesuccess.com

Deany Laliotis, LCSW-C, 4709 Chestnut St., Bethesda, MD 20814, 301-718-9700 (voice), e-mail: dlaliotis@erols.com

Maggie Klee Lichtenberg, P.O. Box 268, Santa Fe, NM 87504, 505-986-8807 (voice), e-mail: MargaretKL@aol.com

Jackie Nagel, P.O. Box 2930, Silverdale, WA 98383, 360-308-0760 (voice), e-mail: info@jackienagel.com

Pam Richarde, 1503 E. Ruscitto Lane, Placentia, CA 92870, 714-996-9911 (voice), e-mail: peacecoach@innerspirit.com

Carol Kurtz Walsh, 4802 Montgomery Lane, Bethesda, MD 20814, 301-656-6420 (voice), e-mail: cwalsh@skipjack.bluecrab.org

Patrick Williams, Ed.D., 7 Wembley Place, Palm Coast, FL 32164, 904-447-0802 (voice), e-mail: doccoach@therapistu.com

Index